International Nietzsche Studies

Nietzsche has emerged as a thinker of extraordinary importance, not only in the history of philosophy but in many fields of contemporary inquiry. Nietzsche studies are maturing and flourishing in many parts of the world. This internationalization of inquiry with respect to Nietzsche's thought and significance may be expected to continue.

International Nietzsche Studies is conceived as a series of monographs and essay collections that will reflect and contribute to these developments. The series will present studies in which responsible scholarship is joined to the analysis, interpretation, and assessment of the many aspects of Nietzsche's thought that bear significantly upon matters of moment today. In many respects Nietzsche is our contemporary, with whom we do well to reckon, even when we find ourselves at odds with him. The series is intended to promote this reckoning, embracing diverse interpretive perspectives, philosophical orientations, and critical assessments.

The series is also intended to contribute to the ongoing reconsideration of the character, agenda, and prospects of philosophy itself. Nietzsche was much concerned with philosophy's past, present, and future. He sought to affect not only its understanding but also its practice. The future of philosophy is an open question today, thanks at least in part to Nietzsche's challenge to the philosophical traditions of which he was so critical. It remains to be seen—and determined— whether philosophy's future will turn out to resemble the "philosophy of the future" to which he proffered a prelude and of which he provided a preview, by both precept and practice. But this is a possibility we do well to take seriously. International Nietzsche Studies will attempt to do so, while contributing to the understanding of Nietzsche's philosophical thinking and its bearing upon contemporary inquiry.

—RICHARD SCHACHT

Nietzsche's Sister and the Will to Power

Nietzsche's Sister and the Will to Power

A Biography of Elisabeth Förster-Nietzsche

CAROL DIETHE

UNIVERSITY OF ILLINOIS PRESS

URBANA AND CHICAGO

♾ This book is printed on acid-free paper.

Illustrations appear with kind permission of the Goethe-Schiller-
Archiv, Weimar.
Library of Congress Cataloging-in-Publication Data
Diethe, Carol, 1943–
Nietzsche's sister and The will to power : a biography of Elisabeth
Förster-Nietzsche / Carol Diethe.
p.   cm. — (International Nietzsche studies)
Includes bibliographical references and index.
ISBN 0-252-02826-0 (cloth : alk. paper)
1. Förster-Nietzsche, Elisabeth, 1846–1935. 2. Nietzsche, Friedrich
Wilhelm, 1844–1900—Family. 3. Philosophers—Germany—Biography.
4. Nietzsche, Friedrich Wilhelm, 1844–1900. Wille zur Macht. I. Title.
II. Series.
B3316.D54   2003
193—dc21   2002015639

Contents

Preface

Blessed with robust good health, Elisabeth Förster-Nietzsche (10 July 1846–8 November 1935) outlived her brother Friedrich Nietzsche (15 October 1844–25 August 1900), who was always plagued by ill health, by thirty-five years. In fact, if we regard the loss of his mind in 1889 when he was forty-five as his "real" death, Elisabeth actually enjoyed an active lifespan twice as long as her brother's, for when she died in her ninetieth year, she was still in possession of all her faculties. The only affliction she shared with her brother was, in the latter half of her life, extremely bad eyesight. The central event in the Nietzsche family as the children grew up was the death on 30 July 1849 of their father, Pastor Carl Ludwig Nietzsche. Thereafter the head of the house was Elisabeth's grandmother Erdmuthe Nietzsche, who undermined her daughter-in-law by spoiling her grandchildren and marginalizing their mother. The line of descent on the Nietzsche side contains sufficient indications for us to conclude that Nietzsche and his father were not the only ones who experienced mental problems: Erdmuthe Nietzsche and Aunt Rosalie both displayed an overexcited nervousness exacerbated by being coupled with a dominant will.

Carl Ludwig's widow Franziska filled the vacuum in her life by directing every ounce of motherly love, bereaved distress, and evangelical religious fervor at the two people nearest to her, her son and her daughter. Neither was ever quite able to recover from the onslaught, though they tried to cope by forming a pact in which they always conspired against their mother should the need arise. This pact held intact until Elisabeth aroused her brother's anger when she meddled in his affair with Lou von Salomé in 1882. Their relationship was never the same after the "Lou Affair." But for most of their childhood, first at Röcken and then in Naumburg, where the family moved in 1850,

Friedrich and Elisabeth Nietzsche were inseparable companions and play-mates. Deprived of a father and resistant to the intensity of their mother's control, their relationship was inordinately close and undoubtedly damaged their later attempts to find marriage partners. Neither had any children and, though Elisabeth was married for four years, both died quintessentially alone.

Elisabeth, at Nietzsche's behest, used her housekeeping skills to help her brother when he was a professor in Basel (1869–79), a decade during which he was often too ill to look after himself. Through Nietzsche, Elisabeth became friendly with the Wagners and began to develop a taste for making grand friends. When the Wagners snubbed Nietzsche because of the content of *Menschliches, Allzumenschliches* (*Human, All Too Human,* 1878), Elisabeth was much more concerned that the Wagners might cut her out of their circle than she was about the anti-Christian diatribe in the book. In the event, she remained friends with the Wagners. It was at Bayreuth in 1870 that Elisabeth met her future husband, Bernhard Förster, whom she married in 1885. To Elisabeth, with her increasingly megalomaniac tendencies, her husband's idea of founding a racially pure colony in Paraguay seemed an excellent idea, though Nietzsche, appalled at Förster's anti-Semitism, predicted that the venture would ruin them both. Nietzsche's fears were more than justified: Förster died in 1889, possibly by his own hand, and Elisabeth, mistrusted by the colonists of Neu-Germania and pursued by creditors, found it expedient to return to Germany to investigate the news of her brother's mental illness.

If Elisabeth and Friedrich Nietzsche had grown apart for a variety of reasons by the time of Nietzsche's mental collapse, they were now thrown together again. From 1897, when their mother Franziska died, Elisabeth, now ensconced in Weimar, had sole charge of her brother until he died in 1900. Elisabeth nursed her brother with apparently unflagging devotion, though she was also motivated by expediency in taking charge of his literary legacy at the very moment when he rose to fame. Ironically, he himself was too ill to reap any benefit. Elisabeth Förster-Nietzsche, as she now styled herself, virtually invented public relations when she founded the Nietzsche-Archiv in Villa Silberblick: publicity and marketing were her forte, and she did not shrink from dragging her enemies through the courts. She increasingly saw people in simplistic terms as either friends or foes. Not surprisingly under these circumstances, she was constantly short of cash. Yet from the turn of the century, Elisabeth employed a team of men who did her bidding, even though they grumbled among themselves about her imperious behavior and, like Peter Gast (alias Heinrich Kösclitz), expressed qualms about her tinkering with Nietzsche's *Nachlaß* (posthumous writings). The team set to work to make sense of the rough jottings, which were published by Elisabeth in

1901 as *Der Wille zur Macht* (*The Will to Power*), giving the false impression that it was a properly constituted posthumous text by Nietzsche instead of a random mosaic. With her drive and her capacity to make people believe in her, often against their better judgment, Elisabeth is a perfect example of the operation of the will to power at the human level, though to be sure, Nietzsche did not have his sister in mind when he conceived the notion of the will to power. The 2001 publication of the ninth section of *Friedrich Nietzsche Werke: Kritische Gesamtausgabe* (Friedrich Nietzsche's Works: Critical Complete Edition), edited by Marie-Luise Haase and Michael Kohlenbach, consists of three volumes (of a planned six) that provide a color-coded transcription of Nietzsche's literary estate under the title *Der handschriftliche Nachlaß ab 1885 in differenzierter Transkription* (The Literary Estate from 1885 in Differentiated Transcription). The reader now has a transcription of half the material found in Nietzsche's last thirteen handwritten notebooks, which contained—among other things—the source material for what has hitherto led a charmed life as *Der Wille zur Macht*.

During Nietzsche's lifetime, few people realized that he had made uncomplimentary remarks about women, though Schopenhauer's misogyny was common knowledge. Elisabeth, like some of his women friends, knew that he believed woman's role to be primarily domestic and maternal. He abhorred campaigners for women's emancipation and branded them all as manly, by which he meant lesbian. Though Elisabeth viewed herself as conventional, the way she led her life was certainly emancipated. Nietzsche's views on women and Elisabeth's relationship to the women's movement will be analyzed in chapter 5, which also contains a discussion of Elisabeth's only extended piece of creative prose, to which I have given the title "Coffee-Party Gossip about Nora." The novella is printed for the first time in English at the end of this volume. It is an extremely interesting roman à clef in that it reveals aspects of Elisabeth's virtually incestuous love for her brother, which she would not have dared to exhibit in public, nor indeed in private, to herself. Discouraged in her literary attempts by her brother, Elisabeth put her writing career to one side, only to pursue it with a vengeance when Nietzsche could no longer intervene. At first she turned to polemics on behalf of her late husband. Very soon, she realized that with Nietzsche silenced as well, she could write about his life and work without let or hindrance, altogether a more satisfying pursuit for her than raking over Bernhard Förster's escapades. Most of her readers believed what she said about her brother, though some of it is as fictional as her novella. For the forty years from 1895, the year of publication of the first volume of her biography of Nietzsche, *Das Leben Friedrich Nietzsche's* (Friedrich Nietzsche's Life), until 1935, when she published *Friedrich Nietzsche und die Frauen seiner*

Zeit (Friedrich Nietzsche and the Women of His Time) only months before she died, she wrote on one topic only: her brother.

Elisabeth went on to found a veritable Nietzsche cult in Weimar. For everyone interested in culture in the first three decades of the twentieth century, Nietzsche was a writer one *had* to have read. Philosophers were slower than writers in coming to the conclusion that Nietzsche was dynamite, but every creative artist or writer in Germany during the first three decades of the twentieth century had a position on Germany's *Bürgerschreck*. For true Nietzsche enthusiasts, a trip to the Nietzsche-Archiv in Weimar was de rigueur. Elisabeth sought to dominate posterity's view of Nietzsche in various ways, for example, by making him out to be a friend of war when hostilities began in 1914. Her own position on matters such as anti-Semitism, which she first embraced through her husband's activities, was largely one of expediency. Expediency led her to deny her former anti-Semitism when she needed money from Ernst Thiel, who was Jewish, and then to stress her proto-Fascist credentials when she needed money from the National Socialists. It is indeed sobering to unravel Elisabeth's dealings with the Adolf Hitler, Wilhelm Frick, and other National Socialists in the 1930s. These dealings later encouraged those with only a casual knowledge of Nietzsche to assume that he, too, had been a proto-Fascist. To be fair to Elisabeth, she never became a member of the NSDAP, though she did join the Deutschnationale Volkspartei when it was formed in 1918.

Though Elisabeth was emotionally attached to her brother to an extraordinary degree, she was incapable of realizing the harm she did to his reputation. Hence her recklessness in her dealings with her brother's legacy. What made Elisabeth a dangerous ally to Nietzsche was the extent of her willpower in dealing with his affairs when he was no longer able to do so himself. Although on one level, Elisabeth still idolized her brother, just as she had done all her life, when he became mentally ill she exploited the situation to manipulate his ideas so that at last she could tell him what to do and say, rather than the other way round. At last she achieved the meeting of their minds to which she had always aspired. It was a grotesque and terrible revenge, and others close to Nietzsche who tried to persuade Elisabeth to adopt a more scrupulous approach were swiftly cast aside. Not surprisingly, in later life she often quarreled with former friends and even, in 1896, bitterly with her own mother. Growing up as a child, however, "Lisbeth" or "Lama" to Nietzsche and "Lieschen" to her mother showed few signs of the ego-driven personality discussed here. When Elisabeth became the custodian of Nietzsche's posthumous papers, she stooped to forgery to try to show that Nietzsche had always maintained his affection for her, when in fact this affection had cooled in the wake of the fiasco with Lou von Salomé and Elisabeth's marriage to Bernhard Förster. Yet although Nietzsche wrote disparagingly of his sister from 1882 onward, this does not mean that he ceased to love her. Even his invective in *Ecce Homo* (which appeared posthumously in 1908)—directed at both Elisabeth and Franziska—shows how upset he was that he could no longer respect them; they still mattered enough for him to passionately dislike. In fact, it was precisely because Elisabeth was so important to him that he cared when she espoused religious or political views that he was forced to reject.

By the same token, the fact that Elisabeth damaged her brother's reputation, especially from the outbreak of the 1914–18 war on, does not mean that she set to work with deliberate malice aforethought. The contrary is true: her overt intentions always appear to have been good, just as her efforts for the Nietzsche-Archiv were indefatigable: she worked very, very hard. Two things spoiled these exertions, and they are connected: first, her faulty education both at school and at Franziska's hands, so that banalities and religious platitudes became second nature to her when her good mind deserved better training, and second, her reckless disregard for scholarly accuracy, which was in many ways a result of her faulty education. Nietzsche had tried hard to guide Elisabeth's mind, though given his hostility toward scholarship in women he was not always the right man for the task. Though Nietzsche had unwittingly taught Elisabeth how to bluff her way in learned society, she was intellectually out of her depth for most of her adult life. Yet as we trace her life in six chapters, we shall see that she aspired not just to social status but to academic *recognition.* Her ambitions led her very far from Nietzsche's thought: in the end, expediency mattered much more than integrity, though in her own way, Frau Dr. Phil. H.C. Förster-Nietzsche was fulfilled and happy when she died. To avoid confusion, I usually refer to her as simply Elisabeth throughout the present work. All translations of German are my own.

Acknowledgments

I would like to thank the Stiftung Weimarer Klassik for providing me with a *Stipendium* in 2000 to enable me to consult the archives in Weimar, and I would like to express grateful thanks for the wonderful help from everyone at the Goethe-Schiller-Archiv. Staff at the Herzogin Anna Amalia Bibliothek and the Schloßbibliothek Anna Amalia have also been invariably helpful and pleasant. Much of the material printed here is taken from manuscripts in the Goethe-Schiller-Archiv, in particular, the manuscript for "Coffee-Party Gossip about Nora." I was allowed to consult the transcription of this but I take full responsibility for overlooking any discrepancies there might be between the manuscript and the transcriptions. With this proviso regarding the possibility for small flaws, I hope readers will agree that the chance to print Elisabeth Förster-Nietzsche's only extant novella (discussed in chapter 5 and given as the Appendix) ought not to be missed. All the illustrations are printed by kind permission of the Goethe-Schiller-Archiv, Weimar.

In particular I would like to thank my patient and loving family, Jürgen, Tom, and Rachel, for their support.

Nietzsche's Sister and the Will to Power

1 Lieschen-Lisbeth-Lama

Circumstances conspired to create the most unsuitable family conceivable for a girl like Elisabeth to be born into. Her mother Franziska was only twenty when her daughter was born in 1846: her first child, born on King Friedrich Wilhelm's birthday and named Friedrich Wilhelm after him, was then approaching two, and another boy, Josef, named after the duke of Altenburg, was born in 1848. The father of the three children, Carl Ludwig Nietzsche, pastor of the small village of Röcken to the southwest of Leipzig, would die the following year at the age of thirty-five, swiftly followed by Josef in 1850. These bald facts are sufficient to indicate the horror that Franziska must have experienced from the onset of her husband's illness in 1848 to the death of her baby two years later. Elisabeth, still a toddler, can have imbibed the atmosphere only at an unconscious level, but Friedrich clearly remembered some of the traumatic events surrounding the two deaths. Franziska was distraught, but she was not alone in her grief: All her short marriage had been spent with her husband's mother Erdmuthe and his unmarried sisters Auguste and Rosalie. During this time she had been unable to assert her rights in the household, as the three older women, with Erdmuthe firmly at the head, had established a strict regime in the Röcken parsonage that came with Carl Ludwig's position. He, however, was too weak to confront his mother or unseat his sisters even had he wanted to. It is a sign of his priorities, and Franziska's lack of confidence, that the latter was actually *grateful* to Erdmuthe for agreeing with her son that Franziska would make a suitable wife.

Carl Ludwig Nietzsche's choice of a very young wife was not unusual for the day, when, in arranged marriages, a groom was often old enough to be his bride's father. But this was a love match. The age gap of twelve years was not excessive in itself, and Franziska's grandmother had also married at the age of seventeen. However, the couple was worlds apart in outlook and experience. Having studied theology, Carl Ludwig first found employment as tutor to the three princesses of Altenburg, Elisabeth, Therese, and Alexandra (Elisabeth Nietzsche was christened with all three names in their honor). At court, he had acquired polished manners and an immaculate manner of dress, something that was bound to impress Franziska, who was very much a shy teenager with one best dress when she became betrothed. Through the patronage of none other than the King of Prussia, Friedrich Wilhelm IV himself, Carl Ludwig was able to secure the Röcken living, and with his talents he could expect it to be a stepping-stone to something grander. Yet although Carl Ludwig was a committed Christian with good intentions, there was an element of fussiness and pedantry in his makeup that meant that though he was respected in his capacity as the village pastor, he was probably not *loved*.

By contrast, Carl Ludwig's father-in-law, Pastor David Oehler, to whom Carl Ludwig suddenly developed a strong dislike shortly after his marriage to Franziska, possessed the affection of his parishioners. A cheerful man compared with the melancholy Carl Ludwig, David Oehler was devout but not fanatical. In a typewritten manuscript that formed the basis for his book *Nietzsches Mutter* (1940), Adalbert Oehler (Franziska's nephew) let it slip that his grandfather David Oehler "was a member of a Masonic lodge."[1] He expunged this from the published version, a book that he sanitized in other respects to please the National Socialist regime, as we shall see below. Nevertheless, it is not the sort of thing one makes up. If it was true, Pastor Oehler probably took his commitments as Mason as seriously as his commitments as pastor. At all events, he read widely, loved poetry and music, and was active in hunting and horticulture. He was relaxed about preparing the Sunday sermon, often speaking off the cuff.

Erdmuthe Nietzsche had also mixed in high circles, first in Weimar during her brief first marriage, and then in Naumburg, where she lived with her brother (Johann Friedrich Krause, a preacher at the cathedral) until she remarried in 1809. Her only son born to her first husband, Carl Krüger, a lawyer at the Weimar court, had died in infancy shortly before Krüger himself fell ill in 1806 and died in 1807. Erdmuthe's second husband, Friedrich August Ludwig Nietzsche, a pastor at Eilenburg and the ecclesiastical head of his region, already had a number of children when he married Erdmuthe, by whom he had three more. In all, he had twelve children, but two died in infancy. Elisabeth and Friedrich thus had a wide circle of Nietzsche stepaunts and uncles besides Rosalie and Auguste. With the death of her second husband, Erdmuthe had become emotionally dependent on her son, just as Franziska would become emotionally dependent on Friedrich. What made matters worse for Franziska was that she and her ten siblings at home in the Pobles parsonage were used to a warm and cheerful atmosphere, in contrast to the hushed atmosphere in Röcken, where the daughters avoided unnecessary noise because of Erdmuthe's oversensitive hearing and addressed their mother with the formal *Sie*. This stiff formality was calculated to alienate Franziska even without her husband's irrational dislike of her parents. At least when he died, Franziska was able to take her children to see their maternal grandparents at Pobles whenever she wanted. Franziska followed her mother's habit of giving everyone pet names. She called her children Fritz and Lieschen and rechristened the Nietzsche matriarchy Erdmuthchen, Augustchen, and Rosalchen, the latter in spite of a feud that swiftly developed between Franziska and her irascible sister-in-law. Fritz called his sister Lisbeth and they both called their grandmother Großmütterchen, which was shortened to Großchen.

The string of pet names makes it sound as though all was well in the Nietzsche household, all-female except for Nietzsche himself, but of course, the death of Carl Ludwig was a catastrophe that left a mark on everyone, especially his two children. Acting in the sense of Lacan's now-famous "nom du père,"[2] Franziska made sure that the patriarchal veto reached from her husband's grave into her own humble rooms, perhaps forbidding her to marry again (for why did she not?), and placing a weight on the young Friedrich from which he arguably never freed himself—for was not his rejection of God his own way of coming to terms with the Oedipal taboo? By overcoming the Oedipal taboo, Nietzsche freed himself from Franziska, or tried to: for once he had announced his skepticism to the world, he swept away the necessity to believe in anything Franziska said. It is no accident that from 1878, the year of publication of *Menschliches, Allzumenschliches* (*Human, All Too Human*), his view of women became more outspokenly jaundiced, and that was four years *before* his humiliation at the hands of Lou von Salomé. If Nietzsche suffered from the lack of a father figure, we can surmise, without probing too deeply into psychoanalysis, that Elisabeth's personality, too, was darkened by the lack of a father. (Indeed, Freud's terminology seems to have faltered when discussing the erotic development of little girls.) With Franziska's libido targeted at her children lest any wisp of sexual desire should escape and find fruition in a second marriage with a good burgher of Naumburg, Elisabeth turned to her brother as her father figure and, later, substitute spouse, especially during the time they spent keeping house together in Basel, as we shall see in the next chapter. Any explanation of her behavior as disturbed, cranky, or worse is justified only to the extent that she had a proprietary view of Nietzsche that was unhealthy for them both. This explains her otherwise irrational behavior when Nietzsche dared to step out of line to court the attractive Lou von Salomé, injuring Elisabeth where it hurt most: at the level of her unconscious desire for her brother.

When Erdmuthe moved to Naumburg in 1850, Franziska moved with her out of financial necessity, having decided not to return to her parental home. The difficult domestic arrangements, thinly papered over by the pet names and other signs of affection, continued well beyond Carl Ludwig's death, and Franziska accommodated herself to them. Perhaps the severe hairstyle with center parting and bun, which she always wore from her marriage onward, was a visible expression of her inhibited emotions. As a girl, she had followed fashion, at sixteen matching her hairstyle to the intricate pattern of Clara Schumann. By seventeen, she had changed the style to looped plaits. It is as though everything superficial, like fashion, froze for Franziska after the death of her husband. This does not mean that she remained bitter and unfulfilled: In Naumburg, she became part of genteel society, though her main social life revolved around the church. She never remarried, and her chaotic diaries—which are full of cookery hints and other snippets of gossip and casual information—give no indication why she did not. Elisabeth Nietzsche thus grew up in a home where the only male was her brother and the rules were set by her grandmother. The meals were cooked by her Aunt Auguste and the newspapers were read by the redoubtable Rosalie, who was also the most theologically minded member of the family (as distinct from merely pious). All Franziska could usefully do in the Röcken *ménage* was look after her children and sew.

In Naumburg, Franziska's living quarters—two small back rooms—were even more cramped and darker than her quarters had been in Röcken. It is an indication of the selfishness of the Nietzsche matriarchy that Franziska was expected to bring up her children under these conditions. Elisabeth later blamed her own poor eyesight and that of Fritz on their dark *Kinderzimmer:* "Our dark children's room in the old flat was really not hygienic and was definitely the cause of our bad myopia, my brother's as well as my own, even if a hereditary disposition for it was present."[3] But to the young Elisabeth, things must have looked very different. Petted by her grandmother who lived in the best rooms in the house and regaled her grandchildren with treats (though Franziska and the children were only ever there on sufferance—toys and Franziska's sewing table were banned), it must have dawned on Elisabeth that Franziska's status in the household was not very high. She probably never quite realized how much Franziska had to struggle, as she herself would inherit from various relatives. Franziska's income—a widow's subsistence grant and charitable donations from the princesses of Altenburg—was fairly meager. Franziska thus had no choice but to accept the charity of her

Figure 1. Franziska Nietzsche as a seventeen-year-old bride, 1843.

mother-in-law. Only after the death of Erdmuthe did she rent her own quarters finally, in 1858, moving into what was later to become known as no. 18 Weingarten, her home for nearly another forty years and a valuable base for her peripatetic children. Elisabeth was oblivious to the difficulties her mother had to face in bringing her children up. She resented being scolded as a chatterbox when others in the house were eager to listen to her. When she looked back on her childhood, she perceived her mother as overstrict in retrospect. It was irrelevant to her that her mother had merely been exerting herself to bring the children up as her husband would have wished. Elisabeth's pent-up fury at being constantly corrected by Franziska spilled out decades later in a number of thinly veiled negative comments in her books.

Forgive Us Our Sins

During the nineteenth century, German Christians, whether Protestant (Lutheran) or Catholic, were periodically exposed to fundamentalism. The reason for this is that a wave of religious revivalism had swept through Germany as a precursor to the revolution of 1848. Right-wing Protestant revivalism dubbed itself Pietism, though the term neo-Pietism should be used, since this movement had little to do with the inward-looking quietism of sects such as the *Herrenhuter* founded by Graf Zinzendorf in Saxony in 1772 and up to this point known as Pietists. Pietists developed their own rituals and vocabulary, in which the use of the word *child* acquired central importance. The true Pietist referred to himself or herself constantly as a child as a matter of deep religious principle, based on Christ's instruction: "Verily I say unto you: Except ye be converted, and become as little children, ye shall not enter into the kingdom of heaven."[4] Though the neo-Pietists claimed to base their beliefs firmly on the Bible and an inner search for faith, in reality there was something ostentatious about their readiness to confess to a multitude of sins, and their public exultation in conversion or *Erweckung* ("Awakening"). The fact that the new Pietism was popular among the Berlin aristocracy, from Friedrich Wilhelm IV down, gave it an air of superiority even without its missionary zeal to acquire converts, quite out of step with the original practice of Pietism. The Lutheranism that had prevailed hitherto was seen as sound and dubbed *Rationalismus* by its adherents and as lacking in evangelical fervor by those with a neo-Pietistic bent. Hence Adalbert Oehler's insistence that his grandfather was "free of Pietism, devoted to the rationalism of that time."[5]

Clearly, confusion has been caused from the mid-nineteenth century right up to the present day by the use of the term *Pietism* when neo-Pietism is meant. Lacking a colonial culture, Protestant revivalism in Germany did not necessarily insist upon the urgent need to "clothe the naked" in Africa, as was the case in Britain, for example. There, the hugely influential evangelical movement, not Catholicism, was the chief rival to the established Church of England. Its strength during the nineteenth century was such that it left an indelible impression on the architecture of Britain: The vast Sunday schools built beside Methodist and Baptist chapels, sometimes with dozens of classrooms, bear witness to the tremendous emphasis placed by these sects on providing Sunday school instruction for children. In the pit villages of Wales or the mill towns of northern England, this was all the education most children received during the Industrial Revolution. The slower pace of German industrialization meant that religious revivalism did not have the same social dimension, either at home or abroad. In its place, it took on aspects of a sanctimonious nationalism: Chauvinists increasingly used the term *deutsch* to designate something or someone morally good, as though no further qualification were needed.

Traditional Lutherans of the old school had little patience with the revivalist awakening, which helps to explain why Erdmuthe Nietzsche was perplexed by her new daughter-in-law. Franziska had a deep, unforced religious faith when she entered the Röcken household. She was not bigoted herself at that time, but it is fair to say that her husband was. As an archconservative, he was reactionary and monarchist to an extraordinary degree and had a natural affinity with the new Pietism, some of which rubbed off on his impressionable wife. He had friends in the movement from his student days but was too wary to confide his sympathy with the movement to his mother since, according to Elisabeth, Erdmuthe "could not get along with this obtrusive sanctimoniousness and confession of sins."[6] For her part, Franziska thought that a review of one's sins each day constituted piety, as did constant reference to the Bible. This was an ideology she found in Wilhelmine Oeynhausen's *Worte mütterlicher Liebe an meine Tochter* (Words of Motherly Love to My Daughter, 1835), which went into a second edition in 1844, the year of Nietzsche's birth (Franziska's copy of the second edition is found in Nietzsche's personal library). Subtitled "A Gift for Christian Maidens," which by 1844 Franziska manifestly was not, the book recommends the quarterly publications of the Basel Missions-Institut, which was the center point of European evangelicalism from its foundation in 1815: "In these publications you will find extremely interesting and up-to-date things on the geography and history of foreign parts and, what is of even more value, you will be strengthened in your faith at the same time."[7] The book also heavily stresses the importance of daily self-examination to an extent we would now criticize as intended to break the individual's will:

Remember today that you must:
1. Praise God.
2. Remember the mercy you have received.
3. Escape from Hell.
4. Save a soul.
5. Seek and give atonement.
6. Repent and turn away from sin.
7. Reach Heaven.
8. Believe in the Savior and copy his example.
9. Beg for mercy and a godly life in earnest prayer.
10. Kill the works of the flesh through the Spirit.
11. Be vigilant and sober.
12. Use time to the full.
13. Strengthen another in the faith.
14. Perform labors of love.
15. Fear the world and yet overcome it.
16. Yes, perhaps even expect death itself.
17. And that you will appear before judgment.[8]

We can see why Franziska placed such emphasis on confession and atonement, but as Elisabeth points out in *Das Leben Friedrich Nietzsche's,* her mother-in-law Erdmuthe thought very differently: "we used to rejoice over our virtues and those of other people, but now one just rejoices over one's sins and those of other people. The more sinful the better."[9] Eventually, as Nietzsche realized with increasing dismay, Franziska did move toward that type of stiff inflexibility evinced by the neo-Pietists and indeed any sect that believes it exclusively holds the key to salvation, rather like born-again fundamentalism today.

Clearly, the young Franziska's religious fervor was somewhat unconventional and unique to her. Through her focus on Holy Scripture as a continual reference point and her determination to be a humble child before God, not much separated her from the Pietist in the original sense of the term, for whom, as Claude Welch has pointed out, "Christianity was not doctrine but life,"[10] until the bigotry deplored by Nietzsche took hold. A Romantic theologian like Friedrich Schleiermacher, brought up in the Moravian brotherhood, would have understood her brand of piety. Yet her veneration of her dead husband's memory and conviction that his spirit was watching over his children are more akin to Catholicism than Protestantism, though Franziska herself was profoundly intolerant of Catholicism. A similar dichotomy can be detected in Bettine von Arnim's *Goethes Briefwechsel mit einem Kinde* (Goethe's Correspondence with a Child, 1835). Though Protestant, Bettine had absorbed a taste for Catholic ritual during the time she spent as a child at the convent in Fritzlar; later, though, she became a close friend of Schleiermacher when she lived in Berlin. She was therefore well versed in his liberal theology, which was so different from the neo-Pietism under discussion. Schleiermacher's cult of inwardness did not even insist on a person's belief in God. Bettine's reference to herself as a child in the title of her work is therefore highly loaded. Bettine deliberately used the trappings of Pietism to cloak her (largely invented) confessional account of her friendship with Johann Wolfgang von Goethe with a veneer of authenticity in a way that would be viewed as cleverly ironic today. There was no irony in Franziska's beliefs, however, a quirky amalgamation of Pietism and neo-Pietism. It is really no wonder that the firmly rationalist Erdmuthe looked askance at Franziska's unconventional brand of religious fervor.

The essence of the matter is that Elisabeth thought her mother overdid religion, though she regarded herself as a good Christian. As a young woman, Elisabeth dutifully attended church, sang in the choir (the "Naumburger Gesangverein"), and helped Aunt Rosalie with her efforts to fund African missionaries. Until she married in 1885, her home was with her mother in

Figure 2. Elisabeth Nietzsche as a girl, date un-
known.

Naumburg, though she was frequently away on visits to relatives, especially
her brother. She expressed shock when she realized the sacrilegious bent her
brother's religion was taking (first broadcast to the world with the publication in 1878 of *Menschliches, Allzumenschliches,* and their ways thereafter
began to part. Her increasingly megalomaniac tendencies as a mature woman
suggest that any true faith was only skin deep. Nevertheless, Elisabeth retained
the trappings of the believer. Like her nephew Adalbert Oehler, she never used
the word *Pietist* in its correct sense. Her frequent stress that the Oehler grandparents were not Pietists—as a covert disclaimer that they were responsible
for Franziska's intense and bigoted religiosity—begs the question of her own
father's clandestine neo-Pietism.

A Fabulous Childhood

The three-volume biography of Nietzsche written by Elisabeth Förster-Nietzsche which appeared between 1895 and 1904 under the title *Das Leben
Friedrich Nietzsche's* gives early examples of her propensity to fudge issues:

when an inconvenient fact is not embellished it is simply brushed aside. The first volume, which is the first major work Elisabeth wrote, is indeed largely a fable, as Franziska's comment on the text makes plain: "She's making things up to an extraordinary degree . . . for I lived through it all, too," she wrote to her nephew, Adalbert Oehler, on 23–24 June 1895.[11] Franziska was persona non grata with her daughter at that time for reasons connected with Elisabeth's demand that the royalties of Nietzsche's books should in future be paid to her, not Franziska. (The ensuing quarrel will be fully discussed in chapter 4.) Suffice it to say that since Elisabeth was conducting a veritable campaign against her mother at the time of writing the first volume of her book, she registered her anger with Franziska by scarcely mentioning her in it. The impression gained is that Franziska had a marginal role in Nietzsche's early years and that Erdmuthe virtually brought the children up. This was patently untrue, but this type of reinvention of the past would become standard in Elisabeth's writing. Not only did Franziska have to swallow the bitter pill that her daughter had deliberately set out to hurt her, she was also forced to accept the full extent of her daughter's capacity to fib. Franziska's nephew Adalbert Oehler, then coguardian with her of Nietzsche, was so dazzled by all his cousin Elisabeth did that he took her side against her mother in 1896 in their quarrel over who should have the rights to Nietzsche's works. In effect Franziska was ambushed by her daughter and her nephew. As though to salve his conscience, some time prior to 1940 Adalbert Oehler wrote a typewritten memoir entitled "Die Mutter von Friedrich Nietzsche: Lebensbild einer deutschen Mutter," which formed the basis for his book *Nietzsches Mutter* (1940).

In both the typewritten manuscript and the printed book, Oehler tried to suggest that Franziska and Elisabeth were always on excellent terms (even *after* the biography came out, as he specifically mentions in the manuscript, but expunges from the book). In the manuscript, he went on to concede that it was unfortunate that Franziska was mentioned so sparingly in the biography, suggesting rather lamely that as both grandmothers were dead when Elisabeth wrote her work, she probably found it easier to write about them than about her own mother, who was still alive. Oehler continued: "Her mother found the book 'wonderfully well written,' but she felt she had come off badly in it. She talked about this to relatives and friends, who agreed with her as they knew that the upbringing of the two children had almost entirely depended on her, and that she had constituted the central point in their cheerful and happy childhood. None of this emerged from the book."[12]

In *Nietzsches Mutter,* the whole question of Franziska's objections to her daughter's biography is omitted, no doubt because Oehler wished to please the National Socialists, for whom Elisabeth Förster-Nietzsche had become a useful icon: a self-sacrificing sister and, though not a mother in her own right, a mother figure whom Hitler could "borrow" for useful photo opportunities which projected the image of a caring son. This probably explains why, in *Nietzsches Mutter,* Oehler expands the typewritten manuscript to praise the heroic German Bernhard Förster, who gave up his post (actually he was dismissed!) for his political ideals: "What finally made the young pedagogue give up his post was a cause for which he had become active, but with which he was far too much ahead of his time: anti-Semitism."[13]

Elisabeth begins *Das Leben Friedrich Nietzsche's* by lauding her father Carl Ludwig's brilliant academic career, a career that prompted his posting to Röcken as pastor, and soon we are abruptly told that his first son was born on 15 October 1844—without there having been any mention yet of his marriage to Franziska in 1843. Elisabeth hurries on with her narrative, briefly mentioning herself and Josef as Nietzsche's siblings before asserting that her father died as a result of a fall and not *Gehirnerweichung* (softening of the brain—a term commonly used in the nineteenth century for a variety of degenerative brain diseases). She insists that his death was caused by injuries sustained upon returning home in August 1848, when he "stumbled and fell backward down seven stone steps onto the paved yard."[14] She had every reason to insist on this story, since the diagnosis which the doctors had pronounced as the cause of Carl Ludwig's death seemed to point to a hereditary factor that might plausibly be linked to Nietzsche's own mental collapse in 1889. Although the fall might well have precipitated Pastor Nietzsche's death, Elisabeth clearly wished to hush speculation about mental illness in the family and, in fact, one of her chief objects in writing the book—written, we should recall, to show Franziska née Oehler just who was boss—was to reveal the "real" Nietzsche family in the best light possible.

Much to the detriment of her mother, whose significance for Nietzsche is passed over in *Das Leben Friedrich Nietzsche's,* Elisabeth describes her grandmother Erdmuthe as the sweetest and devoutest person imaginable, to whom Nietzsche was totally devoted, though it was probably the case that Elisabeth rather than Nietzsche doted on her grandmother. Erdmuthe's tales of her time spent in Weimar with her first husband impressed Elisabeth and could have influenced the latter's choice to settle in Weimar in 1896, a year after the publication of the first volume of *Das Leben Friedrich Nietzsche's.* The book continues in a quasi-chronological progression, devoting many pages to the childish games played by Nietzsche and Lisbeth, as he called his little sister. The friendships with Gustav Pinder and Wilhelm Krug are also described, before the book settles down into a straightforward biography of Nietzsche's schooldays at Schulpforta and his student years. Much of the text consists of quotations from Nietzsche's letters and works, a technique Elisabeth habitually used. She continually rehashed material she had already printed for new publications.

It is instructive to compare Elisabeth's 1895 text with the revised version she wrote in 1912, *Der junge Nietzsche,* which deals with Nietzsche's biography in shortened form up to the breach with Wagner in 1876. (The companion volume dealing with his later life and works, *Der einsame Nietzsche,* appeared in 1913.) In *Das Leben Friedrich Nietzsche's,* Elisabeth appears to give some credence to the myth, peddled by Nietzsche himself, that the Nietzsches were originally of aristocratic Polish extraction. By the time she wrote *Der junge Nietzsche,* Elisabeth was at pains to show Nietzsche as a "true German," and she therefore distances herself from the story; stating that all the documents have been lost: "My brother often mentions his Polish descent, for which even latterly he initiated inquiries with good results. I myself know nothing definite about it, because some of my brother's papers became lost after he fell ill in Turin."[15]

Der junge Nietzsche is also very different in its handling of Franziska. With the passage of time, Elisabeth no doubt thought it politic to speak more generously of her mother. In *Der junge Nietzsche* she does, it is true, introduce Erdmuthe first because she is dealing chronologically with the family forbears, but she soon moves on to a rather cloying characterization of her mother as a "fair maiden." Even then, she cannot resist mentioning that Franziska had only recently given up playing with her dolls when she met her future husband: "In spring 1843 our father met our mother, who had just turned seventeen and a year previously had still been secretly playing with her dolls. . . . When our father came to visit our grandparents that spring with an elderly colleague, godfather to Franziska, the latter, who was fast becoming a fair maiden, came in with a spray of carnations to ask her elderly godfather for advice on what she had to do to make it come up to the standard of his blooms."[16] (The Freudian implications of this little scene in which a girl, ripe for deflowering, symbolically holds a sprig of flowers, will not be gone into here.)

In *Der junge Nietzsche* Elisabeth admits, with some guile, that Franziska had in later life spoken about how much she had suffered as a bride from the repressive atmosphere produced by the female Nietzsche triumvirate in Röcken, Rosalie in particular: "Our dear mother later vehemently denied that it had been at all easy for her to get used to her new living conditions. She was particularly provoked to argument by lectures from her sister-in-law, that is, to us children, the much-loved Aunt Rosalie."[17] Elisabeth never seems to be able to give her mother wholehearted credit for anything—even here, she seems to insinuate that there was nothing wrong with Rosalie, as she and Fritz were so fond of her. Decades later, in *Friedrich Nietzsche und die Frauen seiner Zeit* (1935), Elisabeth repeats more forcefully the apparently charitable observation that Franziska was put under pressure by the stiff formality of the Röcken regime, though we are now told that instead of the information coming from Franziska, she herself never spoke on the subject. Again, Elisabeth hedges her bets by stressing that it never occurred to her that anyone might find her wonderful grandmother difficult: "As our grandmother Nietzsche was so uncommonly popular, we thought it must be happiness itself to live with her. Our dear mother never said what she felt about that, but as she was often away, and was often invited out, especially since we were well looked after by our grandmother and aunts, I think she might well have felt under a certain amount of pressure, for she had to stem her own charming, kind personality and lively temperament somewhat in the presence of the others in the house."[18]

There is also a hint here that Franziska often left the children in order to go on trips alone, which was certainly not the case. At least, in this late text published in the year of her own death, Elisabeth is on her best behavior where Franziska is concerned, declaring "the adornment of our home was our very pretty and much-loved young mother."[19] Such economies with the truth may seem small in themselves, but it must be remembered that they shocked Elisabeth's mother, who died in 1897, two years after the publication of *Das Leben Friedrich Nietzsche's.* They also show that if Elisabeth could be so inaccurate about biographical details, she really was the most unsuitable person to write about Nietzsche's philosophy, the ambiguities of which defy a casual approach, to say nothing of her hubris in bringing out a work, *Der Wille zur Macht,* composed from his discarded notes.

If Elisabeth spoke about her mother more in *Der junge Nietzsche,* the additions often betray her opinion that Franziska was too strict. In *Das Leben Friedrich Nietzsche's* we read: "My brother and I were, during the six years 1850–1856, the recipients of a program of general and special education, but in the main we were left to the care of our dear mother."[20] In *Der junge Nietzsche,* the passage is repeated verbatim with a revealing addition (indicated with brackets): "left to the care of our dear mother, [who brought us up with the same Spartan strictness and simplicity that was the custom at the time, and especially in her own family.]"[21] By stressing Franziska's strictness even in a passage where she is ostensibly *praising* her mother, Elisabeth immediately snatches back most of the credit she has just given to Franziska.

In sum, Erdmuthe Nietzsche ruled the roost and dispensed favors in the home in which Elisabeth grew up. It is hard to banish the suspicion that in her leniency toward her grandchildren, Erdmuthe Nietzsche, who had been extremely strict with her own children, deliberately marginalized her daughter-in-law. The death of Erdmuthe in 1856 was clearly a seismic event for Franziska and her two children. Elisabeth had lost someone by whom she felt understood, whereas Franziska had been liberated from the necessity of sharing her home with her mother-in-law. She now parted company with Rosalie, renting rooms in the house of a pastor's widow whom she knew. In *Das Leben Friedrich Nietzsche's,* determined to talk about anything rather than her mother, Elisabeth relates that the house had a wonderful garden in which she and her brother had endless fun. Seldom does she write so lyrically about any of her experiences:

> Fritz and I lived in the garden from early till late, making the swing fly into the highest treetops; we played the loveliest games, ate and drank and studied in the deep shade of the bushes, and told each other horror stories at dusk. I still have particularly tender memories of two tree trunks that stood by the wall and that had grown together in such a way as to provide a little nest in the interior. Often Fritz occupied one nest and I occupied the other. When Fritz told stories and I just heard his voice without seeing any part of him, it created a wonderfully dreamlike and mysterious atmosphere.[22]

Elisabeth and Fritz were clearly not grieving overmuch for their grandmother at this point! In *Der junge Nietzsche,* Elisabeth repeats the passage about the fun in the garden almost verbatim up to "horror stories," after which the rest is axed to make room for a passage informing the reader that Franziska thought it was high time she had her own *ménage:* "Aunt Rosalie took a flat for herself, as our dear mother absolutely insisted that now at last, in her thirtieth year, she would be quite independent and would remove herself from the very well intentioned tutelage of her eldest sister-in-law. We children were very sorry that Aunt Rosalie no longer lived with us, as there was great affection between her and us."[23] Even here, one detects a grudging tone, yet it was demonstrably good for the three of them that Franziska could at last provide her family with its own home. Elisabeth concedes this in *Friedrich Nietzsche und die Frauen seiner Zeit:* "Perhaps our dear mother's own personality came into its own only when, after the death of our grandmother Nietzsche, we moved into the house of a friend of our mother's. The house was surrounded by a gorgeous big old-fashioned garden. I recall with delight how happy and cheerful we all were then, and in sum, we looked on our dear mother, who, as already mentioned, was very young, more as a dearly loved, if severe, older sister, who understood what we youngsters felt and participated in our activities."[24] It took Elisabeth four decades to acknowledge that her mother, far from being the marginalized figure encountered fleetingly in *Das Leben Friedrich Nietzsche's*, actually *mattered*.

Learning to Be a Lady

Until the formation of the Reich in 1871, after which certain reforms were brought in to lengthen a girl's schooling and broaden the curriculum for girls, even the brightest girl would have to leave school after she had been confirmed, which was usually when she was fourteen. At that age Louise Otto-Peters, who went on to found German feminism, pleaded successfully with her parents to allow her to delay her confirmation so that she could stay at school until she was fifteen, but this was a very great exception. There were no Gymnasien for girls until the end of the century at the earliest, and universities had the same stringent requirements then as now. To pursue higher education, boys took the *Abitur* (high school exit examination) after attending school for a certain number of years. Girls' schooling, being shorter, precluded them from taking the *Abitur*. Even if the universities would let women attend lectures as *Hörerinnen* as Elisabeth did in Leipzig at Nietzsche's suggestion, women could not sit for university qualifications. Toward the end of the century, when a girl's compulsory schooling had been lengthened by two years, a certain number of women were having private tuition for the *Abitur* and studying in foreign universities that admitted women, Zurich being a very popular choice for German women because there was no language barrier. As we shall see in relation to Elisabeth's school exercises, reading, writing, and arithmetic, as well as religion, made up most of the curriculum. When they left school, girls were expected to perfect their sewing and, if they were lucky, they might have private lessons in playing the piano and painting.

Everything in a respectable middle-class girl's education was geared to keeping her expectations within the horizon of imminent marriage. A typical text on girl's education when Elisabeth was of school age was *Die Erziehung der Mädchen* (Education for Girls) by the evangelically Lutheran Karl von Raumer (1853). This little book was written as a guide for mothers of daughters primarily to persuade them of the advantages of teaching girls at home rather than sending them to school: "School instruction is subordinate to domestic instruction in that it is not interrupted by labors of love, since lessons, the essence of instruction, last for several consecutive hours—that is not suitable for girls."[25]

Von Raumer has critical words for society ladies who are too busy attending tea parties and soirées to educate their children. Little girls should be encouraged to help their mothers in the home, and when mature (i.e., after confirmation) they should become fully involved in helping in the house. Von Raumer has no objection to their further acquisition of cultural finesse, since that embellishes the home, but he draws the line at academic study for the older girl: "Education for girls should never degenerate to include science, otherwise it ceases to be a delicate, feminine education. A girl cannot and should not immerse herself in anything scientific with the kind of hard-headed, manly tenacity that makes her oblivious to everything else. Only a completely unfeminine girl could strive to emulate man's thoroughness in science, and her efforts would be in vain because she lacks man's strength and talent."[26]

In short, the book gave a conventional outline of a woman's role as future housewife and mother, laying great emphasis on "religiös-sittliche Bildung" (religious and moral instruction), a long section of the book comprising forty-two pages, compared to the "Unterricht" (lessons) section of sixty pages. Von Raumer's book was really swimming against the tide, as other books on education that appeared a little later, such as Gotthold Kreyenberg's *Mädchenerziehung und Frauenleben in Aus- und Inlande* (Girls' Education and Women's Lives at Home and Abroad, 1872), took it for granted that girls would attend school up to confirmation: "Precisely in school, rather than in the narrow confines of the home, is the best instruction to be found."[27]

It is disappointing but understandable that there were few texts by women on women's education. Betty Gleim's *Erziehung und Unterricht des weiblichen Geschlechts* (Education and Instruction for the Female Sex, 1810) is something of an exception. In her call for women to prepare themselves for work outside the home—though she meant work as nursemaids and the like rather than as qualified professionals—she argued that education had to be goal-oriented and "dynamic yet formal,"[28] and in this respect she was far ahead of her time. In other respects, such as her religious approach to her topic and her belief that women were by their nature (and moral sensibility) different from men, she was very much of her time: "Furthermore, woman has a greater capacity to endure, persevere, renounce than man, whose strength lies in doing and producing. Man's predominant strength lies in action, woman's lies in being. But as action is determined by being and not the reverse . . . , it follows that woman is not at all inferior to man in terms of moral value, in fact, her nature is capable of a higher and more complete development than that of man."[29] Gleim's view is closely echoed in the entry for "Frauen" in the ten-volume *Damen-Conversations-Lexikon* (1834–38) edited by Carl Herloßsohn, where the pious tone is also present:

Woman *complements* man; the unification of the two is the definitive example of divinity in man. He is the elm, she is the vine; he strives upward, full of strength and marrow, casting broad shadows; she is delicate, scented, with an inner glow, easy to bend but full of a glorious flame, she brings forth fruit and inspires: elm and vine only make a picture together, not as separate entities. . . . If man possesses greater creative power, woman has more imagination, is more contemplative; if man is more prepared to speculate, woman tends to idealize; if man is levelheaded in repose, woman is decisive in danger. He thinks before he feels, she feels before she considers.[30]

Now it will have become patently obvious to the reader that these descriptions of woman's character have almost no rapport with Elisabeth Nietzsche's later difficult personality. She was not spoiled by Franziska, nor was it necessarily the treats given to her by her grandmother and aunts that encouraged her to be selfish and (later) extravagant. It was more the fact that the Nietzsche matriarchy undermined Franziska's mothering that "spoiled" Elisabeth. The only way for Elisabeth to have a truly secure upbringing was for Franziska to be happy and relaxed. This was never going to happen while she shared a house with three difficult women who fundamentally resented her presence. No doubt they would have made life difficult for any wife Carl Ludwig had brought home. It is all the more to Franziska's credit that she made sure that both her children had the very best education she could provide at that time. Thus, in spite of Elisabeth's later attempt to give the world the impression that Erdmuthe Nietzsche was more important for herself and her brother than their own mother, the young widow Franziska devoted herself to bringing up her son and daughter with single-minded determination. She worried about such things as whether and how much she ought to read to them and refused to listen to her own father's suggestion for a school for Fritz. It turned out that she was quite correct to do so, as he did well at Naumburg's elementary school for boys and spent a few years at a private school before proceeding to the *Domgymnasium* (cathedral high school) where his talent was recognized. In October 1858, having been awarded a scholarship, he became a pupil at the prestigious Schulpforta, a boarding school a short distance from Naumburg.

Franziska wanted to do the best for her daughter, too. Her friend Mme. Laubscher advised her to send Lieschen to Fräulein von Paraski's school for young ladies in Naumburg, which she then duly did. While Fritz set about reading Greek and Latin texts in the original, Elisabeth received an education which demanded infinitely less of her good brain. The syllabus consisted of German, French, history, geography, biology (*Naturkunde*), arithmetic, drawing, and singing. There was considerable accent on good conduct. Elisabeth soon became adept at French, and her talent in the other subjects was recognized, too; she often received praise. Great stress was laid on handwriting, and Elisabeth exerted herself to become proficient, though she never came near to Franziska's neatness. Spelling mistakes had to be written out in a "Correction Book," and work was practiced in a rough book before the fair copy was made in the neat book. One exercise book from 1857 has a certificate "For immaculate conduct" pasted to the front and one giving "Commendation of Good Progress" pasted to the back. A large number of these exercise books are stored in the Goethe-Schiller Archive in Weimar, so that we can see, for example, that while Nietzsche grappled with the classics, Elisabeth was asked to write essays with such inane titles as "May This Year" or "My Methods of Saving Time."[31] In her school reports, Elisabeth usually had the comment "Good" for every subject, although in her earliest school report from the *Volksschule* in 1854, the pastor's daughter received her worst grade, "satisfactory," for scripture.[32]

The exercise books are a fascinating source for information on women's education in the mid-nineteenth century, much better than all the dry books on theory. It is also interesting that in spite of the pious precepts of academic pedagogues, Elisabeth's exercise books indicate that there was not a religious slant on *everything* the girls were asked to learn: although one way of teaching handwriting was to make the children write out pious sayings, poems on a variety of topics were also deemed suitably instructive material for copying out. In one exercise book, the last she used at Madame Paraski's, the last few pages contain a neat copy of a poem ("Friendship"), after which Elisabeth has added for good measure, as the book was now full, "*Finis coronat opus!!!*" ["the end crowns the work"].[33] Her teacher's comment was: "Very nice." Clearly neither the poem, nor the teacher, nor indeed the school could quite match up to Elisabeth, but she was obviously happy there, since on the very last page of the same book she has written with a flourish: "Farewell then, you dear school!" Elisabeth left school in 1861.

The Goethe-Schiller Archive also possesses a number of Elisabeth's diaries, invariably started with every good intention, only to be abandoned. Unlike Franziska's diaries, the entries are not so much chaotic as sporadic. A diary which starts in 1856 has, after a few pages, a dried leaf sewn into it with the inscription that it was picked on 30 June 1858! A new attempt to rekindle interest in keeping a diary frequently merited a new book. In one special book with a hard cover and (broken) lock, which she entitled "Aus meinem Leben" (From My Life) on the flyleaf, Elisabeth provides invaluable information about her confirmation. On the first page, dated 27 December 1860, we read: "I am now only 14½ years old and naturally I still go to school, and am therefore a prospective teenager. At Easter I shall be confirmed, and from then on I want to write [in the diary] whenever I feel the urge."[34] Incidentally, the photograph taken to mark her confirmation depicts Elisabeth as anything but a teenager: the extremely décolletée fashion seeming particularly out of place in the context of a young girl's celebration of a religious rite. It is interesting to note that Nietzsche was also confirmed (later than was usual) at Easter 1861 at Schulpforta. Elisabeth remained at school in the "Selecta" class (for final-year pupils) until she was confirmed. The next entry on the second page of this "special" book is dated 11 April 1861, and Elisabeth prefaces her remarks with: "A good deal of time has elapsed!" With obvious regret she continues: "I have finished my last term at school. . . . Oh, now I no longer attend the school I love so much, oh so much."[35] But her Aunt Sidonia had been on a short visit and Elisabeth speaks enthusiastically about her little cousins. Several pages later, in an entry written in Dresden and dated 1 April 1862, Elisabeth confesses her guilt at not keeping up with her diary, especially as so many exciting things had been happening to her.

When Elisabeth went to finishing school in Dresden for six months, beginning in February 1862, she was taught French and some English. Not much could be achieved in the allotted period, which contained a good deal of social activity as well as academic instruction. The language instruction seems to have consisted largely in copying things out, but Elisabeth was also set simple essays and was asked to compose letters. She also had to translate from German into French and English, a pedagogic practice now frowned on for all but the most competent. The teachers in Dresden set some fairly stringent tasks for their charges. For instance, Elisabeth was given Aesop's fable "The Lion and the Mouse" to translate into English, a tale in which a lion spares a mouse and is in turn saved by the mouse when caught in a net (Elisabeth translates this as "filet"), as the mouse is able to gnaw through the net. At the end of the translation, Elisabeth had to explain not only that "this fable is an example of goodness for goodness" (the teacher corrected "goodness" to "kindness"),[36] she then had to suggest how the story might be told if it was "wickedness for wickedness," "noblety [corrected to nobleness] and generosity for wickedness" or, alternatively, "ingratitude for noblety [*sic*]." This was asking quite a lot, but Elisabeth rose to the challenge. In her proposed version to illustrate the last option, instead of the lion sparing the mouse, he tries to eat it but is interrupted by a stone falling on his head.

Though Elisabeth's efforts in English were more valiant than accurate, this is not true of her French, where her exercise books show she made great progress. Asked to write a letter, she chose to write to her brother (no surprises there!) describing a trip to a château with her school friends: "C'était très dommage que vous n'étiez pas avec nous. Mais alors adieu mon chère [*sic*] frère! Ayez la bonté de m'écrire bien tôt, votre affectionnée soeur."[37] (What a shame you were not with us. Farewell then, my dear brother. Please write back soon, Your affectionate sister.) It is notable that there are just two mistakes here, the second merely the incorrect order of the last two words. The formal *vous* was no doubt insisted upon by the teacher as a mark of good form. Elisabeth also admonished her brother in this letter for not writing to her: "j'étais très fâchée" (I was very cross). This is a refrain in Elisabeth's letters, and although she was having to make them up, it indicates that she was often cross and did not try to hide it. As a young woman, Elisabeth kept up with her acquisition of language skills. In Basel, when not looking after Fritz, she tried to learn Italian (the exercise book is also still extant) and in 1879, she went to Switzerland to perfect her French with several friends from Naumburg.

Though most readers will deplore the state of girls' education a century and a half ago as described above, Elisabeth gave no outward sign of frustration. Aunt Rosalie was, by contrast, overtly neurotic at being held back from intellectual pursuits. She read the newspaper and was something of a theologian, though being a woman she had no outlet for her intellectual interests. Elisabeth had no obvious ambition beyond pleasing her teachers, and of course, her brother. In Dresden, the novelty of being in a *pension* was colossal. In her diary "Aus meinem Leben," four pages are devoted to a description of Herr von Oettinger's *pension* and her activities in Dresden. Nietzsche hoped that finishing school would make Elisabeth improve her handwriting, which was deteriorating to a scribble. He also had high hopes that his sister would be taught to moderate her flowery writing style during her spell at finishing school, but these hopes were not very realistic, as her style would remain incorrigibly affected to the last: "If only she could learn to write better! And when she narrates something, she must leave out all the 'ahs' and 'ohs' 'you won't believe how lovely, how wonderful, how enchanting etc it was.'"[38] Elisabeth was lucky in that she had a clever older brother who took an interest in her education. He made it his business to point his sister in the right direction in her choice of reading matter. The result of his tutelage, though not intended, was that she could bluff her way in any learned society.

From today's perspective, the restricted syllabus fed to girls under the name of education during the nineteenth century was little short of a scandal. Certain subjects such as the sciences were barely taught at all. What one can say with certainty is that Elisabeth was bright and eager to learn but was taught very little, simply because she had been born a girl. Her education was a complete flop if judged by the criteria of the time, since it certainly did not prepare her to be a demure young lady who would marry young and devote

Figure 3. Friedrich Nietzsche as a student, 1862–63.

herself to rearing a family. It was a flop if judged by more modern criteria, too, because she was certainly at least a potential candidate for further education. On the other hand, though she showed certain gifts, there is no early evidence of the creative flair we see in her novella "Coffee-Party Gossip about Nora." Her school essays lapse very quickly into descriptions of wilting flowers and falling leaves, as though she could not think of anything more original to say. To be fair to her, when she did refer to Greek heroes and similar cultural material gleaned from her brother, Nietzsche told her not to put such topics into her essays. Perhaps he thought that such references would seem obviously cribbed, but the main reason was that they were not ladylike. And being a lady was ultimately the young Elisabeth's burning ambition.

Fritz and the Llama

Elisabeth was devastated when she learned that Nietzsche was going to attend Schulpforta. She was staying with her grandparents in Pobles at the time.

Her grandfather broke the news to her and told her to be brave, giving her a book to read to comfort her. It is possible that this was a natural history book with a description of the llama, because within the context of her inconsolable grief over the news that Fritz was leaving home, she tells us in *Das Leben Friedrich Nietzsche's*: "I, poor llama, felt ill used by fate, refused to take nourishment and lay down in the dust in order to die."[39] In *Der junge Nietzsche,* Elisabeth informs readers in the following passage that the nickname came from a natural history book: "The llama is a remarkable animal: it carries the heaviest burdens of its own free will, but if compelled or badly treated, it refuses to take nourishment and lies down in the dust in order to die."[40] The above description of the llama is *not* taken from Fritz Schoedler's *Buch der Natur* (Book of Nature, 1840) as has commonly been supposed: Klaus Goch writes: "The source for the description of the llama was Fr. Schoedler's *Buch der Natur,* which she and her brother read together."[41] Though everyone is agreed that "Lama" (the spelling in German) was a fitting nickname for Nietzsche's stubborn sister, Schoedler says nothing about the llama lying in the dust to die, but he does highlight another habit of the animal, that of spitting food in its enemy's face:

> It [the camel] is encouraged to great feats less by blows and ill-treatment than by being spoken to by the handler; song and music are said to have a particularly encouraging effect on it. In contrast to the voices in praise of the camel there is the account of one good observer who, on his travels in the desert, found the camel to be a most disgusting beast because of its stubborn nature, foul smell, and ugly voice. The camels in Peru, namely the llama (Auchenis lama) [Schoedler at this point refers to figure 98, given here as figure 4] are smaller and lack the hump, the size of a stag, brown, and tamed as house pets or beasts of burdens. . . . It is noteworthy that as a method of defense, the llama spews its spittle, mixed with half-digested food, at its enemy.[42]

Possibly something from another book, such as *Kleine Naturgeschichte für Schul- und Selbstunterricht* (A Brief Natural History for School- and Self-Tuition, 1848) by Dr. Harald Othmar Lenz, remained in Elisabeth's memory, though the work is neither in her library nor that of Nietzsche. Lenz describes the camel's refusal to carry too heavy a load: "If it (the camel) finds it too heavy, it shrieks lamentably and no force can make it stand up."[43]

In the first volume of *Das Leben Friedrich Nietzsche's,* Elisabeth printed a letter from Nietzsche to her in which the word *Lama* is encoded. During Nietzsche's summer vacation in Plauen in 1863 he visited Kirchberg, which he had visited once before with Elisabeth when they were still children. Elisabeth prints the whole letter from Nietzsche, dated 4 August 1863, and gives the full

Fig. 98.

Figure 4. "The Llama," from Schoedler's *Buch der Natur,* first published in 1840.

anecdote, but the point is that in his letter, Nietzsche asks Elisabeth in parenthesis if she remembers the former visit by saying, "can you recall it, my . . . ?"[44] Elisabeth explains, also in parenthesis: "the four dots were supposed to be 'Lama'; Fritz was making a tactful reference to the nickname as I could not stand it at the time."[45] The original letter contains only *three* dots, not four.[46] However, Elisabeth is right to stress that at this period, Nietzsche's written references to her as Lama are sparing. In his letters to his sister as a girl and young woman, he invariably addressed her as "Dear Lisbeth," an exception being the rather good Italian joke in his letter from Basel of 29 November 1869: "Cara Mamma, cara Lamma,"[47] his euphoric mood explained by the prospect of his spending that Christmas with the Wagners at Triebschen.

In 1876 Nietzsche acquired, and annotated in his usual style (pencil marks in the margin), Schoedler's *Buch der Natur,* which had appeared in the twentieth edition in 1875. This could well have refreshed his interest in his nickname for his sister. On 28 July 1876, Nietzsche, newly arrived in Bayreuth and looking forward to Elisabeth's arrival there to join him, ended his letter: "Farewell my good Lisbeth, giddy up, fine Lama!"[48] Illness soon forced him to decamp without seeing Elisabeth, leaving her to deal with the unused tickets for *Der Ring des Nibelungen.* On 4 September 1876, he wrote a note to Elisabeth to thank her for "rescuing him," once again using the nickname: "Many thanks to the good L.A.M.A. for her long and interesting letter from B[ayreuth]."[49] Thereafter he referred to his sister as Lama more frequently within his letters, probably because she no longer objected, and on 14 March 1879 he began his letter with "Beloved Lama,"[50] but it was not until mid-July 1883, when he had made a half-peace with his sister after the Lou-fiasco in 1882, that he started to address his letters to her as "My dear Lama" regularly. From then on, this became Nietzsche's characteristic form of address in his letters to Elisabeth, and we can assume that he registered a level of censure thereby. Though Elisabeth, in *Das Leben Friedrich Nietzsche's* of 1895, is clear on the fact that she did not like this nickname as a girl, in *Der junge Nietzsche* of 1912 she clouds the issue by saying that she loved Fritz to call her by the pet name Lama. This is a pertinent reminder that one can never take a quotation from the pen of Elisabeth Förster-Nietzsche at face value. All her comments and quotations have to be checked against the authoritative sources for authenticity. Once she took control of Nietzsche's posthumous writing, she thought nothing of inventing forged documents to support her version of the unclouded relationship she had enjoyed with her brother.

Because of Elisabeth's relaxed attitude to learning and—later—the strategic distance she kept between herself and the campaign for women's rights (discussed in chapter 5), it is impossible to gauge just how much she resented the fact that her brother had received an excellent education while she was given the mediocre education considered fitting for a young lady of the period. She laughs off the fact that the "Quintaner" (eleven-year-old student) Nietzsche, having gained a place at the *Domgymnasium* in 1854, looked down on her as a "little girl": "I still remember very well that my brother seemed to me to be someone quite splendid."[51] She excuses him by explaining that he was big for his age while she was "small and delicate"—as though that were really relevant, when everyone can understand that a "Quintaner" usually tries to keep little sisters at a distance. In this, Nietzsche was not very successful, for if Franziska idolized him, so too did Elisabeth. From being a small child she had looked up to him almost as a substitute father figure as well as a brother—without the strictness of a father. She relied on his support against Franziska in any conflict. As we have seen, it was as hard for her when he decamped to Schulpforta as it was for Franziska—Nietzsche, too, had terrible qualms about leaving his much-loved home, and his letters were pounced upon with an almost unnatural interest. These letters reveal that although Nietzsche needed the closeness of his mother and sister, their efforts to exert control from a distance were often extreme. For example, Franziska sent him a list of things he was to wear for best and second-best occasions and told him to study it regularly so that he did not forget anything, while Elisabeth reacted jealously to his first stirring of interest in a girl (Anna Redtel, the sister of one of his friends), as though it were a personal slight.

Whenever he could, Nietzsche hurried home to Naumburg. When Elisabeth attended finishing school in Dresden, Nietzsche did not just write letters to his mother expressing the hope that Lisbeth would benefit from her stay there, he paid her a flying visit during his own vacation just before Easter. He continued to write her affectionate letters while she remained in Dresden and complained that she did not write home often enough. To the envy of her friends, he sent her his own musical compositions, saying that he looked forward to hearing her play them on her return. When they were all together again for Christmas 1862, Franziska insisted that Fritz should write verses as part of the *Bescherung* (the giving of gifts); Fritz duly wrote an affectionate poem "An die Schwester" (To My Sister). It is fair to say that during his childhood, Friedrich Nietzsche loved his home almost too much, and during her childhood, Elisabeth loved her brother almost too much. Nietzsche does not appear to have been spoiled, but he was allowed to act like a little professor well beyond his years. This encouraged a certain propensity for solitude in him that was not necessarily in his best interest. He did not write voluminous biographies of his family, as did his adoring sister in her later life, but as we have seen, what he did write during his childhood manifests his heartfelt affection for his little sister.

Nobody could have foreseen that this pert and precocious girl would turn into a writer capable of forgery and other forms of manipulation. This "will to power" only asserted itself in her personality much later, from about 1878 onward, when the relationship between brother and sister had begun to change, something that indicates that Elisabeth's subsequent willfulness could have been exacerbated because she felt cheated out of the security that her brother's love and support had provided up to that point. As though to convince herself that Nietzsche had always loved her, Elisabeth spent the latter half of her life writing about the past. When she revised and shortened *Das Leben Friedrich Nietzsche's* into *Der junge Nietzsche* and *Der einsame Nietzsche,* she went over very much the same material, adding a paragraph here and cutting a page there. One could almost say that she constantly plagiarized herself—it is as though she only ever wrote one work, the life story of her brother. When she purported to offer a critique of his thought, this invariably consisted of long quotations from the work in question. Nietzsche's criticism of her "ahs and ohs" was extremely pertinent, as she never learned to write without a certain affectation, as we see in her novella "Coffee-Party Gossip about Nora." Her whole manner of thinking gradually left behind the desire to please others that characterized her early years, to be replaced by ruthless and headstrong traits. There is no guarantee that an excellent education would have prevented her from some of the excesses of her later life, such as her support for her husband's anti-Semitism, and, in her old age, her admiration for the Fascists Mussolini and Hitler. Furthermore, as we shall see repeatedly, expediency always won over moral position in Elisabeth's scale of values. But what would she have been like if she, like her brother, had received an education that truly taught her to think for herself?

2 Fräulein Nietzsche

There is a huge gap in the literature on Elisabeth Nietzsche between the years 1864 and 1869, from the age of eighteen to twenty-three. Her mother had given birth to three children, lost one of them, and was widowed during that time span of her own life. In contrast, Elisabeth had fewer responsibilities. She was able to perfect her pencil drawing technique, at which she became proficient, and continue with her language study when social engagements and other duties permitted. One can, however, view this apparently pleasant lifestyle as part of the enforced impoverishment of the life of a young, unmarried woman in the nineteenth century, for whom most careers were barred. Some of Elisabeth's drawings of 1862–63 are dated, so that we can ascertain that it could take her four days to finish a piece—no doubt with many interruptions. Sometimes, as in a very handsome drawing of flowers (figure 5), she did not actually finish the work. Others are so good that if they were not very clearly in Elisabeth's private sketchbook one would doubt their authenticity. The carefully sketched landscape with church (figure 6) shows talent, as does the drawing of the coffee jug (figure 7), though here the pencil strokes are rather thick, and as the work took several days (she dates it rather quaintly 24 April, 25 April, 1 May, 29 May 1863), Elisabeth was obviously not very inspired by the subject matter, though she was very fond of the real thing—a coffee party, or *Kaffeeklatsch*.

As her novella "Coffee-Party Gossip about Nora" shows, Elisabeth was a good observer of small-town attitudes and manners. If she was better than average at drawing and, with time and effort, could perhaps have been more than a dilettante, the same is undoubtedly true of her creative writing, though her poems, which nearly always consisted of humorous variations on the

Knittelvers (tetrameter couplets) made no claims to literary merit. In the following poem, the lines do not scan and the central thread is provided by that most hackneyed of metaphors, the sunbeam, but she is very good at debunking rhyme itself—she uses an anarchic rhyming scheme in the full knowledge that Nietzsche, an expert in these matters, would be amused. Written on 20 December 1864 as a Christmas present for Fritz when he was a student in Bonn, the poem sets out to match the wit of Fritz's short poem "An die Schwester," written for Elisabeth at Christmas 1862, and can even be said to *outwit* Nietzsche by poking fun at his student life. Elisabeth lists the things Nietzsche spends time on before adding the study of philology to the list: theology, for which he was still officially inscribed until he changed his course to philology at Easter 1865, is not even mentioned. Nietzsche is teased as a wastrel who stays in bed all morning, getting up at midday to fritter the rest of the day away.

Figure 5. Sketch of flowers by Elisabeth Nietzsche, ca. 1862–63.

Figure 6. Sketch of landscape with church by Elisabeth Nietzsche, ca. 1862–63.

Figure 7. Sketch of coffee jug by Elisabeth Nietzsche, 1863.

Es war ein schöner Morgen am Rhein!	*It was a lovely morning on the Rhine!*
Es tanzte lustig der Sonnenschein	In merry dance, the sun was shining
Auf wogenden kräuselnden Wellen,	On the crinkled waves a-billowed,
Die Sonnenstrahlen flogen umher	Rays of sunlight flew all round
Und wo ein Herz war trüb und schwer,	And if a gloomy heart was found
Da suchten sie's zu erhellen.—	They tried to make it lighter.—
Ein Sonnenstrahl tanzt ganz allein	A lonely ray of sunshine, dancing
Auf ganz besondern Stoecken	Singles out a certain room,
Zu einem Fenster lugt er hinein	Through a window comes a-glancing
So an der Bonnstraßenecke.	At a street corner in Bonn.
Die Glocke zwar ist schon halb neun,	Half past eight, the chimes declare,
Doch drin, da scheint's noch früh zu	But in the room, it's earlier,
sein,	
Denn unser Schläfer sich nicht regt,	Or so it seems. Our sleeper there
Er schnarcht und schläft, sich nicht	Snores as he sleeps, and does not stir,
bewegt,	
Und da er musikalischer Art,	And since he's musically gifted,
Sein Schnarchen zur Musik gar ward	Snores to music all have shifted,
Zu'ner Aria aus der Iphigenie!	Iphigenia's Aria!
Kein Wunder ist's das lang er ruht,	No wonder that he lies abed
So viele Arbeit er ja thut.	So long. The man is overworked.
Er phantasiert und componiert,	He improvises and composes
Er kritisiert, politisiert,	Gives critiques, politicizes,
Er disputiert, polemisiert,	Polemicizes in dispute,
Er debattiert und abonniert,	Subscribes, and takes part in debate,
Er commerziert und renommiert,	Talks commerce, seeks for good repute,
Er auskuriert und debreziert	Relaxes well, eats sausages,
Er fein diniert und gut soupiert	He lunches well, enjoys his dinner
Auch philologia er studiert,	All this, and studies philologia.
Und was er alles noch vollführt	And there is a whole lot more
Was unsereines nicht kapiert.—	That ladies like me must ignore.—
Gar still ist's in dem kleinen Raum	It's quiet in the little room
Doch jetzt aus seinem süssen Traum	But now, awakened from his dream
Herr Ritter Glück fährt rasch empor	Herr Ritter Glück[1] sits up in bed
Er ruft mit ärgerlichem Ton	And calls aloud with angry yell
"Was trifft mein schlummervolles Ohr	"What has my sleepy ear just heard?
Die nimmer müde Glocke schon	Already chimes the tireless bell
Wo steckt denn nur die Taschenuhr	Where is my watch? This is absurd,
Ich sehe nirgends eine Spur	It can't have simply disappeared.
Und spät muß es wahrhaftig sein	And that it's late, is clearly true
Denn da guckt schon der	Because the sun is peeping through.
Sonnenschein.	

Ja wenn ich nur vor meinem Bett
Ein paar hübsch warme Schuhe hätt
Da könnte ich es eher fassen
Dies liebe Bett jetzt zu verlassen,
Doch so—zwar habe ich keinen
        Kater—
Kann's werden noch ein wenig später.
Kolleg ist heute punkto acht
Zu spät ich dazu aufgewacht.
Drum will ich noch ein wenig harren
Bis ich hör' eine Thüre schnarren."
Er legt sich auf das linke Ohr
Und träumt so lieblich wie zuvor.
Doch plötzlich klopft es an der Thür:
"Was geht da draußen denn herfür:
Herein! Herein!
Wer's auch kann sein.—
Herr Stiefelfuchs was ist die Uhr?"

"Ich glaube es ist halb elfe nur!"
"Halb elf? Was habe ich denn
        geträumt
Den Morgenschoppen gar versäumt?
Ei da muß ich mich tüchtig tummeln,
Um mich zu machen recht hübsch
        fein
Denn zu dem Trottoirenbummeln
Muß ich wohl auf dem Damme
        sein.—"
Der Sonnenstrahl vom Fenster geht
Fliegt über Berg und Thale,
So weit, so weit ist er gewest
Bis endlich er nun stille steht
In Naumburg an der Saale.
Er strahlet hell jetzt auf ein Haus
Ein Mädchen späht zum Fenster raus,
Die bittet den lieben Sonnenstrahl
Um Gruß und Kunde jedesmal;

Und nun zur Antwort hat er ihr
Dies kleine Lied gesungen:
Sie hatt's in diesen Zeilen hier
Zu einem Reim geschlungen.

Beside my bed I'd like to see
Two nice warm shoes awaiting me.
Why, then I would have better reason
To quit my bed so out of season.
—No hangover, it's true. That said,

I think I'll just remain in bed.
College on the dot of eight
Is out, as I have slept too late.
I'll hang around a bit, therefore
And listen out for someone's door."
On his left ear he lies again,
Re-entering his dreams' sweet train.
But not for long. A knock is heard,
What's going on now, there outside?
"Come in! Come in!
Who's making such a din?
Herr Stiefelfuchs, what hour has
        struck?"

"I think it's half past ten o'clock."
"Half past ten? I nodded off

And missed my early morning quaff?
And now I really must make speed,
Put my best bib and tucker on,

Because my promenade will need
My full return to normal soon.—"

The ray of sunshine quits its post
To fly o'er hill and valley,
It traverses a long, long way
Until at last it comes to stay
At Naumburg on the Saale.
At last upon a house it shines,
A young girl from the window leans,
She greets the lovely beam of sun
Each time, and asks for news from
        Bonn.
In answer to her question keen,
It sang this song, as we have seen.
In fashioning these lines, she tried
To tell the story, versified.[2]

In the original German, Elisabeth writes with a certain aplomb and, indeed, the whole poem is upbeat. She refers gaily to the "hangover" (*Kater*) and "morning quaff" (*Frühschoppen*) as an essential aspect of student life, but her reference to "ladies like me," though made in jest with just the right amount of coyness, reminds us that she was excluded by her sex from joining in this kind of student life. In contrast, her time in Naumburg was spent visiting relatives and friends and shadowing her mother in her social round and church occupations. The fact was that Franziska Nietzsche had been welcomed by Naumburg society with open arms, and naturally, Fräulein Nietzsche was included in invitations to social gatherings. The family's financial situation had gradually improved, too, and in 1868, Franziska was able to purchase her home (later 18 Weingarten) outright. The only cloud on the horizon was Nietzsche's wavering religious faith. Franziska, so proud of Fritz when he went to Bonn to study theology, was horrified when he changed to philology. Learning of his religious doubts, she tried to reassure her son in the only way she knew, exhorting him to trust in the "Dear Lord God" in a letter written on 12 November 1865: "Surrender your heart right truly to the true dear Lord God. . . . You more than anyone have reason to be content, since the good Lord has been so merciful to you since your heavy loss, and has led and directed us all; surely you young people above all ought to be most receptive and grateful to Him?"[3]

This letter and others in the same vein, though well meant, simply made Nietzsche realize the gulf between himself and his mother, and he gradually distanced himself from his home. Elisabeth was not willing or not able to do this; convention dictated that she should remain under Franziska's roof unless she married. She remained reticent on why it was that she did not meet a marriage partner until she was approaching forty, though it is probably fair to say that there was no man she felt more comfortable with than her brother. Franziska was puzzled by the likelihood that Elisabeth would remain a spinster. After all, was she not good looking, with money of her own? But this is not how Elisabeth saw herself. In Dresden, she confided to her diary in an entry dated 1 May 1862 that she had come to the conclusion that money ruled the world, something that worried her enormously: "for what do I have to look forward to in life? Nothing! I'm not pretty and I'm not rich and what chance is there without these? This is a topic that really never ceases to bother me, naturally in silence. Oh, if I were rich, really terribly rich, it would be so magnificent. I think I would then be quite heartless with regard to men. I would never marry because my husband would only be marrying me for my money!"[4]

Elisabeth then (presumably it was she) ripped the next page out of her diary—and she removed several other pages that might have revealed too much—so that, as usual, we can only guess at the really private aspects of her life. It should be mentioned here that we only know about these missing pages because her mother made a copy of "Aus meinem Leben," in all likelihood before Elisabeth went to Paraguay. Franziska gives her copy of the diary the heading "From the Diary of My Daughter Elisabeth Nietzsche" and explains: "It begins a few days after I had given each of the children, at their express wish, a diary with a lock and key, a few days before Christmas."[5] The original diary with its broken lock can be studied side by side with Franziska's transcript. The only explanation one can venture for why Franziska would later want to copy out her teenage daughter's diary was that she thought it possible that neither she nor Bernhard Förster's mother (the latter with good reason) would ever see their children again.

Elisabeth, like her mother, was disappointed when Fritz changed his course to philology under Professor Friedrich Wilhelm Ritschl, but she did not react in the same way as Franziska. She briefly flirted with the idea of becoming an atheist, but she found that to doubt one's faith meant staring into the abyss. It was far too uncomfortable and disturbing, as she wrote to her brother on 26 May 1865, especially as Franziska criticized her for "being another one who's too clever . . . and yet, since I cannot forget my llama nature, I'm completely confused, and prefer not to think about it, because I just come up with nonsense."[6] Elisabeth's *Daseinsangst* lasts only for a page, however. She then tells her brother that she is having English conversation lessons, though on her own admission she is a thoroughgoing dilettante: "it's really ever so nice. Naturally the lesson is just conversation, 'no text book.'"[7] She also recounts her meeting with a certain Schneider family in Kösen, where she befriended their teenage daughter, after which she was sent a poem in thanks. Elisabeth composed a long and very gay poem in doggerel in reply, suggesting another outing together:

Ob Morgen *if it is very fine*	Tomorrow, *if it is very fine*
Bei klarem Himmel und Sonnenschein	With clear blue skies and with sunshine,
Wir könnten uns nicht wiedersehn	Could we not meet again? It would
Das wäre doch so wunderschön!	Be truly, wonderfully good![8]

After this mixture of gaiety and seriousness, Elisabeth signed herself "Your tender loving Lama or Lieschen Nietzsche," as though she was not really quite sure which one she was. Nietzsche replied to Elisabeth at length. He took Elisabeth's stirring of doubt seriously and was prepared to give her every encouragement to cross over to skepticism, as he had done: "Here the ways of man part; if what you want is peace of soul and happiness, then believe, if you want to be a disciple of truth, then seek [after it],"[9] he replied on 11 June

1865. In spite of this encouragement, Elisabeth decided that she wanted to keep the prop of religion, and that she could not follow her brother down the road of religious doubt.

When Ritschl moved to Leipzig in 1865, Nietzsche followed him, much to Elisabeth's satisfaction. Leipzig was easy for her to get to and she was able to visit her brother and enjoy some of the student activities in his company. Now nineteen years old, she also made other trips to see relatives, but most of her time was still spent in Naumburg with Franziska at 18 Weingarten, where she was exposed to Franziska's unease over her continued spinster status. Elisabeth probably felt trapped and hoped for broader horizons. Her hopes were raised when Nietzsche met Wagner in Leipzig in 1868 and even more when, in February 1869, Nietzsche surprised his mother and sister with the news that he had been offered the post of professor of classical philology in Basel. To Elisabeth it was clear that the more time she spent in her brother's company, the better, as he was not only Herr Professor, he actually knew the music

Figure 8. Friedrich Nietzsche in his early twenties.

phenomenon of the age, Richard Wagner. Before Nietzsche took up his professorship in summer 1869, he asked Elisabeth to help him with a card index he had promised to make of the twenty-four volumes of the learned journal *Das Rheinische Museum.* This was scissor-and-paste work and Elisabeth enjoyed collaborating with Fritz, who could think of no bigger reward than for her to attend Leipzig University as *Hörerin.* Elisabeth agreed to this and so, more surprisingly, did Franziska. Elisabeth stayed with Professor Karl Biedermann and his wife Therese, where Nietzsche had also lodged as a student in Leipzig. For reasons that are not clear, Elisabeth cut short her planned stay— the venture lasted only from May to July—though one can surmise that the insuperable problem with Leipzig was that Fritz was no longer there, as he had begun his duties in Basel.

Basel: Looking after Fritz

Nietzsche found it difficult to settle in Basel. Plagued with stomach problems, he could not find anywhere suitable to eat inexpensively, and he was lonely; he found the Swiss more reserved than he had bargained for. Things improved immensely, however, when on 22 May 1869 the Wagners invited him to Triebschen for Wagner's birthday. He had to decline because of pressure of work, but Wagner was insistent and converted it to an open invitation. Nietzsche was soon on such a friendly footing with the Wagners that he spent Christmas 1870 with them, and—having just completed *Die Geburt der Tragödie* (*The Birth of Tragedy*) that November—Christmas 1871 as well. By then, he had also made the acquaintance of the Bachofens and Jakob Burckhardt and, most important, for his lasting friendship, Franz Overbeck. Everything should have been perfect, but he was constantly ill. Elisabeth, learning from his letters that he was plagued by migraines and obviously could not run his own household, responded to his pleas to join him in Basel and in 1870 made the first of several long trips to live with him and manage his affairs. She stayed with him for four months in 1870, six months in 1871, and several months in both 1872 and 1873. In 1874 and 1875 they spent the summer vacation together. To cap it all, Elisabeth set up house for the pair of them from August 1875 until March 1876. With a joint ménage they were able to entertain Nietzsche's cosmopolitan friends like Malwida von Meysenbug, whom Nietzsche had met at the laying of the foundation stone for the Bayreuth Festspielhaus in May 1872. She became a motherly influence in his life, sympathizing, like Elisabeth, with his many afflictions, and she was well disposed toward Elisabeth.

In the second volume of *Das Leben Friedrich Nietzsche's* (part 1), Elisabeth mentions her housekeeping for Nietzsche in Basel only in passing, though one can read between the lines that she was very happy to do it. Certainly, Nietzsche was extremely pleased to have her with him in Basel, though they had to persuade a reluctant Franziska to part with Elisabeth. In a letter dated 1 March 1871, Nietzsche duly thanked his mother: "It *was*, for me, *a very great relief* that you let Elisabeth go" (emphasis in the original).[10] With none of the routine duties of Naumburg, Elisabeth was also able to continue with her language study—her Italian exercise book, dated Basel 1875, is still extant (GSA 72/1039a). One can see at a glance that the method of instruction is the usual one of copying out, and there are corrections by an unknown hand. Elisabeth was encouraged to learn Italian by Nietzsche, who was still intent on improving her mind. From Sorrento he sent her a postcard dated 20 January 1877 to tell her he was reading Benoni. "You must, above all, learn Italian!"[11] he added. Once she had returned to Naumburg, Elisabeth pursued various activities to enliven her humdrum life, including further study in English, French, and Italian. Franziska, writing to her son on 27 November 1876, found that it was all too much:

> I think it's too much, as she has English, French and Italian classes and has to study and prepare for them, besides, she attends the instruction given by the clergyman for everyone involved with the Sunday School, telling them what they have to teach the children (that's every Friday, and on Saturday there is Darning School for children of the poor), in short, every day apart from Tuesday has its own nuisance, but to her it's a pleasure. I just think "every man has his meat," and have to put on a brave face.[12]

Elisabeth no doubt felt some pressure from the expectations Franziska placed on her. Franziska for her part thought that learning languages was a hobby, whereas teaching Sunday school was a duty. It was at this juncture that Bernhard Förster came into Elisabeth Nietzsche's life.

Bernhard Förster was a schoolteacher in a Berlin Gymnasium, but his mother lived in Naumburg and knew Franziska. Nietzsche had already met Bernhard's brother Paul, as a letter to Elisabeth from Basel of 8 July 1875 recounts, and had taken an instant dislike to him: "In this state of health [Nietzsche had been ill], I received a visit from a gentleman from Berlin by the name of Dr. [Paul] Förster, and had a reasonable (in his case, unreasonable) chat. He insisted that he had once spent some time with our dear mother, in Großjena, if I recall correctly."[13] He would not meet Bernhard Förster until after Elisabeth married him in 1885.

Like Nietzsche, Bernhard Förster admired Wagner's music, but unlike Nietzsche, he fully supported Wagner's nationalism and anti-Semitism—the two amounted to the same thing, Förster argued (as the National Socialists would later do), since the presence of Jews on German soil poisoned the land. He argued the need for an Aryan Christianity uncorrupted by the presence of Jews. He was also a zealous vegetarian, though when he and Elisabeth settled in Paraguay, this principle did not last for long. Hans Paul von Wolzogen, the editor of *Bayreuther Blätter,* gave him enthusiastic publicity. Elisabeth did not immediately undergo a "road to Damascus" experience with regard to Bernhard Förster when she met him at Bayreuth in 1876, though she was aware that he was eligible. Obnoxious though Förster's views were to her brother, Elisabeth found them congenial and not nearly as perplexing as her brother's new way of thinking. She no doubt registered that Förster was handsome and available, but at this particular point in her life, the most important person for her was undoubtedly her brother. Two things happened to bring about a cooling of their relationship: the publication of *Menschliches, Allzumenschliches* (*Human, All Too Human*) in 1878 and Elisabeth's involvement in her brother's humiliation at the hands of Lou von Salomé in 1882, discussed in the final section of this chapter.

Bernhard Förster had visited Elisabeth during the Christmas vacation in 1876. On 20 January 1877, in the same postcard discussed in relation to Elisabeth's acquisition of Italian, Nietzsche pronounced his verdict on the news that Förster had called on Elisabeth in Naumburg to pay his respects: "Pleased to hear about Dr Förster's visit (we don't think much of his *Brethren*)."[14] He swiftly came to dislike Bernhard Förster and all he stood for as much as he had disliked his brother Paul, although he did not meet his brother-in-law in person until mid-October 1885. No doubt Nietzsche would have disliked any man who wanted to marry Elisabeth, given the unusually close relationship the siblings had. By the same token, Elisabeth's reaction to Lou von Salomé shows that although her search for a wife for Fritz during the years of his professorship in Basel was a standing joke between them, she would have made life difficult for any wife if he really had decided to marry. Förster first entered into correspondence with Elisabeth in 1877. Writing to her in Basel on 25 November that year, he apologized for not sending her some books he had promised her. He had tried to give them to his mother to pass on to Elisabeth, only to learn that she now lived in Basel, though this situation was soon to change. By mid-July 1878, after frequent quarrels over *Menschliches, Allzumenschliches,* it had become clear that Fritz and Lisbeth could no longer live together. Elisabeth helped her brother to find another apartment and returned to Naumburg in high dudgeon. She spent the late summer of 1879 as companion to the Swiss aristocrat Fräulein Meta von Planta and remained in Chur that winter. In 1880, she returned to Naumburg, where she picked up the threads of her humdrum life.

Elisabeth's exit from Basel had great significance for both the Nietzsche siblings. Once she had gone, Nietzsche, who had been propped up by her careful management of his life, was forced to realize that he simply could not carry on with his post. He spent another wretched year in Basel, which proved to be his last in paid employment. After his ménage with his sister in Basel, he never had a proper home again until he returned to 18 Weingarten in 1889, following his mental collapse in Turin. For the moment, though, being homeless and godless was liberating for Nietzsche. Freed from his university duties in 1879 and no longer in thrall to the master, he set off to find the most congenial spots in Europe where he could eke out his invalid's pension. For the next ten years, permanently in transit, he wrote his major works. Elisabeth now had to review her options for how to spend the rest of her life. She had enjoyed keeping house for Fritz, and if circumstances had been different she might well have kept house for him indefinitely. But she had to accept that her brother was no longer his old self. During the course of 1879, Elisabeth had begun to look toward Bernhard Förster with some interest and, by 1880, they were good friends, though still on formal terms. In May 1880 Förster sent Elisabeth a copy of his anti-Semitic petition to Bismarck and asked her to collect signatures. That Elisabeth was still a fairly remote friend when Förster wrote a note to her on 21 February 1882 can be deduced from his mode of addressing her—"Most esteemed Fräulein"—and the cool farewell, signed with his initials: "With best wishes, B. F."

Elisabeth and Cosima

Not all the magic that attracted Elisabeth to Basel emanated from Nietzsche. In June 1870 Nietzsche had taken her to Triebschen on the shore of Lake Lucerne to meet Richard Wagner and Cosima, who was still officially von Bülow until her marriage to Wagner on 25 August 1870. When Nietzsche first met Wagner, he immediately fell under the spell of his genius, while Wagner, who was used to being virtually deified by Cosima, found it flattering to provide a role model for such a promising young academic. Something rather similar happened between Elisabeth and Cosima Wagner, which made Naumburg seem tame and stuffy to Fräulein Nietzsche. It is fair to say that she ingratiated herself with the older woman, but Cosima was a willing partner—from the first, she found Elisabeth useful and asked her to do errands for her. Elisabeth became so well integrated in the Wagner's inner circle of friends that in 1875 she looked after their children for them in Bayreuth when they went on vacation. Cosima had first written to Nietzsche on 16 January 1875 to see whether there was any point in asking this large favor of Elisabeth.

The problem was Franziska, whose possessiveness would, Cosima feared, force Elisabeth to refuse the request, whether she wanted to or not. As usual, Cosima is the soul of tact:

> Before I make the desperate decision of a convent, I want to ask you whether your dear sister would show me the great kindness of visiting us here at the beginning of February and staying with my children as mother after my departure (on the 15th). . . . I did not, however, want to write to your sister directly, to spare her the trouble of having to refuse, you will know best, whether what I desire is *feasible*. I know all the various difficulties everyone has to combat, and how constrained everything is. The fact that I am asking such a great favor of you and your dear sister will demonstrate to you how much I value our friendship.[15]

Cosima's letter to Nietzsche obviously had the desired result. He reasoned with Franziska and wrote a note to Elisabeth to tell her that it was his particular wish that she should comply with Cosima's request: "I absolutely request you to *do* what is asked of you, our dear mother will be pleased to say yes!"[16] This was a clear command from Nietzsche to his sister, and we can perceive how much he was under the Wagners' spell at this time. In a letter to Cosima written on 19 June 1870, incidentally the only extant letter from this period of intense collaboration with the Wagners, Nietzsche had joked: "Having thought over matters concerning Baireuth [*sic*], I think it would be the best thing for me if I were to defer my professorial duties for a few years in order to join your pilgrimage into the Fichtelgebirge. These are hopes I love to entertain."[17] (This letter will be discussed in context in chapter 4.) It is ironic that for Nietzsche at least, Bayreuth did not live up to its expectations, but as the Wagners were moving ever closer to the political right, he would have grown away from the Wagners in any case, even had they remained at Triebschen.

Finally, after an illness led Elisabeth to fear that she would have to let Cosima down after all, she recovered in time to travel to Bayreuth and relieve the Wagners, who had delayed their departure. Almost thirty at the time, and a woman who in another dozen years would be founding a colony in Paraguay, Elisabeth must have felt frustrated by the restrictions Franziska imposed on her freedom of movement. At all events, she arrived at Bayreuth and was put into "Nietzsche's room." She promptly wrote to him on 17 February 1875: "Please, please write to me soon, my dear, ah, if only you were here!"[18] Thrilled to be in Bayreuth in the capacity of substitute mother to Cosima's children, Elisabeth performed her task well, in spite of trouble with the servants, for which Cosima apologized in a letter written on 2 April 1875. That Cosima was grateful is quite clear: by looking after the children—who thought Elisabeth was wonderful—Elisabeth made herself so indispensable to Cosima that she was now addressed as *du*: "A thousand thanks for your kind letter, and please thank your dear mother truly and sincerely from me for permitting you to perform such an indispensable service for me."[19]

Cosima's discreet reference to Franziska reminds us again of the subterfuges necessary to make this trip possible. In *Der junge Nietzsche* (The Young Nietzsche), Elisabeth related that Franziska resented being without Elisabeth for the summer as well as the winter: "As I mentioned earlier, there had always been little differences at a jocular level between mother and son about him monopolizing me for the whole summer, and now she would be without me in the winter as well—that was a bit much for her. Besides, she had all sorts of objections to make against a stay in the Wahnfried establishment."[20]

The first performance of Wagner's *Ring des Nibelungen* in 1876 was an important watershed for the Nietzsche siblings. For Nietzsche, *Der Ring* (as much as he heard of it) was a disappointment, and he fled from Bayreuth in dismay, though one must also add that he had fallen for a young woman, Louise Ott, without realizing that she was married. The flight from Bayreuth was thus a strategic necessity and gave him a chance to lick his wounds in secret. There was also a deep schism between his thinking and Wagner's, which the rehearsal he heard of *Der Ring* forced him to confront. He had already become acutely conscious of the atmosphere of nationalism and anti-Semitism in the Wagner circle, orchestrated by Richard and Cosima themselves. The very notion of the Rhine belonging exclusively to Germany, let alone demanding its treasure from a cluster of Rhine maidens, was the sort of chauvinist extravaganza he decided he could no longer tolerate. For Fräulein Nietzsche, the performance of *Der Ring* at the 1876 Bayreuth festival was where she met Bernhard Förster, who would become her husband. Trouble would soon bedevil the relationship between the Wagners and the Nietzsche siblings, since Nietzsche's admiration for the master was cooling at precisely the time that Elisabeth wished to consolidate her friendship with Cosima. It is ironic that at this juncture, Elisabeth was the one who felt insecure, whereas in years to come, Cosima expressed regret that Elisabeth did not seem to want to keep in touch. The reasons are discussed in chapter 4. Meanwhile, Elisabeth received a letter from Cosima in Bayreuth written on 17 February 1877, Eva's birthday, addressed to "Dearest Elisabeth": "How are you? Have you had good news from your brother? It must seem strange to you, not keeping house for him any more. As you know, I have seen the living quarters in Sorrento and everyone seemed satisfied with them."[21] Cosima is referring to Nietzsche's stay in Sorrento for the winter of 1876–77 with Malwida von Meysenbug, Paul Rée, and Alfred Brenner. Cosima and Wagner had stayed in Sorrento for the month of November. They had no idea that Nietzsche had fled from the first performance of *Der Ring* for any other reason than ill health. Wagner and Nietzsche had met in Sorrento, giving Wagner a chance to describe his plans for *Parsifal* to a shocked Nietzsche, who had admired Wagner as a free thinker if nothing else. Now Wagner's life was to be crowned with a work in which man fawningly seeks redemption from God: Nietzsche could not believe his ears.

"God Is Dead."—Nietzsche / "Nietzsche Is Dead."—God

Nietzsche's religious doubt, as boldly expressed in *Menschliches, Allzumensch-liches* upset Elisabeth more because it threatened her relationship with the Wagners than because his rejection of Christianity brought shame on the family, though that too was thrown at Nietzsche in arguments. With the Wagners, a trend toward religious belief had become predominant. Cosima Wagner had developed a fervent Protestant faith, having been brought up a Catholic; Wagner, reneging on his atheism, was now gearing up to write his overtly Christian finale, *Parsifal,* as already discussed. Since Elisabeth's admiration for Cosima Wagner was deep and apparently permanent, while her religious faith was permanent if not deep, she was prepared to side with Cosima against Nietzsche on the perfidious content of *Menschliches, Allzumenschliches.* Perhaps Nietzsche had underestimated the impact that *Menschliches, Allzumenschliches* would have on his sister and the Wagners; he was overcome by disappointment when he realized he had simply been *dropped.* According to Peters, "It was Wagner's total silence that unnerved Nietzsche."[22] However, knowing the Wagners' propensity for piety, he ought to have realized what their reaction would be to his anti-Christian invective in *Menschliches, Allzumenschliches,* since the argument insults the intelligence of those who cling to the Christian faith. For Nietzsche, Christianity weakens man by making him feel guilty at not living up to the expectations of a perfect Almighty. If only the idea of God could be abandoned, Nietzsche argues, man could lose the debilitating burden of guilt. He would be healthier in mind and body, and the whole culture would benefit. In short, people are Christians through a misunderstanding, as it were *by mistake:* "Well: a particular false psychology, a certain kind of fantasy in interpreting motives and experiences, is a necessary precondition for a person to become a Christian and feel the need for salvation. With insight into this confusion of reason and fantasy, a person ceases to be a Christian."[23] Nietzsche's attack on Christianity in *Menschliches, Allzumenschliches* was merely an opening salvo in a vendetta against Christianity that he would pursue with vigor in the rest of his works.

Nietzsche abhorred the arrogant certainty by which Christians claimed salvation—for him, Christianity produced a slave morality by which the priest manipulated the unthinking flock. Nietzsche subsequently inveighed against "the ascetic priest" (really any priest who *officiated* in any religion) for using trickery to achieve blind obedience. He expressed these ideas metaphorically in *Die fröhliche Wissenschaft* (*The Gay Science,* 1882) where, in a symbolic enactment of what Nietzsche himself was about, a madman rushes to the marketplace to tell everyone the news: "God is dead! God remains dead! And we have killed him!" However, nobody can or will understand the

Figure 9. Friedrich Nietzsche in 1882.

madman: "'I come too soon,' he said, 'for my time has not yet come. This great event is still approaching and on its wanderings.'"[24] For Nietzsche it was axiomatic that priestly precepts are lies at best. It must have made him wince every time Franziska peppered her letters to him with references to the Lord. If Franziska's eclectic version of religious fervor infuriated her son, we can be sure it irritated and confused her daughter in equal measure. Even so, Elisabeth opted to keep faith with the church, at the same time uneasily distancing herself from her mother's sanctimonious piety. Fritz's openly skeptical publication was thus in every way unwelcome to his sister, as it made her dealings with her mother and with the Wagners more difficult.

On 20 February 1878, Cosima reassured Elisabeth that their friendship remained intact in spite of the contents of *Menschliches, Allzumenschliches*, which Nietzsche had sent to the Wagners from Basel at the beginning of the year. In their increasingly pious mood as *Parsifal* progressed, the Wagners were shocked at Nietzsche's newly published affront to the Christian religion. Cosima put it all down to Nietzsche's bad health and patronizingly declared that she did not envy Elisabeth, who she assumed would now have to care for the invalid: "Yet you must be patient, very patient, you will need a lot of time! Ah! . . . I think your brother ought to have used his vacation for a proper, medically directed cure instead of going to Italy—but what use is it to say 'I think' and 'he ought?'"[25]

Ten years *before* Nietzsche's mental collapse, Cosima speaks about him as though he had already lost his mind. Letters from Cosima to Elisabeth continued in this vein during 1879. Of course, although the Wagner circle was moving ever more to the right, there were plenty of people in it whom Nietzsche could admire, like Malwida von Meysenbug, but the fact remained that Wagner was increasingly gathering round him a group of people whose nationalism was bigoted and who were openly anti-Semitic. Soon, in spite of Cosima's reassurances, Elisabeth would feel marginalized in the Wagner circle; Nietzsche himself was already as good as dead for the God of Bayreuth.

Enter the Devil: Elisabeth versus Lou von Salomé

Since this book is about Elisabeth rather than Nietzsche, suffice it to say that Nietzsche had been summoned to Rome in April 1882 by Malwida von Meysenbug, who wanted him to meet her young protégée, Lou von Salomé, for she thought Lou might be a good disciple for him. The complications turned out to be legion, since Nietzsche and his friend Paul Rée, who was also Meysenbug's guest in Rome, both found themselves in love with Lou at the same time. Neither had any inkling of her frigid attitude toward men, but both swooned over her brilliant mind. When Lou expressed a desire that the three of them should spend the winter of 1882–83 in Paris in a chaste ménage à trois, both men hurriedly agreed, each secretly hoping to make Lou his own. Fate seemed to smile on Rée, who got on well with Louise Salomé, Lou's mother. The latter was the widow of a Russian general and it appears to have puzzled Nietzsche and his sister to an extraordinary degree that she allowed her daughter such liberty. To sum up, Nietzsche hoped that Lou, who had spent a good deal of time with Rée during the summer, would spend some time with him in August before they all met up in Leipzig in the autumn of 1882 to make plans for Paris.

Having allowed the rift with the Wagners to become permanent, Nietzsche did not feel welcome to turn up at Bayreuth that July, though he sorely wanted to be there on account of Lou von Salomé. Nietzsche had kept up with his membership of the Wagner Patrons' Society (originally purchased for him as a present from Elisabeth); this society had been formed in 1877 as the Patronatsverein zur Plege und Erhaltung der Bayreuther Festspiele (Society of Patrons to Support and Further the Performances at Bayreuth); in 1883 it was renamed Allgemeiner Richard-Wagner-Verein (General Richard Wagner Society). Nietzsche thus had a right to tickets, and he asked Elisabeth to make use of them and to make friends with Lou so that she could escort the latter to Tautenburg, where he had rented lodgings for the month of August. Lou and Elisabeth were to sleep at the local pastor's house. Thus Elisabeth attended Bayreuth at the same time that Lou von Salomé made her début and was painfully aware that she herself was a less fêted guest than in former years. She wrote a postcard to her mother from Bayreuth on 26 July 1882 to say that she had arrived safely: "I have not yet met many people I know, but it was very amusing at dinner, though really expensive. As a joke, we are all going to eat at the vegetarian table tomorrow."[26] Leaving aside the irony that three years later, Elisabeth, schooled by Förster, would be intoning against the dangers of eating meat, one can see that Elisabeth was not the center of attention at Bayreuth and she must have felt especially marginalized at the spectacle of Lou's social success.

During the three weeks that Nietzsche managed to scrape together with Lou he experienced the most intense emotional and intellectual relationship he ever had with any other human. Unfortunately, it does not appear to have been a mutual delight. The loss of Lou's friendship, largely through Elisabeth's coarse interference, was the worst blow Nietzsche suffered in his life. Ida Overbeck later pointed out to Nietzsche that it was foolish of him to entrust the mission of chaperoning Lou to Elisabeth. Nietzsche himself was forced to confront the fact that Elisabeth had grown distant from him and that she had willfully chosen to ignore how much the friendship of Rée and Lou meant to a recluse like him. Perhaps, without Elisabeth's meddling, things with Lou might have been different. First of all, Lou did not care a fig for convention and might not have minded being in the rented house alone with Nietzsche. Second, it was a foregone conclusion that Elisabeth would be jealous of Lou even had the latter been a shy and sweet young woman who looked up to Nietzsche's sister.

What had really shocked Elisabeth even before she realized Nietzsche's attachment to this rival was not that Lou had spent the month of July 1882 flirting with her compatriot Paul von Joukowsky in Bayreuth, but that she had also made a good deal of capital out of showing the now notorious photograph of herself, whip in hand, in the cart pulled by Nietzsche and Rée, for which the "Holy Trinity" ("Heilige Dreieinigkeit"), as they blasphemously dubbed themselves, had posed in Lucerne that May. Elisabeth's feelings of jealous affront were later rationalized into the assertion, examined below, that Lou was trying to take advantage of Nietzsche's ideas to use them to her own advantage. Elisabeth could not resist adding slanderous remarks about Lou's morality. To Lou's face, Elisabeth cautioned that if her behavior did not improve, she would lose her good name, a sententious remark that Lou, who prided herself on her personal liberty in all things, found hilariously funny. When Elisabeth heard about the Holy Trinity's plan to spend the winter together, she was appalled. She tried to give Lou some impression of her perfidy in leading a respectable pastor's son astray, but here Elisabeth went too far. Lou was prepared to be civil to Elisabeth but she was not prepared to be patronized by a narrow-minded and provincial bigot. Elisabeth, who could have no concept of Lou's sexual difficulties (actually, on Lou's own admission she did not even sleep with her husband throughout their marriage), had certainly witnessed her free *lifestyle*—not the same thing as a free morality—and felt duty bound to protect Fritz from a woman she saw as an immoral adventuress.

Nietzsche had no idea that his wonderful "find" had fallen afoul of Elisabeth, though he would soon be disabused of his ignorance and made to rue his rashness at involving Elisabeth in the affair. He had wonderful discussions with Lou in Tautenburg while keeping a respectful distance. If he had admired Lou before she came to Tautenburg, he was besotted now that he had had a chance to get to know her and her mind (which amounted to the same thing for Nietzsche). Meanwhile, Elisabeth seethed with hatred for the Baltic demon. When Lou left to rejoin Rée at his estate at Stibbe, Elisabeth remained at Tautenburg because she did not want to be in Naumburg at the same time as Fritz. She had apprised Franziska of the whole affair, and Franziska met her errant son with a wall of hostility when he arrived in Naumburg, still thrilled to death at having been able to pour out his thoughts to someone who was receptive and responsive. It is too easy to say that he was madly in love, though this is probably true. He was so bowled over by Lou that he would have accepted her friendship on any terms—as indeed her husband Fred Andreas would do. Not only had Elisabeth soured the atmosphere in Tautenburg, she saw to it that Fritz was frozen out at home, and she wrote poison-pen letters to Lou herself, of which Nietzsche heard only later.

After the fiasco between Elisabeth and Lou von Salomé, the gloves were off between Elisabeth and Nietzsche. Once her brother had taken himself off to Leipzig to lick his wounds, Elisabeth returned to Naumburg and commiserated with Franziska about Fritz's complete lack of morality. Writing to Overbeck on 9 September 1882, Nietzsche complained: "The 'virtue' of Naumburg is at my throat, there is a real *breach* between us—and my mother so far forgot herself with one word she said that my cases were packed, and I left for Leipzig early next morning. My sister (who did not want to come to Naumburg while I was there and is still in Tautenburg), quips ironically 'Thus began Zarathustra's downfall.'—In fact, it is the *commencement* of the *beginning*."[27] At that time, Nietzsche still had the firm belief that the ménage à trois was going to take place, and he was looking forward to it, though the huge rows at home over his immoral plans had unsettled him. He was also not hearing much from Rée and Lou, but he did see them in Leipzig, though not, one gathers, on a very intimate footing.

It must have occurred to him that he might need his own premises in Paris, since he wrote to Louise Ott at this time asking her to find something suitable for him (and not for three people). She replied on 10 November 1882 that she was looking forward very much to seeing him after six years and signed herself "Looking back and *looking forward,* your friend Louise Ott."[28] On 15 November Nietzsche wrote to Louise Ott to call everything off: "Oh, my esteemed friend, hardly have I said that I'm coming, and I have to tell you that I won't come for a long time,—that at least a few months will have to elapse."[29] Clearly, Nietzsche was still toying with the idea of *eventually* going to Paris at that point. It remains an open question why he did *not* go in any case, since Louise Ott had found him a suitable room. No doubt the realization that his friends were cold-shouldering him had made him ill; he was ill all winter, as it turned out. In Leipzig in mid-November, though, he was merely shocked that the old comradeship seemed to have disappeared, and it was with a sort of horror that he realized that his friends had left for Paris without him, obviously opting for a ménage à deux. Gradually and painfully Nietzsche realized that he had been jilted. He never saw either of these friends again, and he always blamed it on one level on Elisabeth. The draft of a letter to Elisabeth (probably sent but destroyed by the recipient) written in September 1882 reads "I do not like the type of soul that you, my poor sister, possess: and I like them least when they even try to bleat out morals, I know their narrowness of mind.—I much prefer it if you disapprove of me."[30]

Meanwhile, Franziska had entered the fray to save her son from the devil. Though Nietzsche was not writing to her, she had plenty to say to him in her letter of 15 November 1882: "If she [Lou] is something so 'special,' she would surely demonstrate that without your [i.e., Nietzsche's and Rée's] help, but it is probably the case that she can't achieve anything by herself, and her chief talent lies in pumping other people's minds for information and then presenting it as her own coin, that's also why she goes from one relationship with a man to another."[31]

In November 1882, still not on speaking terms with Elisabeth or Franziska, Nietzsche fired off urgent letters to Lou and Rée, which were not answered, and a letter to Lou's mother, which was. We can glean important information about Lou from her mother's reply to Nietzsche's letter, dated 10 November 1882, since she speaks of Lou as someone with absolute freedom—and this at a time when it was not considered proper for a girl to go for a walk in the countryside unchaperoned: "*Rules* and *compulsion* have never been brought into operation with my daughter, a young girl has seldom had such freedom as she has had to do as she wished, but whether she will find her true happiness in this completely free life will only be shown in the future."[32]

If her own mother had absolutely no control over Lou, what hope was there for anyone else? Nietzsche, cut off from colleagues by ill health and from his mother and sister who had otherwise smothered him with love, fled from Leipzig to Genoa, where, in deep despair, he spent a terrible winter racked with pain. He found emotional conflict with those close to him extraordinarily upsetting. On 6 March 1883 he wrote to Overbeck from Genoa: "I don't like my mother, and I find it very unpleasant to hear the sound of my sister's voice."[33] Yet when Elisabeth, who had not heard from Fritz all the winter of 1882–83, made contact with him in Genoa, Nietzsche seems to have been genuinely glad to be back on speaking terms with his dear Lama again, though their relationship was never the same. They arranged to spend the month of May 1883 together in Rome with Malwida von Meysenbug. After this reconciliation, Nietzsche took himself off to Sils Maria, where he began to write his poetic masterpiece, *Also sprach Zarathustra* (*Thus Spoke Zarathustra*).

It is a mystery that Franziska's letters to Elisabeth for the years 1880–84, which must have been legion since they corresponded whenever they were apart, are not in the Goethe-Schiller Archive in Weimar, where everything

Figure 10. Elisabeth Nietzsche holding her fan, 1881.

else is found. It would have been very interesting to read the correspondence between the two of them for autumn 1882. True, Elisabeth was with her mother in Naumburg for a good deal of this time, but not all. We could reasonably expect to find a number of notes from Franziska to Elisabeth during this period. The very large number of undated "fragments" of letters from Franziska to Elisabeth in the archive—usually with the first, dated, page missing—make it impossible not to suspect Elisabeth of destroying the evidence of their complicity in making sure Lou stayed clear of Fritz. These fragments await transcription. Another possibility is that Franziska herself destroyed Nietzsche's letters to her at this time, perhaps without opening them, even though she herself bombarded her son with ever-new calumnies about his friend after the "Lou Affair." In a draft for a letter to Franziska written in January–February 1884, Nietzsche chided his mother: "and then you told me in letter after letter things that were quite new to me, and threw more filth on those months of self-sacrifice *afterward,* I call that despicable."[34] It is not important whether Nietzsche actually sent this draft; what is important is that it reveals that Franziska had sent him "letter upon letter." Apparently, Nietzsche began to worry that his letters to Franziska were not getting through: at one point, at the beginning of June 1884, he sent Overbeck a note for Franziska, asking his friend to write the envelope and mail it from Basel: "I have finally begun to have suspicions about which I do not want to say any more."[35] He was obviously deeply hurt by the barrage of criticism from his mother.

In the second volume of *Das Leben Friedrich Nietzsche's* (part 1) in the chapter "Bittere Erfahrungen" (Bitter Experiences), Elisabeth vented her spleen against Lou von Salomé in the first of a series of attacks, which she would hone to precision in the coming years. According to Elisabeth, she discovered in Tautenburg that Lou von Salomé and Rée were hypocritically mocking Nietzsche's ideas behind his back. She mentions the terrible scene she had with Lou of which Nietzsche learned nothing until the following late spring and draws a picture of Rée as a weak man, very much in thrall to Lou von Salomé. She mendaciously recounts that Nietzsche was bitterly disappointed with Lou's mind and accuses Lou of seeking shallow pleasures, interpreting the latter's concept of "sich ausleben" (living one's life to the fullest) as just another term for idleness: "But Fräulein Salomé did not in the least covet a high aim, she wanted to lead an 'enjoyable life' with Rée, to live life to the fullest (*sich ausleben*); she just thought about amusing herself, even if this was in another manner to that otherwise practiced by young women."[36]

It is worth noting that Elisabeth's account of these bitter experiences in *Das Leben Friedrich Nietzsche's* gains very much from the fact that Elisabeth had not yet quarreled with the Overbecks (an event discussed in chapter 4). Therefore she gives a reasonably concise account of the debacle—though obviously from her own perspective—and correctly assesses the effect it had on Nietzsche when she states "However, the worst thing was that as a result of these experiences, he [Nietzsche] became conscious of *how* lonely he was, nobody understood him, and that there was in fact nobody with any concept of how terribly difficult a task lay upon him and of which goals he was pursuing."[37]

Returning to the topic of "Bittere Erfahrungen" again in *Der einsame Nietzsche* (The Lonely Nietzsche) in another chapter with that same title, "Bittere Erfahrungen," Elisabeth asserts that Nietzsche feared Rée and Lou were mocking his ideas. In this connection she again berates Lou von Salomé's concept of "sich ausleben," equating this with a willful misunderstanding of Nietzsche's thought: "From this experience he could already fully predict what would later happen, that his philosophy would be exposed to the worst misunderstandings, that cold egoists who think of nothing but their own amusement and enjoyment of life would take his philosophy as a pretext to justify their own low personal qualities, 'sich ausleben,' as the disgusting expression goes, and thus debase his most exalted thoughts."[38]

Let us say at this point that never was there a clearer case of a pot calling a kettle black, in view of Elisabeth's own misinterpretations of Nietzsche's philosophy. Indeed, Lou von Salomé's interpretation of Nietzsche's philosophy in *Friedrich Nietzsche in seinen Werken* (Friedrich Nietzsche in His Works, 1894) was sensitive and just, though many have found her psychological approach tendentious, especially as she insisted that Nietzsche was deeply religious all his life, in spite of the self-inflicted wound that his breach with the church produced: "The first transformation that Nietzsche battled through in his intellectual life lies far back in the twilight of his childhood, or at least his boyhood years. It is the breach with the faith of the Christian church."[39]

Predictably, Elisabeth was outraged by Lou von Salomé's book: "What I reproach her for [however] is that after Nietzsche became famous and had fallen ill, she had the boldness, not to use a sharper word, to present herself as a friend of Nietzsche's, and as such, to write that untrue book about him."[40] Incidentally, the Overbecks were critical of Lou von Salomé's book for the same reason. As usual, when Elisabeth did not like something, she projected her displeasure onto another person, and so it is not at all surprising that she views Lou von Salomé's book "as an act of wounded female vanity's revenge on the poor invalid, who could no longer defend himself,"[41] whereas it is very clear that at least part of Elisabeth's motive in throwing herself into making propaganda for Nietzsche from 1893 onward represented the channeling of various thwarted ambitions, including her thwarted literary aspirations, and was one way of settling scores with a brother who had not always realized how wonderful she was.

In *Der einsame Nietzsche,* all the aspects of the "Lou Affair" that so tortured Nietzsche in 1882 are rehearsed, and a new chapter, "New Adversities," is added to expand upon Nietzsche's humiliation. Malwida is brought into the argument, having been the instrument of Nietzsche's discomfort by summoning him to meet Lou in spring 1882. Paul Rée's brother George is brought in for having threatened Nietzsche with libel action over a letter Nietzsche sent to Paul Rée in mid-July 1883 (only the draft of Nietzsche's letter remains, but Elisabeth quotes it extensively and then piously hopes that Nietzsche toned it down before he sent it). The very idea of Nietzsche considering a duel with Rée because the latter purportedly called him an "egoist" would be absurd if it were not tragic. It is revealing to see what the beleaguered Nietzsche, at work on *Also sprach Zarathustra* in Sils Maria, wrote to Ida Overbeck in mid-July 1883, precisely the same time that he was trading insults with Paul Rée: "My sister wants her revenge on that Russian woman—well all right, but so far I have been the victim of everything she has done in this matter. She can't even see that I'm within an inch of drawing blood and the most brutal possibilities—and I live and work up here this summer like someone 'who is putting his house in order.'"[42]

Finally in this section of *Der einsame Nietzsche,* Elisabeth settles down into what had become a favorite theme with her, the berating of Ida Overbeck. The latter is dragged in for daring to contact Nietzsche in 1883 over the question of Lou: "Above all, Frau Overbeck, in her ignorance of what had happened, hoped to damage me in my brother's eyes and in general and has tried to do this right up to the present day."[43]

Nietzsche was certain that Elisabeth's behavior and interventions had driven Lou completely out of his life, though we should not forget that with Lou's theories on free living, it would have taken very little for her to keep some friendly link with Nietzsche, whoever she was living with. No doubt she thought that a clear break was the only way to shake off Elisabeth, though in this she was mistaken: both women lived to a ripe old age (Lou died in 1937) and even in 1935, the year of her death, Elisabeth in *Friedrich Nietzsche und die Frauen seiner Zeit* (Friedrich Nietzsche and the Women of His Time) gave vent to her hatred of "the Russian," as she called Lou. The fateful scene between Lou and Elisabeth is played out once more, and after more than fifty years, Elisabeth can still raise her voice in indignation at the memory of Lou's disrespectful attitude toward Nietzsche: "she continued with her defamation of my brother's character, saying the most extraordinary things."[44] Elisabeth never fully realized the harm she had done to her brother: She always felt quite proud that she had delivered him from Lou's clutches. She was impervious to the direct attempts Nietzsche made to explain to her what the friendship of Lou and Rée had meant to him. In mid-July 1883, he wrote to her from Sils Maria: "Finally, finally, my dear Lama, *I* am left as the only one 'who behaved badly';—after the steps you took, from which it was concluded that my nearest relatives did not believe in my 'idealism' in the matter, everything turned to my disadvantage."[45]

During the vicissitudes of the "Lou Affair" in 1882–83, Elisabeth had continued to correspond with Förster, even though his political activity had made his position at the Berlin Gymnasium where he worked untenable, forcing him to resign. Perhaps fearing—with good reason—that her quarrel with Fritz over Lou von Salomé might never be properly made up, Elisabeth wrote Förster a particularly flattering letter dated 17 January 1883. Here, she addresses him as "Dear Friend" and closes with "In hearty friendship, your Elisabeth Nietzsche." Förster, a true pioneer, had decided that his future lay in trying to found a colony of racially pure Germans in South America, and in February 1883, he set off to Paraguay in search of suitable territory for such a colony. He sent Elisabeth a farewell greeting on a postcard from Hamburg dated 1 February 1883.

When he left Germany, Förster probably did not have the remotest notion that Elisabeth would eventually become his wife. From Paraguay, he wrote many letters to friends and collaborators to tell them how his colonial plans were progressing—starting them with "Dear Friends"—so that they could go the rounds. From Asunción on Easter Sunday 1883, Förster responded to Elisabeth's letter of 12 February 1883 by addressing her as "Dear Friend!" He went on to outline his activities and explain the problems that he faced: "My plan is the following: to acquire a good territory, with a view to buying it,"[46] and he ended by saying that in spite of the difficulties: "I am very happy to be at work here." He ended his letter: "Well, goodbye" ("Also auf Wiedersehen"), a valediction peculiar to him. (He would use it to extremely poignant effect, blackguard though he was, at the close of his final note to Elisabeth, fired off from Asunción on 2 June 1889, the day before he took his own life— or so we presume.)

In order to raise the necessary capital for his venture, he explained in his Easter Sunday letter, he would need 100 families, but so far only 20 had expressed an interest. This poker game with immigrant numbers would be Förster's undoing, though his negotiations over the territory that he eventually acquired and called Neu-Germania (as Nietzsche informed Heinrich Köselitz in a letter dated 20 May 1887) also failed because he let himself believe that the land there was more productive than it was. Disregarding his politics, one can surmise that had Elisabeth sounded a note of caution—as his own mother did—he might have been saved from himself, though Elisabeth probably realized that the only way to his heart was to appear as fanatical as he was himself; and once Elisabeth had convinced herself of something, there was no point in making remonstrances, as Nietzsche knew from many years of experience of her "llama nature."

From Nice in spring 1885, Nietzsche glowered as Elisabeth's wedding day approached. As we shall see in the next chapter, he repeatedly tried his best to turn her away from this step. He even felt that he might have contributed to it by not showing her enough affection. But after the "Lou Affair," he had been too angry to behave otherwise, as he tried to express in a draft letter dated March 1885:

> It is one of the puzzles I have thought about a number of times, how it can be possible for us to be blood relatives. . . .

If I raged against you, it was because you forced me to give up the last people to whom I could speak without hypocrisy. Now—I am alone.

With whom I could speak, without a mask, about things that interest me. I really didn't care what they thought and said about me.—Now I am alone.[47]

If Nietzsche felt isolated and lonely, Elisabeth was about to enter a heyday of activity, though many might think in retrospect that she sold herself to the devil when she placed herself under the protection of Bernhard Förster. How *could* she be fooled by this anti-Semitic agitator, even if he *was* handsome and available?

3 Frau Eli Förster

Most Esteemed Fräulein . . .

While Nietzsche raged and sulked over the damage his sister had done to his private life, an unrepentant Elisabeth carried on a cordial correspondence with Bernhard Förster, whose colonial exploits she was actively promoting. During 1883 she wrote him a dozen letters, some long. One letter from Rome, written during the period April–June, relates her joy at meeting the celebrity Levin Schücking several times "with his daughter and her friend,"[1] but the best part of the trip was the proximity of Malwida von Meysenbug and, of course, Nietzsche; thrilled that he had apparently forgiven her, it took Elisabeth two weeks (from the end of April to 10 May) to write the letter, as she blithely told Förster at the top of the page. At the turn of the New Year 1883–84, Elisabeth sent a postcard to Förster to wish him a happy New Year. She had to send it care of "Consulade de Inglaterra Asunción," and was still "Sie" to her friend and still signing herself "Elisabeth Nietzsche" at that point, while his letters usually began with "Most esteemed Fräulein." Though I would not go so far as to suggest that Elisabeth bribed Förster, her letters to him in Paraguay did put the idea into his head that she was prepared to fund his colonizing efforts with her own money. She expressed concern that he was struggling with deprivations that she had the means to ameliorate; depressed and lonely, his thoughts took a romantic train.

On 30 November 1883, Förster sent Elisabeth a letter from Asunción, which he prefaced with a subtly revised extract from Goethe's sonnet "Die Liebende abermals" (The Loved One, Yet Again, 1807):

Dearest Friend!
Why I should start to write a note again,
Is something better not to ask, my dear;
I've really nothing more to say, 'tis clear;
Except that your dear hands will hold it then![2]

He then said how impatient he was for news from her, adding the next day (1 December), in a postscript, that her letter and the enclosed copy of *Also sprach Zarathustra* that she had sent with it had just arrived. However, he added "Since 1877, a great deal separates me from your brother, whose whole worldview has become alien and incomprehensible to me in the meantime,"[3] before he launched into an anguished statement that the Germans will be lost as a "Volk" if German society is not restructured. He added that he was pleased to learn that she had enjoyed reading his *Über nationale Erziehung* (On National Education). For Elisabeth, what was important was not Förster's attempt to engage her in politics, but the extract from the sonnet— a little token that released a flood of emotion. She responded by pouring out her affection and support for her absent friend. She then wrote to apologize for having been too profuse with her sentiments, though she blamed this tactically on Förster because the sonnet had spoken directly to her heart. On 31 March 1884, Förster was still only "Dear friend," with Elisabeth signing herself "Yours, Elisabeth Nietzsche." Warily, the would-be lovers continued to edge closer to one another by letter.

Two months later, in a letter from San Bernardino dated 15 May 1884, Förster declared his love for Elisabeth, but he asked her to consider very carefully before she decided to do anything rash. He knew she was well settled in Naumburg, and he probably could not imagine that she would be able to adjust to life in Paraguay, where he felt his future lay. He also felt qualms about his own reliability, having been duped for some years by a woman whom he had trusted. He asked Elisabeth, underlining the words with deliberation, "*Of what value is the friendship, the love of a man who could be so mistaken?* Consider this well!" What value, indeed? But Elisabeth was in no mood to look for weaknesses in Förster, whose letter continued:

In the meantime, the fact nevertheless remains that we both, E. and B., feel an inclination for one another and in our thoughts and feelings are drawn to each other. For the present, nothing can alter these facts, we must let them stand, guard them well and, in good time, draw the logical consequences from them in summer 1885, when we see each other and speak to one another again.

For the moment, your friendship remains, beside my mother's love, my dear-

est possession on earth . . . *believe* in my love for you, don't ever lose this belief, and believe in my devotion, as well! In love and devotion, devotedly yours,
always your friend, B.F.[4]

In spite of Förster's Oedipal reference to his mother in this love letter, which
would make most young women pause in these post-Freudian times, Elisabeth was enraptured by his declaration that he would return to Germany to
marry her. It is also noteworthy that she persuaded him to bring the wedding plans forward in a way he had not anticipated in his letter of 15 May 1884.
By the summer of 1885, when he had next planned to be in Germany, he was
well into his honeymoon. Perhaps Elisabeth still hoped to be able to have a
family, in which case every minute counted: she was nearly thirty-nine when
she married. As it happened, the marriage remained childless, and no light
has ever been thrown on this issue. Having declared their mutual love, Elisabeth and Bernhard became more affectionate in their letters, with Förster
taking the lead and demonstrating that he really did hold Elisabeth in high
regard, and Elisabeth appearing more modest, as she probably felt was fitting.
On 2 August 1884, she now addresses Förster as "My beloved friend," while
he addresses her as "Beloved!" in his letter of 14 October 1884 from San Bernardino. He ends the letter by spelling out the qualities he sees in her, inspired
by her name, ELISABETH:

Edel
Liebevoll
Innig
Stolz
Anmuthig
Beharrlich
Ernst
Treu
Hochherzig[5]

[Noble, Kind, Profound, Proud, Graceful, Persevering, Earnest, True, Generous]

It would be very easy to make cheap jokes at the expense of the lovers in
question. Their effusions of affection were not based on solid knowledge of
each other's whims and foibles, which meant that each would find it difficult
to live up to the romantic ideal of the other. However, I do not quite agree
with Peters that Elisabeth was simply out to catch a husband and that she was
"forced to capture him by correspondence."[6] Förster had given Elisabeth a
certain degree of encouragement to think that they had an understanding;
it was only because he was so focused on his colonial project that he failed
to think through their relationship. He regarded himself very much as a

missionary who forfeits the right to comfort and luxury. In her letters, Elisabeth had asserted that she would like nothing better than to share this lifestyle, but he knew her circumstances in Naumburg and he knew Paraguay.

Förster *ought* to have known that life there would never be acceptable to her. Instead, he wildly exaggerated the economic prospects for the colony and thus blinded himself and others to the doomed nature of the venture. For Elisabeth, Förster was less a missionary than an *expatriate*. She probably knew that English wives of expatriates in India took "tiffin" (a light lunch) and were addressed as "mem sahib." Whatever she said to flatter Förster's fanaticism, her vision of life in Paraguay was one of pleasant indolence—and he had done much to cultivate that impression by regularly embellishing his descriptions of the country. Förster should have realized that Elisabeth had expectations (largely aroused by himself) that could not possibly be fulfilled. He could, of course, have married Elisabeth and dropped his crackpot scheme to make Neu-Germania an enclave of racially pure Germans: but for this he was too arrogantly confident of his own abilities and too zealously anti-Semitic to turn his back on the cause. That said, critics have all underplayed the physical attraction of this pair: Förster was a handsome man, and Elisabeth was still a good-looking woman.

For some months, the courtship proceeded by means of a loving exchange of long letters. Förster brought forward the date for his return to Germany by several months, arriving home in March 1885. His letters became increasingly passionate as he approached Naumburg and Elisabeth, revealing his inclination to idealize his bride in such a way as to invite disappointment. From Grabow on 24 March 1885, Förster wrote to Elisabeth addressing her as "Dearest, quite Inexpressibly Beloved!": "And do you know *how much* I look forward to seeing you? I shall not be able to tell you because I'm not eloquent, but you ought to feel it, you magnificent woman!"[7] At the end of this letter his feet touched down briefly as he gave Elisabeth the choice of whether to meet him at the station in Leipzig. "Write to tell me if and whether you want me to stay in L[eipzig] for longer than one day." Already one can detect a propensity to defer to Elisabeth, a trait that would become much more pronounced when things became difficult in Paraguay. As usual he ended the letter: "*Goodbye then!!* Yours, completely yours, B" ("*Also auf Wiedersehen!!* Dein, ganz dein B" [emphasis in the original]).

The Antipodes: Nietzsche and Förster

Nietzsche tried from the first to warn his sister of the dangers of associating with a man with such warped views. Podach writes that it is understandable that Elisabeth wanted to escape from the stuffy atmosphere in Naumburg that she shared with her mother. He also adds that Nietzsche's habitual demands on his family, especially Elisabeth, had stored up trouble for the future: "In view of the demands that Nietzsche made on those nearest to him, it is beyond doubt that he would have construed his sister's marriage to anyone as "disloyalty." His sister, in her temporary adulation and the assurances of their closest unity, had probably nurtured strong illusions in him, as well.[8] However, the fact that Elisabeth chose to marry Förster was a terrible blow for Nietzsche. He did not hate Förster for himself, but for what he believed in and stood for. "Nietzsche would never have had dealings with a man like Förster, whose feelings and ideas made him the antipode of Nietzsche, virtually to the level of caricature. . . . Bernhard Förster was an agent of Bayreuth,"[9] Podach writes. But Nietzsche found to his dismay that no amount of appeal to his Lama could wrench her away from her determination to marry Förster: She was quite capable of going out to Paraguay and marrying him there. Förster and Elisabeth were married in Naumburg on 22 May 1885, which was Wagner's birthday, and Nietzsche could not bring himself to attend the wedding.

When Nietzsche learned that Förster called Elisabeth "Eli," he sneered that this was originally a Jewish term—"at any rate *Hebrew*, which surprises me with an old anti-Semite: Eli means 'my God' or probably, in a special case, 'my goddess.'"[10] Before and after the marriage he expressed his dismay to Elisabeth that she had taken a wrong turning in allowing herself to make common cause with the anti-Semites. In a letter written on 7 February 1886, Nietzsche ends with the lament

> I pull myself together as best I can, but an incomparable melancholy takes possession of me every day, and especially in the evening,—always on account of the fact that the Lama is running away and is completely abandoning her brother's way of thinking [*Tradition*].—The chief court musician in Carlsruhe (to whom I had written at the request of poor K[öselitz]) has just informed me that my letter of introduction ("the letter of introduction from a man whom I enthusiastically respect") aroused in him the most favorable impression for the work, and while I am heartily pleased by this, it occurs to me that you would both say: "but he's only a Jew!" And that, I think, expresses how far off course from her brother's way of thinking the Lama has jumped:—we are no longer pleased by *the same thing*.[11]

In *Friedrich Nietzsches Briefe an Mutter und Schwester* (Friedrich Nietzsche's Letters to Mother and Sister), which appeared in 1909, nine years after Nietzsche's death, Elisabeth provides a footnote to this letter after the word *Jew* to say "That was an error," but she does not say whether it was an error that she and Förster would make a comment like that or whether it is an error that Hofkapellmeister Mottl was a Jew.[12] In either case, she has completely missed Nietzsche's meaning, since the letter is his vehicle to point out that Elisabeth has taken a path directly contrary to his beliefs—this was definitely *not* "an error."

In *Friedrich Nietzsches Briefe an Mutter und Schwester,* Elisabeth stooped to cannibalizing or even inventing letters to her from Nietzsche in order to make their correspondence during her stay in Paraguay appear bulkier than it actually was. The forgeries can be checked against the letters in *Briefwechsel: Kritische Gesamtausgabe,* edited by Colli/Montinari, which contains the full complement of Nietzsche's extant letters. True, the *content* of any forgery is usually much as Nietzsche would have written, though Elisabeth cannot match his style. Sometimes it *is* what he wrote, but he addressed it to someone other than Elisabeth, more often than not Franziska. There was a regular flow of letters from Nietzsche to Elisabeth in Paraguay for the years from 1886 until 1889, the year of Nietzsche's collapse, but this did not satisfy Elisabeth: he wrote on average four times a year, and not necessarily at length. The following letter, purported to be dated 21 May 1887, has no traceable original and must therefore be seen as pure invention, since Elisabeth herself was the jealous guardian of Nietzsche's correspondence:

> You say that Neu-Germania has nothing to do with anti-Semitism, but I know for certain that the colonization project has a distinctly anti-Semitic character from that "Correspondence circular" that is only sent out secretly and only to the most reliable members of the party. (I hope my brother-in-law does not give it to you to read, it is becoming ever more unpleasant.) However, it seems to me that is it quite possible, even probable, that the party may well talk about this, but does nothing. . . .
>
> Ah, my good Lama, how did it come about that you got mixed up in such adventures? If only it all ends well! Whenever I am depressed, all sorts of worries plague me; for if I know my dear sister, she would rather die than leave something in the lurch. But that is Nietzschean![13]

This passage shows Elisabeth's talent for reinventing the past. Nietzsche is made to conveniently surmise that Förster's influence led Elisabeth to her anti-Semitic stance. He utters a banal "Ah!" that betrays the hand of the true author, before the Lama's obstinate nature is touched upon and the sigh goes out that this, too, is "Nietzschean." It will be seen in chapter 5 that Elisabeth's inventions were taken at face value by admirers like Luise Marelle, who in good faith quotes the above (spurious) letter in her biography of Elisabeth.

It is highly ironic that Elisabeth's invented reference to Lama-like persistence as "Nietzschean" should thus acquire a life of its own.

Nietzsche foresaw that Elisabeth would abandon his teaching to take on her husband's mantle and said so in his letter to her of 20 May 1885, in which, brooding over her imminent marriage (two days later), he set down a record for his sister of what his views were and what he had tried to achieve, pointing out that he had never found any kindred spirit. Predictably, Elisabeth took no notice. Under Förster's guidance, she jettisoned her former love of fun for the very unfunny task of preaching for their racist colonial venture. Although she did not share her mother's taste for religious fervor, her support for Förster's campaign bears all the hallmarks of a religious conversion. Robbed of a father and now turning away from her brother, who had been everything to her for nearly four decades, she set her eyes on Förster as the Messiah, but a very special kind of Messiah. Not only was he going to save Germany from itself, but he was going to take the place of the missing father and brother in Elisabeth's life. It was also a master stroke against Lou von Salomé and all those who, like Elisabeth's own mother, had thought that Elisabeth was "on the shelf." All this was asking too much of a humorless and deluded former high school teacher like Bernhard Förster.

Dr. Förster

Though it is clear that Nietzsche was vigorously opposed to Förster's anti-Semitism, at a superficial level the two men had several things in common. Förster believed passionately that German culture was going rapidly downhill and blamed this on the deteriorating grammar school system and an over-centralized government. Nietzsche, too, criticized the system of education in the *Gymnasien* (Förster preferred the term *höhere Schulen,* or "higher schools"). Förster's ideas on education were outlined in his pamphlet *Über nationale Erziehung* (On National Education, 1882). As he says on the flyleaf, the ideas expressed are heavily based on Paul de Lagarde's *Deutsche Schriften* (Writings on Germany, 1879). Förster berates the falling standards in the grammar schools and lays the blame squarely on Prussia: "The 'higher schools' have been thoroughly ruined by Prussia during this century."[14] He argues that too much stress is laid on practicalities to the detriment of the education of the whole person, not just at the academic level but at the physical and aesthetic level as well. He believes that Prussia has brought a cash value into education that robs it of its core value. Since Prussia is the chief culprit in the deterioration of educational standards (for the élite, it must be added—and then only boys!), he goes on to describe what can be done to improve the running of the state. Nietzsche also disliked the Prussian state under Bismarck. His sister even compiled a slim volume of his sayings on the matter: *Nietzsche: Worte über Staaten und Völker* (Nietzsche: Words on States and Peoples, 1922), which by its very nature gave a false impression of its subject matter, since Nietzsche wanted to see as little state control as possible.

Leaving aside Förster's spectacular failure to run a small colony of thirty families, there were several aspects of his thinking that would certainly find approval in some circles today. His support for vegetarianism and "green" issues (forest despoliation, for example—at least as far as German forests were concerned) and implacable hostility to cruelty to animals, especially vivisection, of which more later, place him within the "back to nature" movement of the *Wandervögel* or scout's movement. He argues for a brand-new social system, with taxes levied locally in regions where all will, or should, own their own houses. And this is the moment when we realize he is completely mad, for in his utopia, local taxes are to be used prohibitively to curb what one can only describe as *pleasure:* "these taxes can, for example, be levied so high on items like tobacco, alcohol, rented apartments, public houses, and so on, that they actually amount to the prohibition of the same;—taxes can obviously have an *ethical* dimension as well."[15]

This was a man with no sense of humor who in all seriousness wanted to close down the *pubs*—and we have not even reached his anti-Semitism yet, which is only touched on in this brochure. Förster intones that his ministates will need military provision and their own health service or *Sanitäts-Korps,* whereupon he praises nurses and launches into his plans for girls' education. He has nothing but abuse for the type of girls' school attended by Elisabeth: "The existing '*schools for the daughters of gentlemen,*' as the most offensive nonsense ever peddled with regard to pedagogy, would have to be shut by the police on the first day of the new regulations" (emphasis in the original).[16]

Förster, part ascetic priest and part Fascist *avant la lettre,* wants to *use the police* to shut schools that he thinks are unsuitable. Again one asks of Elisabeth, how could she? One of the answers could lie in Förster's remarkably forward-looking posture on women's career opportunities, in spite of his annihilating comments on the current state of education for girls in Prussia. A Greek scholar and no doubt mindful of Plato's guardian women, as described in *The Republic,* Förster argues that society cannot afford to let good potential go to waste: a country should capitalize on the intelligence of its citizens, be they male or female: "Among women there are some powerful, heroic, brilliant natures who have the desire and capacity to achieve more than what the common norm would like to assign. Though they are exceptions, such individuals are too valuable for the national system of education not to pay particular attention to them. What I said earlier with regard to men applies to women, too: whoever feels drawn to a career must be put in the position of being able to pursue that career."[17]

With views like this, which were avant-garde for Germany in the 1880s, Förster put clear water between himself and Nietzsche, who held conventional ideas on woman's domestic role. Förster returned to the topic of education in *Zur Frage der "nationalen Erziehung"* (On the Question of "National Education," 1883), though here he did not put forward his plans for decentralized states but concentrated on his argument for a properly thought-out curriculum in the "higher schools." His slogan is: "*Nature never lies*" (emphasis in the original) and he elaborates by calling for children to be taught to value animals: "It seems to me that the educational power inherent in an amicable relationship between young people and nobler animals has not yet been sufficiently appreciated."[18]

When Förster was not grinding a political ax, the pedagogue in him came to the fore. And just as there is no show without Punch, nothing written by Förster neglects to pay homage to the master. In *Richard Wagner als Begründer eines deutschen Nationalstils mit verschiedenen Blicken auf die Kulturen indogermanischer Nationen* (Richard Wagner As Founder of a National Style with Diverse Mention of the Cultures of Indo-Germanic Nations, 1880), Förster praises Wagner for reclaiming Germany's lost brilliance, thus bringing a new "national style" to Germany. The same theme of Germany's need for cultural renewal is found in *Der deutsche Prosastil in unseren Tagen* (German Prose Style in Our Time, 1880). Förster not only signed Elisabeth's copy with the words "Fräulein Elisabeth Nietzsche with the author's friendly greeting," he also changed the text (indicated by italics below) so that Nietzsche, whose style he greatly admired, could be included in the sweeping praise he awarded originally only to Burckhardt: "Jakob Burckhardt's/*and Fr. Nietzsche's* style, just to give *two* [changed from one] random example/*s* [changed to plural] that occurred to me, is so expressive, rich and pertinent, while perfectly correct, that I can confidently include it among the true art forms."[19]

Förster would have dearly liked recognition from Nietzsche in return but had to resign himself to the fact that this would never be forthcoming in spite of Elisabeth's repeated assurances to the contrary. As Elisabeth would subsequently do, Förster, having once set out his views, tended to regurgitate the same material; the only real exception to this is his description of the grave inscriptions in Greece in *Olympia: Ein Blick auf den allgemeinen Kunst- und Kultur-historischen Werth der Grabungen am Alpheios* (Olympia: A Look at the Artistic and Cultural-Historical Value of the Excavations at Alpheios, 1886). Thus in the pamphlet *Der Vegetarismus: Ein Theil der sozialen Frage*

(Vegetarianism: A Part of the Social Question, 1882) and the eight-page brochure *Die Frage der Vivisektion im Deutschen Reichstage: Ein Stück Kulturkampf* (The Question of Vivisection in the German Parliament: A Piece of Kulturkampf, 1882), Förster lays down ideas that he will repeat in chapters 5 and 6 of *Parsifal-Nachklänge: Allerhand Gedanken über deutsche Cultur, Wissenschaft und Kunst, Gesellschaft u.s.w.* (Parsifal Resonances: Miscellaneous Thoughts on German Art, Science, Society, Etc., 1883); a truncated second edition of this work was given the title *Richard Wagner in seiner nationalen Bedeutung und seine Wirkung auf das Culturleben* (The National Importance of Richard Wagner and His Effect on Cultural Life).

Though Förster was authoritarian, humorless, and eccentric, this does not detract from his passionate campaign against cruelty to animals. In his polemic *Die Frage der Vivisektion,* he castigates for their specious argument that it can benefit humankind those in parliament who have agreed to the legalization of vivisection: "So, supposedly to help prolong human life—it is not yet proved—man is to be permitted to rage in the most merciless and cruel way possible against the life and feelings of animals? I have never yet heard a more demonic argument."[20] Förster's argument is still used as a valid objection to vivisection by contemporary campaigners for animal rights.

We come now to Förster's anti-Semitism, an essential aspect of his character and the motivating force behind his colonial endeavors. After Heinrich von Treitschke's founding of the Verein Deutscher Studenten (German Students' Association) in 1880, anti-Semitism was rife in certain clearly defined sections of the German population, such as the academic world. Förster was a main player in the formation of the anti-Semitic Deutscher Volksverein in 1881. This was only one of many splinter groups that depended as much on personalities as on programs. They had very little success, and virtually no support for Förster's colonial venture was forthcoming, a constant source of complaint by Elisabeth, who later often railed indiscriminately against "die Antisemiten" or the "antisemitische Partei," complaining that her husband was let down by his colonial and political backers. When the Antisemitenkongreß was held in Bochum in 1889, Förster had died a few days previously in Paraguay. This congress, which drew together all sections of the anti-Semitic movement in Germany, demanded that Jewish emancipation should be rescinded: Jewish men should be deprived of the vote, Jews should be excluded from the legal and medical professions, Jewish immigration from the east should be halted, and unnaturalized Jews should be expelled. The Deutschsoziale Partei (founded in 1889, the year of Förster's death) rivaled the Antisemitische Volkspartei (founded 1890), but they merged in 1894 after winning 16 of the 407 seats in the 1893 general election. Their impact was negligible.

To understand this upsurge in anti-Semitism that Förster had done much to incite, we have to realize just how liberated the Jews in Germany had become during the nineteenth century. At the beginning of the century, they possessed virtually no civic rights, but were given legal equality in Prussia in the Stein-Hardenberg reforms of 1811–12, when Prussia was still under French occupation. After the battle of Leipzig in 1813, which drove Napoleon out of Germany, conservative elements in Prussia began to pick apart the concessions awarded to the Jews, and Jews experienced further setbacks in 1819 after the murder of Augustus von Kotzebue. The "Hep Hep" riots, during which Jews were mocked with a bastardized version of the cry "Hierusalem est perdita," led to the repressive Carlsbad Decrees. When Friedrich Wilhelm IV ascended the throne of Prussia in 1841, Jews in Prussia saw what rights they had achieved eroded further. The rights of Jews in other German states varied considerably, but by 1869 all German states had approved constitutions giving Jews equal legal status. Bismarck sought to put an end to the unjust and piecemeal situation once and for all when he declared that citizens of all religious persuasions were equal before the law in the new Reich, founded in 1871.

Throughout the nineteenth century, many Jews circumvented the manifest injustices to which they were exposed by converting to Christianity. There were also two sects that welcomed Jews, converted or not: the "German Catholics" (Deutschkatholiken[21]) and the Lichtfreunde, or "Friends of the Light." Since the latter were tolerated as a Protestant sect from 1847, they filled the vacuum left by the disbanding of the German Catholics after the failure of the 1848 revolution. After the foundation of the Reich, it struck many Jews as unnecessary that they should continue to feel under pressure to convert to Christianity. They therefore followed their own rituals while living their lives as law-abiding citizens of the new empire. They exulted in the new freedom, but German nationalists took this as proof that they were not willing to assimilate into German society. Thus, one of the few things one can praise wholeheartedly in Bismarck's Reich spawned an ugly undercurrent of unrest that would simmer until resurrected and intensified by Hitler in the 1920s.

This is the background for Förster's bitter comments on the Jews' failure to integrate into society, the burden of his petition presented to Bismarck on 13 April 1881—which the latter summarily rejected, even though Förster had managed to amass nearly a quarter of a million signatures. The petition began

> Your Highness, most Noble Chancellor and Prime Minister!
>   For some time now, the minds of deeply patriotic men of every class and party have become profoundly alarmed at the overgrown Jewish element of the population in the fatherland. The earlier hopes, cherished by many, that the Semitic element would be assimilated, have proved to be deceptive, in spite of

the fact that there is now complete equality. It is not just a question of placing the Jews on a par with ourselves, but rather that of a stunting of our national excellence through the prevalence of the Jews, whose growing influence springs from racial characteristics that the German nation could neither wish nor dare to accept without losing its identity. This danger is recognizable and is already recognized by many. Already the German ideal of chivalry, uprightness, and sincere religiosity is beginning to be displaced, to make way for the substitution of a Jewish pseudo-ideal.[22]

Though Förster directed his anti-Semitic attack in the petition at the dominance of Jews in financial institutions, what really rankled with him was their failure to assimilate into the cultural life of Germany. To reject the *culture* of the host nation was something he could neither understand nor forgive. Hence, in *Das Verhältnis des modernen Judenthums zur deutschen Kunst* (The Relationship of Modern Jewry to German Art), a talk he gave to the Berlin branch of the Bayreuth patrons' society in 1881, Förster bitterly lays the blame for Christian antipathy toward the Jews on the Jews themselves:

It is said that the blame for the rift between the Jews and the Germans lies solely with us Germans, the poor Jews were not in a position to become Germans, as we prevented them from doing so. Allegedly we have always treated them too badly, and if we had not persecuted them so much, they would have become good Germans long before now. But if one demands proof for this statement, then those who make the assertion find it hard to answer. For where, in history, can we find the Jews saying: "We want to abandon everything that is particular to us in language and behavior, custom and religion, and be good Germans, it is difficult enough for us poor Jews, but we want to make an honest effort: if we don't succeed, our children and grandchildren will."—Did the Jews ever say anything like that? Have they ever even tried to perform the transformation? Or were we supposed to sacrifice some of our own characteristics?[23]

Of course, the answer to these rhetorical questions was that thousands of Jews *had* embraced Christianity; it was a sign of progress that those who did *not* convert felt secure enough to openly practice their beliefs while still going about their daily business. The bigot in Förster was affronted by the Jews' exercise of what were, after all, their legal rights. Cunningly, he parades his anti-Semitism as though it is a facet of aesthetics, but the applause—included in the text!—at the mention of the Jews and *money* (indirectly, via an allusion to the golden calf) reveals just how political Förster's polemic really was: "I come finally to the worst thing: the most perfidious influence that the Jews exercise on our whole life through the *cult of the golden calf,* which they have known and relied on from the beginning of history. (Lively cheers.)"[24]

By far the most significant of Förster's publications was *Deutsche Colonien*

im oberen Laplata-Gebiete mit besonderer Berücksichtigung von Paraguay:
Ergebnisse eingehender Prüfungen, praktischer Arbeiten und Reisen, 1883–1885
(German Colonies in the Upper La Plata Regions with Particular Regard to
Paraguay: Results of Thorough Research, Practical Work, and Travels, 1883–
1885 [1886]), which he prepared for print during the nine months that he and
Eli, as Elisabeth now liked to be called, spent in Germany before setting out
for Paraguay together in February 1886. The book presented the results of
Förster's investigations during his travels in Paraguay. Dedicated "To my dear
wife Elisabeth," it was first printed privately in Naumburg; a second edition
appeared in the same year with Fock in Leipzig. The book gave a wholly ide-
alized impression of what the potential colonist had to expect. In particular
it appealed to the myth that the true German belonged in the *Urwald* ("virgin forest") and declared—irresponsibly, as it transpired: "the fertility of the
red soil where the virgin forest has been cleared seems to know no limits."[25]
Predictably, Nietzsche and many others found the frontispiece photograph
of Förster (figure 11) in bad taste because it displayed vanity.

Figure 11. Bernhard Förster,
ca. 1884.

Leaving Elisabeth with his own family in Naumburg until they left for Paraguay, Förster went on a hectic tour of Germany to propagandize for his colony. While parted, the newlyweds corresponded with each other with considerable affection and—rather touchingly—on his old notepaper, still headed with "Naumburg," some of which found its way to Paraguay with them. On 18 September 1885, Elisabeth writes to tell her husband that she is cross not to have heard from him: "Dearest Bernhard, Why don't you write to your little wife? I am quite restless and alarmed about it."[26] She really had no reason at all to doubt his affection: His letters show that he was passionately in love with her. On the same Naumburg-headed notepaper from Berlin, Förster addressed his wife as "Dear, magnificent, great one!" and signed himself: "Eli, *completely* yours, Your Bernhard" [his emphasis]. Another undated letter from Berlin starts with "Dear Only One!" Elisabeth responded in kind (still on his old notepaper), addressing him in a letter dated 15 September as "Dearest Bernhard" and signing herself "In heartfelt love, Yours, Eli." On 20 and 23 September 1885, Förster is "My dear Bernhard of my heart" (Mein lieber Herzensbernhard), while Elisabeth signs herself "Your little Eli" and "In tender love, your Eli" respectively.

Such effusions just could not last. The first note of discord was sounded over the publication of Förster's *Deutsche Colonien*. While Förster was on his publicity tour, which did at least bring in a sufficient number of volunteer colonists that the project could go ahead, Elisabeth had tried to make her peace with her brother by asking him for advice about Förster's book. Nietzsche, unimpressed by the fact that he was dealing with an expert on German grammar and the author of "German Prose Style," made some alterations to the text that Elisabeth asked the publisher to put into effect. A furious Förster then countermanded her instructions, which infuriated Elisabeth. She sulked at not being praised for her efforts with the book and made her feelings manifest by saying that she did not need the money Förster had sent her: "Why have you sent me money, then?" she wrote in a letter of 30 September 1885, telling him she has forty-eight marks from the sale of brochures and signing herself "Very distressed, Yours, Eli."[27] Obviously, neither her brother nor her husband wanted to upset her, and so she was able to broker a meeting between her husband and brother on 15 October 1885, Nietzsche's forty-first birthday. On this occasion, the two men behaved with impeccable politeness toward each other.

In spite of the contretemps with regard to Förster's book, Elisabeth and her husband were both thrilled at their belated love match and were certain that things were going to work out. The tragedy was that both of them had a slender hold on reality. Elisabeth, so practical in things like a large wash—

or turning her hand to milking a cow once she arrived in Paraguay—was as fanciful over their prospects as Förster was bigoted and reckless. Nietzsche groaned to himself that the colony was doomed. Though they set sail in the *Uruguay* in February 1886, arriving in Asunción at the end of March, the Försters could not immediately proceed to Neu-Germania: Throughout 1887, Elisabeth bombarded her mother with details of her worries, mainly over money, and Franziska faithfully kept Nietzsche informed of the news. In fact, it was not until 1888 that they finally and triumphantly arrived in the colony. Elisabeth wrote a long, ecstatic letter to Franziska dated 18–28 March 1888:

> Beloved mother of my heart (Geliebte Herzensmutter),
> On 5 March we arrived in our magnificent new homeland and made an entry like kings. . . . In fact, it is wonderful here, everything has a functional and therefore splendid veneer: our administrator and our clerks are gentlemen [in English in the original] and respectable people who are particularly suited to their posts, and one assumes that the colonists are like the clerks. I can't resist telling you that before I go to sleep, I often lie in bed making calculations and asking myself: how did we actually acquire the money for this magnificent undertaking? God has blessed it, he has multiplied every mark we had, or which loving hearts gave to us or lent, into five marks, otherwise it can't be explained at all.[28]

Franziska was so overjoyed to receive this rapturous letter that she copied it out and sent it on to Nietzsche, though not without the odd inaccuracy, deliberate or otherwise—for example, "the money" becomes "the means." Unfortunately, Elisabeth's optimism that their funds would be as prolific (and as miraculous) as Jesus' parable of the loaves and fishes was characteristically misplaced. The problem was that Elisabeth certainly did not have sufficient capital to fund Förster's venture, and Förster should have realized it.

As already indicated, a number of letters in the collection *Friedrich Nietzsches Briefe an Mutter und Schwester* are almost certainly forged. The following spurious letter of 20 April 1887, purportedly written by Nietzsche to Elisabeth, places Elisabeth in a very favorable light and must also be regarded as a forgery: "Up till now, I have not written anything about it to you, but I am not enthusiastic about your whole venture. In my mind I can see these impoverished people, thrown on your pity, greedily pressing themselves upon you to exploit your weakness: your over-generosity. Make no mistake, no colony can flourish with such elements. It would be somewhat different if they were farmers!"[29] Elisabeth's generosity is praised here and an escape route for the failure of the colony—the fact that the colonists were not real farmers—is provided *retrospectively,* since Elisabeth must have invented the letter some time after the collapse of the Paraguay venture, possibly with the publication of the family correspondence already in mind.

One really has to admire Elisabeth's skill in craftily slipping a number of forged letters from Nietzsche among the genuine correspondence. These literary inventions appear to show that Nietzsche understood all too well that the colony would founder through no fault of Elisabeth's. Ironically, in the very same year as the publication of *Friedrich Nietzsches Briefe an Mutter und Schwester,* Elisabeth suppressed the comments Nietzsche really had made about her when she published *Ecce Homo* (1908). In the definitive *Briefwechsel: Kritische Gesamtausgabe* (1975–), letters from Nietzsche to Elisabeth are found for 26 January 1887 and 5 June 1887, with nothing in between. In compiling the letters for publication, Elisabeth was no doubt irked that Nietzsche had written so few letters to her in Paraguay, and in particular had not reacted to the news of her triumphal march into Neu-Germania on 5 March. She therefore alters history by providing letters to herself purporting to be from Nietzsche dated 24 February, 23 March, 20 April, and 21 May. It is as though Nietzsche's prime occupation is to know what is happening to his sister, whereas the opposite is more likely to be true.

What the extant correspondence reveals is that Nietzsche, after a neutral letter in January, appears to have written nothing to his sister until he wrote a very firm letter to her dated 5 June 1887 from Chur, which they had visited together in 1879. This letter, whimsically reviewing the past, also foresees a future where their ways must part: "Everything has deserted me in the meantime: even the Lama has jumped away and gone among the anti-Semites (which is about the most radical method of 'finishing' with me)."[30] Nietzsche's next extant letter to Elisabeth is a note from Venice of 15 October 1887 in which he tells her that he has been kept informed "about the progress of colonization."[31] In another note of 11 November 1887, which accompanied his complimentary copy of his new book, *Jenseits von Gut und Böse* (*Beyond Good and Evil*), Nietzsche repeats that his position had not altered: "Take it [the letter] as an expression of my heartiest wishes for everything you have both so splendidly undertaken: I myself, of course, cannot but remain 'the good European.'"[32]

Finally Nietzsche comes to express his real opinion in a letter written at the end of December 1887 in which he expresses outrage that the anti-Semitic press has published references to his *Also sprach Zarathustra,* but his letter at the end of January 1888 is milder, and again neutral, mostly containing his news, as does a note written on 31 March 1888. Naturally, Elisabeth later felt that this represented a rather flimsy correspondence on Nietzsche's side, which of course it was. That Nietzsche did *not* write to Elisabeth in response

Figure 12. "Försterhof," Neu-Germania, with Elisabeth and Bernhard Förster, 1888.

to her rapturous babbling in the letter of 18–28 March 1888 is clear from Nietzsche's opening sentence in his letter from Sils Maria of 14 September 1888, in which he first apologizes for not having written for a considerable time: "I've been meaning to tell you for ages of my great joy over the fact that you have finally settled in and over the ceremonial ways and means in which this was accomplished!"[33]

It should be explained that although Nietzsche was against the whole Paraguayan venture, once the Försters had actually embarked upon it he could only hope that it would succeed for the sake of everyone concerned. He also felt duty bound to reassure Franziska, who was frantic with worry on her daughter's behalf, that things would work out. Hence his relief about the welcome that Elisabeth had received from the colonists. As mentioned above, Nietzsche did *not* respond to Elisabeth in May 1888, though she would have dearly loved him to; instead, he wrote to *Franziska* from Turin on 27 May 1888 expressing moderate optimism that the venture would not founder: "You really provided me with an extraordinary pleasure with your copy of the Lama-letter: I have read it at least six times and each time I received encouragement anew from it. Now that things have gone this far, one is actually justified in having some faith: even I have begun to have some faith in the matter."[34]

To be fair to Elisabeth, Nietzsche asserts in a letter to Franziska dated 16 June 1888 that Elisabeth has not responded to his letters sent during the previous winter, so the post could share some of the blame for any gaps. That said, the forged letters were obviously intended to suggest that Nietzsche was penning a note to his sister at least once a month. What is astonishing is that Elisabeth did not *destroy* more than she did, for there are many unflattering references to her, especially in the letters, which she had the power to erase. It appears that she *did* operate as a conscientious guardian of Nietzsche's works at one level, though in her judgment, expediency dictated that certain additions and adjustments should be made.

The Collapse of a Dream

The Försters' experiment now began in earnest. The delay in Asunción after their arrival in Paraguay meant that their experiment at living together in the specially built house, Försterhof, lasted not much more than a year. In order to set the colony up at all, Förster had entered into a shady tripartite deal with Cirilio Solalinde, a Paraguayan, and the government, which meant in essence that Solalinde had sold his land to the government for a good profit. Although Förster's signature made it look as though he now owned the title to the colony's land, the title would be invalidated if 140 families were not in residence by August 1889. The letters between Förster and Elisabeth—parted yet again—still bear witness to a remarkably strong affection. On 10 May 1887 Elisabeth, holding the fort in Neu-Germania while Förster is in Asunción, writes, "My dear Bern of my heart, since you went away, my heart has been so terribly heavy."[35] And on 11 June 1888, writing to "My dear good Bern," she ends her letter with a request for chocolate: "Now, my dear Bern of my heart, farewell, *please bring chocolate,* you can't imagine how effective a remedy it is for every form of dissatisfaction. Goodbye until I see you soon, Yours, Eli Förster."[36] Another undated letter tells Bernhard that she is "absolutely out of *chocolate*" [her emphasis]. Such is the essence of colonial life.

On 24 October 1888, Elisabeth writes to "My dear Bern of my heart" (Mein lieber Herzensbern), again in Asunción, to tell him that there have been disturbances and to warn him to be on his guard on his journey home. "Now, my dear Bern of my heart, bring a statute book,"[37] she commands, without realizing how irrelevant that was for his problems. She signs herself: "In great longing and love, Yours, Eli" and frequently stresses that she misses him and wishes to embrace him. In an undated letter, possibly written in February 1889, she writes: "My dear, dear Bern, how I long for you! I hope you will come soon. In true love, your Eli."[38] On a sheet of paper among the undated letters, Elisabeth has written questions for Bernhard to answer in Spanish. His replies are penciled in except for the final answer, in ink. The final question is "Does Bernie [Bernchen] often long for his little wife?" to which the reply is "1000 times yes!"[39] Whatever her husband's faults, she clearly missed him. Förster was away again in San Pedro in February 1889. In a letter to his wife of 22 February 1889 he begins: "Dear Child! We sail from here on Sunday aboard the *Hermann* [a steamship] and hope to be in the colony on Monday afternoon." The letter ends "With a thousand heartfelt greetings, goodbye. Greetings also to Erck and Steckfuß. Your faithful Bernhard."[40]

Though the tone is a little cooler, this does not yet constitute the desperation that had set in by May 1889, when Förster was forced to travel to Asunción to try to head off financial ruin. By this time, Eli Förster had become completely disenchanted with the life of a colonist. The deprivations were depressing her and she found Bernhard unsympathetic when she complained. A new colonist, Julius Klingbeil, had arrived, had swiftly realized the extent to which Förster had lied about the colony, and decamped back to Germany, where early in 1889 he published *Enthüllungen über die Dr. Bernhard Förster'sche Ansiedelung Neu-Germanien in Paraguay: Ein Beitrag zur Geschichte unserer colonialen Bestrebungen* (Revelations about Dr. Bernhard Förster's Settlement Neu-Germania in Paraguay: A Contribution to the History of Our Colonial Efforts), a book showing the struggles of the colonists in Neu-Germania in their true light. Förster's fraudulent claim that those who wished to leave the colony would have their investment returned was also revealed and denounced. Förster was beside himself at this damage to the bona fides of the venture, the success of which vitally depended on the imminent arrival of dozens more families. More important for Elisabeth at this juncture, however, was the news she had received of Nietzsche's mental collapse in Turin. She was mortified at the thought that she had somehow left him in the lurch. She wrote to Franziska from Neu-Germania on 9 April 1889, pouring out her dissatisfaction and disappointment with her life in Paraguay to "My dear, good mother":

> Naturally I am an excellent wife when, as usual, I take every burden upon myself with pleasure, the only reward the success of our enterprise, never desiring anything for myself, but only ever caring about Bern and the colony. . . . But now for the past six weeks I have thought about myself for once, first I had a painful eye infection and then this great trouble, and I am only now discovering that Bern is a terrible egoist, and that hurts me so much. Like Jesus when he asked the disciples: "Cannot you watch with me one hour?" I want to say "Cannot you have some sympathy with what I am suffering and feeling, while I only think of you and your work, year in year out?"
>
> But what use is all the talk, life is hard and difficult, hardly bearable, and every evening I go to bed with the wish: "Would that I did not have to wake up again." Good God, what cares weigh us down in every way, what difficul-

ties, what a workload, what unpleasantness I have to bear and have borne with pleasure, I have done what lay in my powers without wavering, but now I have grown tired. . . .

But I well know that without me, this whole founding of the colony would have been a shady and uncertain affair, I say that without boasting, but simply to excuse myself for leaving my poor Fritz in the lurch: for my life did have a purpose and a great goal, even if I neglected a duty toward the poor lamb.[41]

In contrast, Förster's brief and fraught letters from Asunción, where he was fighting a last-ditch battle against bankruptcy, show his increasing panic, and he complains bitterly of headache. On 15 May 1889, he wrote to tell Eli that he was delayed in Asunción and the only thing to do was to wait "*con patientia!*" Though the letter has a terse ending—"Hearty greetings. Goodbye"—this was his usual way of signing off and can have raised no alarm bells in Eli's mind. The note Förster wrote from San Bernardino on 2 June 1889, the day before he probably took his own life, is particularly poignant:

Dear Child!
A number of letters enclosed.
I am not feeling well; how are you all? I hope to be able to come to you very soon. Most heartily yours, Bernhard.[42]

This note, in large letters, together with a hastily scribbled and smudged postscript on another sheet of paper, gives an indication of what was going through his mind when writing to his wife. He had put her on a pedestal and now they were about to be ruined. And here he was, enclosing letters to her from Naumburg, where their relatives still believed that all was well with Neu-Germania. The irony of the situation will not have been lost on him. In an undated reply to one of her husband's letters sent one "Tuesday evening" sometime in spring 1889, Elisabeth wrote, "I have received your dear letter, it sounded so sad, and I am too my darling, just come back soon, I am so longing for you. Yes, our situation is serious."[43] Knowing full well how serious the situation really was, a desperate Förster died in his hotel room in San Bernardino on 3 June 1889, either through self-poisoning or, as Elisabeth always asserted, through a heart attack; we cannot know for certain unless the body is exhumed. It is sufficient to say that his worries certainly brought about his demise.

One of Elisabeth's main priorities when she rushed to deal with her husband's body was to make sure the doctor gave a diagnosis of heart failure. She either wanted to save face or, quite possibly, sincerely did not believe that he had committed suicide. With Nietzsche, too, she had refused to believe the diagnosis of syphilitic insanity, immediately settling on Nietzsche's abuse of hydrochlorate as a reason for his collapse. Here again, she might have been right, or just trying to save face.

Many years later, Adalbert Oehler, faithful to the memory of his late aunt, repeated the story that "ein Herzschlag machte seinem [Försters] Leben ein Ende,"[44] though from the press coverage at the time, he must at least have suspected that this might not be true. For example, the *Berliner Presse,* having received a wire from Asunción, carried a report the day after Förster's death declaring that he had died of strychnine poisoning. However, in spite of the deceit with which Elisabeth was prone to envelop inconvenient facts, I do not agree with Peters that Elisabeth's grief at Förster's death was necessarily faked: "When the news of his death reached Elisabeth, she displayed all the signs of grief of a loving wife who has suddenly lost her husband, although her love for Förster, never very strong, had declined considerably during her marriage, especially in the months after she heard of her brother's illness."[45]

How can we know that Eli's love for "Bern of her heart" (Herzensbern) was "never very strong"? The letters tell a very different story. Elisabeth's letter to Franziska dated 2 July 1889 clearly shows that she was distraught at the death of her husband:

> My poor dear mother, what have we done, there is a curse upon us. I am shattered, depressed beyond comfort, so full of sorrow and misery that I just don't know at all how to I can go on living. The pain over Fritz was not without hope, but now my only loved one! Without him, how am I to live? And that he died with a sense of outrage, outrage at that villain Klingbeil, that is too hard, too hard.
>
> Or if this meant that he had at least escaped from disgrace and misery, that would have been some comfort, but no, what we are now doing, giving the colony over to the government or to an English company, is also something we could have done earlier, and then we could have lived without worries at last, those dreadful worries that so embittered our happiness. But I ought to have asked myself a great deal more, I lived as though in a dream, it *never* came into my mind that God would not help my only loved one in time, but there is no God, otherwise the villains of the world would not hold sway.
>
> My only beloved certainly thought that God had deserted him, the payment of a large sum was imminent, and then his anger and worries put an end to his life, since his nerves were so affected by the constant worrying. If he had been a business man, the whole affair would not have affected him so much, and if the news had reached him here, that would not have been so bad either, I knew him so well and would certainly have discovered something to lessen his anxiety, or I could have warded off the heart attack, using compresses and foot baths as we used to do.
>
> And now I have to bear the dreadful burden alone, ah! Erck, the good man, actually bears the main burden as I am so broken in body and soul.

Nobody will lose their money, the dear departed made my money secure in his will, there will probably even be a little money over apart from that, please tell Paul [Förster's brother], so that nobody is concerned. If only somebody could lend me 7000–6000 marks, so that I could just make a few payments at once without adding these to the overall debt. There is a dreadful old man here, to whom Bernhard owed money and who nearly plagues me to death, naturally a German. Otherwise, everyone is good to me.

The German community in San Bernardino buried my heart's darling ("Herzensliebling") as a soldier, with all the honors they could muster, sixty horsemen followed [the coffin] and fired a salute over his grave. Yes, he died as a warrior in the struggle against the villainy of this world. Oh, my heart's darling, I wish I were lying with him in his grave.

With a thousand greetings I embrace you and Mütterchen [i.e., Frau Förster, Bernhard's mother],

Your Eli.

Nobody must write to me.[46]

Elisabeth's letter is extremely revealing. First of all, I would argue that it shows that she really did care for Förster. The help she now received from Oscar Erck, after Förster the most prominent of the pioneers and now *de facto* the leader of the colony, shows that she still retained some credibility in Neu-Germania. Her pride in the fact that he was buried "as a soldier" (see figure 13) is obviously genuine. However, in her reference to her despair at not having been able to put compresses on Förster as a cure for a heart attack (cold compresses and footbaths had always been Franziska's cure for any ailment in the family, hence "as we used to"), we witness her capacity to believe her own falsehoods: Even Franziska would know that neither a cold compress nor a foot bath is much use with a man who has had a heart attack, still less one who has taken strychnine. Elisabeth *wills* her version of events to be the truth. Otherwise, why should she make a long letter even longer with such a detail? The ominous remarks that there cannot be a God also belong to the category of fancy: It was not much use telling Franziska, of all people in the world, that there cannot be a God. However, the reminder to Franziska to tell Förster's brother Paul that *nobody* would lose their money shows that she is thinking pretty coolly. This was a huge lie, but it had to be told if the colony was going to have any future credibility. Elisabeth speaks of Bernhard's outrage, but *she* is the one who is outraged: with Bernhard for having killed himself, with God for letting him do it, with all the "villains" who brought her husband to this pass, and finally—with herself.

Eli Förster had tried extremely hard to make Neu-Germania into a success, but she had not been able to second-guess and preempt her husband's (pre-

Figure 13. Bernhard Förster
in military uniform.

sumed) suicide. If it is true that his testament safeguarded her property, it may
well have been the case that Elisabeth was financially better off with her husband dead. This might have been one of the calculations if he did indeed com-
mit suicide. He probably also felt at that point that she loved her brother more
than she loved him, as she had been grumbling about Neu-Germania and
worrying about Fritz in equal measure since she had heard the news of her
brother's collapse. It was irrational for Förster to be jealous of Nietzsche, who
was half the world away and as mad as a hatter by this point, but Förster was
not thinking clearly either. Elisabeth must have reproached herself in her heart

of hearts for having contributed to her husband's death. For a woman as spoiled as Elisabeth these were very tough emotions. I would argue that this letter shows a watershed with Elisabeth Nietzsche. Even allowing for the fact that Elisabeth could not be quite frank with her mother because the letter would be shown around (though this had not stopped her writing openly on 9 April earlier that year), we see here the typical belief in her own fibs that would become so much a part of her subsequent character.

A few months after Förster's death his friends rushed out a memorial tribute, *Bernhard Förster. Eine Schrift zum Andenken und zur Rechtfertigung* (Bernhard Förster: A Memorial Publication and Justification, 1889). For this collection, Elisabeth contributed a fourteen-page essay purportedly written earlier in 1889, when her husband was still alive, entitled "Ein Sonntag in *Nueva-Germania.*" It was written at Neu-Germania, "in the German spring of 1889," she informs us at the end, although she insists at the beginning that in Paraguay it was summer: "It is a midsummer Sunday, half past four in the morning,"[47] she begins idyllically and rather stylishly. After descriptions of happy natives and the food they eat, she turns to answer the questions people have asked her about her own suitability to lead the colony: "Perhaps my activities arouse some amazement, and dear friends might ask how I came to be in charge of things about which I could scarcely have a notion in my former life. . . . Certainly, I would prefer to deal with more intellectual matters, as I used to do, but my poor dear husband is so often away and has such an endless amount to do, that I am only too happy to take some of the work away from him, however thankless and objectionable it might be."[48]

The document contains an attack on Förster's anti-Semitic backers for lack of support, which will be discussed below; otherwise what is remarkable in the above is the near certainty that Bernhard Förster, who is spoken of in the essay as though he were still alive, was already dead when it was written. This would account for the confusion between German spring and Paraguayan summer and would set the writing in January. Elisabeth corrected her mistake in a later version, as will be discussed below. Santiago Schaerer's essay in the same collection was entitled *Erwiderung auf die Klingbeil'sche Broschüre über Neu-Germanien in Paraguay* (Reply to Klingbeil's Brochure on Neu-Germania in Paraguay) and dated "Asunción Junio 4 de 1889," which means that Schaerer, the "General-Commissär der Einwanderung" in Asunción, had sat down to write it on the day after Förster's (supposed) suicide.

If that were all to be said on the matter, the collection would merely seem a tribute put together with unseemly haste. That it was produced as an outright piece of propaganda for Neu-Germania is clear from the next work Elisabeth published in 1891 under the name Eli Förster, *Dr. Bernhard Förster's*

Kolonie Neu-Germania in Paraguay, dedicated "In memory of my dear departed spouse, Dr. Bernhard Förster." The book was thrown together in late 1890 when Elisabeth returned to Naumburg to settle her affairs. At that point she probably thought she would be going back to the colony permanently, and her top priority was to mobilize opinion in favor of the venture. In the first section, "Reports from Paraguay," Elisabeth reprints "Ein Sonntag in *Nueva-Germania*" (pp. 30–52) but makes some very interesting additions (shown below in italics). It is significant, too, that she now finishes the article with the information that it was written in January and February 1889, thus compounding the suspicion that it must have been written *after* the death of her husband in June 1889, as only this could explain the wonderfully idyllic tone, when we know from her letter of 9 April 1889 to Franziska that for the previous six weeks she had been plagued with eye trouble and quarreling with Bernhard. She wants everyone to believe in her sanitized version of the atmosphere at Försterhof, herself most of all. She signs herself Eli Förster née Nietzsche, an indication that her thoughts are beginning to be fixed on Nietzsche and that the double-barreled name is just around the corner. The original of this piece begins with a rather petulant passage bewailing the lack of support for the colony from the anti-Semitic party:

I. And our Neu-Germania? It is slandered, vilified, not supported by Germany, the Cinderella of the Jewish press and nevertheless—the only German community abroad that, though recently established, can call itself a German colony with full justification and that, while vigorously striving ahead, has achieved in all peace and tranquility that which all Germany demands.[49]

II. And our Neu-Germania? It is slandered, vilified, not supported by Germany,—(*ah, you anti-Semites, is that what you call loyalty, courage, to leave one of your most idealistic leaders so shamefully in the lurch?*)—and nevertheless the only German community abroad that, though recently established, can call itself a German colony with every justification and that, while vigorously striving ahead, has achieved in all peace and tranquility that which all Germany demands. *Besides, if anti-Semitism only had a negative side, manifested in the denial of Jewry and in noise and insults, there would not be any reason for it to help out in Neu-Germania and my husband would certainly not have sought their help, as he is infinitely tired of any passionate party allegiance if it were not justified.*[50]

Apart from small changes, the passage starting with: "And our Neu-Germania" remains intact, but instead of the colony being the Cinderella of the Jewish press, Eli now seeks to justify the whole program of anti-Semitism on which the colony is founded. Her tone changes from rebuking fellow anti-Semites for not being of more assistance to the colony to sighing that Bernhard Förster (deceased, so in other words, Eli Förster) was—or she *is*—heartily tired of politics. *Four more pages* castigating "the anti-Semites" have been inserted into the original pastorale, making it much less idyllic. The point she makes, at enormous length given the brevity of the essay itself, is simply that the anti-Semitic parties have not delivered the help they promised: "Let anti-Semitism show at last that it is capable of more than just envious and critical denial. Let it finally demonstrate here in Neu-Germania, *through action,* that it can take part in creating something genuinely German and of the folk."[51]

Elisabeth praises Hans Paul von Wolzogen, the editor of the *Bayreuther Blätter,* for his indefatigable support for Neu-Germania, and she lashes out at the Leipziger Kolonialgesellschaft for squandering money when they ought to have been acquiring land. But it is important *where* they buy land. Anyone considering the possibility of Germans emigrating to North America is firmly discouraged: "North America no longer offers the German émigré any advantages," a statement palpably ridiculous even at the time. South America is, on the other hand, "the land of opportunity,"[52] and further, "above all else, the German there remains German, Germanness can be retained there pure and unadulterated."[53] After this digression, she returns to her original topic of *Neu-Germania* with the disingenuous query: "How did it come about that modest people like us succeeded in having such a fortunate start?"

How, indeed? Knowing what conditions were really like for her, this willful deception, of others but, as it seems, herself as well, is truly staggering. It should also be observed that even without Förster's prompting, Elisabeth is still pumping out nationalistic rhetoric. Clearly, disillusionment had set in with both the Försters some time before Bernhard's death, but as already pointed out, their inflated ideals virtually guaranteed that they would be disappointed with each other and with Neu-Germania. Elisabeth seemed to really believe that if things had gone just a bit better, or if Förster had not been quite so eccentric, the colony might have had some chance of success, though the heavy soil was always going to be a problem.

The shock of the collapse of Elisabeth's Paraguayan dream accentuated traits in her personality that are routinely viewed as neurotic today: repression, denial, projection, scapegoating, and so on, all terms from Freud's repertoire that have entered the everyday vocabulary. She projected all unwelcome aspects of life outward. We have seen her propensity to deny a fact; to lay blame on others that she ought to shoulder herself, with a particular propensity to scapegoat people who contradicted her. Creditors become, for her, unreasonable "villains." Whistle-blowers like Klingbeil become liars. Repression becomes a characteristic coping device. These traits are, in fact, a benign camouflage for what really lay at the heart of Elisabeth's psychological dilemma: a love for her brother that verged on incestuous, a taboo that Elisabeth, the pastor's daughter, would have condemned in others. If she successfully concealed her neuroses, that was because her willpower was such that where others get migraines, or faint, or show psychotic tendencies, she got angry. She could deal with anger. She directed it straight back onto those who crossed her with the full force of her powerful personality. She won almost every fight. Only those like Lou von Salomé, who ignored her, or Cosima Wagner, who understood her, were able to withstand the blast of the will to power as manifested by Bernhard Förster's widow as she set to work in earnest to become a writer and biographer, first of her late husband and then of her brother.

4 The Will to Power

Nemesis in Naumburg

When Elisabeth arrived home in Naumburg shortly before Christmas 1890, Franziska hoped that she would stay in Germany to help her to look after Nietzsche. However, Elisabeth was still very much Eli Förster of Försterhof, as her printed letterhead proclaimed. She continued to propagandize for the colony and had even secured a Lutheran clergyman for Neu-Germania for two years. Yet when she returned to Neu-Germania in August 1892, she soon decided that she did not want to stay there. The wealthy colonist Fritz Neumann had published a scathing critique of the amateurish way Neu-Germania had been colonized in the German journal *Kolonial-Nachrichten*. He was especially bitter that Förster had given settlers the impression that they would be able to clear the forest and grow crops there. This had not been possible, as Förster should have foreseen. What really angered Neumann was that under Elisabeth's direction, more settlers had been sent into the forest in spite of the notorious lack of water, a crime in his view, since it put the health of the colonists in jeopardy. Elisabeth and Erck, who was now perforce the leader of the colony after the death of Förster, mounted a counter-campaign, unwisely as it turned out. Elisabeth also wrote a scurrilous attack on Paul Ullrich, one of the stalwarts of the colony who had been effective in gaining land titles for the colonists. Ullrich now wrote her an open reply, which the editor of *Kolonial-Nachrichten* published. Here he stated baldly, "If anything thorough-going is to happen in Nueva Germania, the first prerequisite is the removal of Frau Doctor Förster."[1] Although the letter was printed after Elisabeth had left Paraguay for Germany for the second and last time in September 1893, she knew of its contents before her departure.

Clearly, Elisabeth had become persona non grata in the colony she had helped to found. Once she had sold Försterhof in the summer of 1893, her money was secure and she was able to bow out of the colony, much to the relief of the majority of the residents. By prior arrangement with Franziska, a telegram had been sent requesting her urgent return to Germany, thus providing her with a perfect excuse to bid the colony farewell. She kept in touch from afar, supported the colony's successful but temporary effort to build a school, and even sent a crate of books over in the 1930s, though her generosity was limited to asking her friends and acquaintances to contribute spare volumes. Gabriele Reuter, residing in a house "Am Horn" overlooking the park in Weimar, gave several dozen, mainly novels by recent writers like Clara Viebig or Berta Traun, though there were also books on the British composer and Nietzsche enthusiast Frederick Delius as well as the Buddha. Elisabeth's own contributions included *Wagner und Nietzsche zur Zeit ihrer Freundschaft* (Wagner and Nietzsche at the Time of Their Friendship, 1915) and her husband's *Richard Wagner in seiner nationalen Bedeutung* (the second edition

Figure 14. Elisabeth Förster-Nietzsche, 1894.

of *Parsifal-Nachklänge*), his book *Deutsche Colonien im oberen Laplata-Gebiete,* and his essay *Über nationale Erziehung* (On National Education). The list also included *Also sprach Zarathustra* and other works by Nietzsche. A motley collection indeed for the stragglers left in the colony to devour in order to improve their minds.

No doubt Elisabeth's visit to Germany from Paraguay (which lasted from Christmas 1890 to summer 1892) was crucial for her later decision to return to Germany for good. Furthermore, by the time she reached Naumburg in September 1893, she had come to the conclusion that it would be more sensible for her to throw her weight behind propaganda on her brother's behalf than on behalf of her late husband. She had had time to reflect on the fact that Nietzsche's name was beginning to be known, while Förster's would have already been consigned to oblivion had it not been for her efforts to keep his memory prominent in the nationalistic press. This demonstrates that the anti-Semitic party was more interested in driving Jews out of Germany than in supporting crazed plans for Germans to emigrate. The *Bayreuther Blätter* continued to print anti-Semitic propaganda, although Wagner himself had died in 1883, and other prominent voices such as the historian Heinrich von Treitschke, for whom the term *Volk* (folk or people) was a nationalistic slogan, made sure that there was an anti-Semitic undercurrent in German society toward the turn of the century. In years to come, Elisabeth would frequently link Nietzsche's name with that of Treitschke because both despaired of German culture; here again she showed a wanton disregard for her brother's repugnance for nationalistic and anti-Semitic dogma.

Undeterred by the fact that she had abandoned her creditors in Paraguay, Elisabeth breezed into Naumburg determined not to be dominated by her mother even though she was once again under Franziska's roof. She found Fritz worse than she had anticipated. She also found it difficult to settle into her mother's regime, having run her own household and servants in Paraguay. She began to call herself by the double-barreled name Förster-Nietzsche and made the change legal with a court order. To channel her considerable energy, she began to sort out Nietzsche's *Nachlaß,* which included *Der Antichrist* and *Ecce Homo* as well as voluminous notebooks, some of them destined to see print under the title of *Der Wille zur Macht.* Here it must be pointed out that it was Peter Gast (Nietzsche's name for Heinrich Köselitz) who first alerted Elisabeth to the idea of publishing the *Wille zur Macht.* Franziska had faithfully kept every single scrap of paper deposited with her by Overbeck, who had escorted Nietzsche back from Turin. Peter Gast was already at work deciphering the notebooks on his own initiative. He wrote to Elisabeth on 6 October 1893 offering her his services as decipherer *extraordinaire,*

Figure 15. Franziska and Friedrich Nietzsche, 1892.

which one had to be in order to read Nietzsche's handwriting: "Only someone who is intimately familiar with Nietzsche's way of thought and wealth of vocabulary can extract this treasure. Everything must be copied onto loose leaves, which must be put into the order which the author will have given to you—or rather, into that order from a presumably great whole which their author will have formed. All in all there will certainly be 5 or 6 volumes each with 400 pages, and in addition the whole undertaking would equate with the planned work 'The Will to Power.'"[2]

Elisabeth now railroaded Franziska into agreeing to have two rooms on the ground floor knocked into one so that a rudimentary archive could be established. Here she not only began to assemble manuscripts by Nietzsche or on Nietzsche—early works of criticism were beginning to appear—she also set about collecting his correspondence, pointing out to those who did not wish to part with their letters from Nietzsche that they were the intellectual property of the newly established archive.

Elisabeth pursued her retrieval of material pertaining to Nietzsche relentlessly and with great success, though at that time she had no legal right to do so. She sacked Gast/Köselitz, the self-appointed editor of Nietzsche's *Nachlaß*, and in his place persuaded a reluctant Fritz Koegel (who liked Gast) to take on the task of editing a collected edition of Nietzsche's works. Eight volumes appeared in 1894. Elisabeth then began to cultivate a circle of prominent Nietzsche admirers like Rudolf Steiner and Gabriele Reuter, who came to visit the fledgling archive from Weimar. Others came to attend her soirées on the ground floor, where Koegel, who was fourteen years younger than Elisabeth, entertained guests on the piano. All this had so far happened with Franziska's consent, but the latter found Elisabeth's social events in the little archive grotesque, with Nietzsche immobilized upstairs and sometimes crying out like a wild beast. Klaus Goch writes: "She (Franziska) must have slowly become conscious of the fact that Elisabeth was using her sick brother as a defenseless instrument and medium to satisfy her own craving for admiration and urge for fame and recognition."[3]

Elisabeth now began the vendetta against her mother in earnest. Although she gave the excuse that Nietzsche needed more spacious living quarters, the motive for the vendetta was financial: Elisabeth was short of funds, and with Nietzsche came his pension. She tried, without success, to persuade the doctors to declare that Nietzsche was not receiving proper care from Franziska. At the same time, she temporarily raised questions about the publication of the fourth part of *Also sprach Zarathustra* by claiming that it might be too blasphemous to print (though Nietzsche had already had it printed privately), which put Franziska into a panic because she had signed a contract with

Naumann for its publication. In effect, mother and daughter were engaged in a "tug of love": Elisabeth was certain that she knew best how Nietzsche should be cared for, and she was just as certain that nobody but herself could handle his literary legacy properly. It is no wonder that Franziska was bewildered and hurt.

Elisabeth soon decamped with the archive to a neighboring street, where she set about writing the first volume of her brother's biography, *Das Leben Friedrich Nietzsche's* (The Life of Friedrich Nietzsche), which appeared in 1895. She wrote the work with a grudge against her mother, to whom she awards a laughably marginal role in Nietzsche's upbringing. Thus Elisabeth launched herself as a writer and would-be Nietzsche scholar while Franziska, still bearing the full brunt of Nietzsche's daily care, descended into despair. She confided her troubles in letters to her nephew Adalbert Oehler. In a letter of 23–24 June 1895, she complained of Elisabeth's "alteration of the facts"[4] in the biography of Nietzsche and in July–August of the same year pointed out that the childless Elisabeth might not be so ruthless if she had children of her own to care for: "It lies in the nature of parents to do what is in their power for their children, and especially when their father has been carried off so early, of course one tries to double up as substitute, to compensate for this dreadful, painful loss as far as it lies in a woman's power so to do."[5]

Franziska's remarks will strike a chord with the millions of single parents today who struggle to be both parents to their offspring, often overcompensating as a result. This Franziska certainly did, and if the adolescent Fritz had not been sent to Schulpforta he might have found it much harder to escape the kind of control which Franziska had still exercised over Elisabeth even when the latter was well over thirty. Franziska now stood aghast as her daughter demonstrated her independence.

The biography was not Elisabeth's only weapon in her struggle to gain the copyright of Nietzsche's works, and hence his royalties, from Franziska. Elisabeth had managed to persuade Adalbert Oehler, Nietzsche's coguardian (with Franziska), that she herself ought to be Nietzsche's literary executor instead of Franziska. Though she minced her words, what Elisabeth really wanted was control over Nietzsche's copyright, though she expressed herself in terms that suggested that Nietzsche was not being adequately cared for. Franziska, in contrast, wanted to keep her son under her protection in her own house, convinced that he was happy there. The doctors agreed, in spite of Elisabeth's bizarre claim that Nietzsche was being neglected. Elisabeth finally bowed to Franziska's desire to keep Nietzsche at 18 Weingarten, extracting in return a severe sacrifice from her mother: Franziska was bullied into signing away her claim to Nietzsche's royalties on 18 December 1895.

However, Elisabeth had to pay 30,000 reichsmarks into Nietzsche's bank account by 1 February 1896, something she was only able to do through the last-minute assistance of Meta von Salis and the good offices of the banker Robert von Mendelssohn. In August 1896 she moved to 5 Wörthstraße, Weimar, complete with the growing archive.

In this way, Elisabeth took control of the *Nachlaß*, something which Franziska could now see as potentially catastrophic for Nietzsche's reputation in view of Elisabeth's increasingly reckless disregard for the facts, which, as we have seen in the last chapter, was well established in Elisabeth's literary repertoire before Franziska herself became aware of it. The strange thing is that although Elisabeth had many detractors—at this time, the chief of these was Franz Overbeck—most people were prepared to give her the benefit of the doubt for decades, awarding her manuscripts a respect for accuracy that they manifestly did not deserve. The God-given chance to get her hands on her brother's *Nachlaß* and, in effect, to write *Der Wille zur Macht*, allowed Elisabeth to see herself as her brother's collaborator again, just as she had been with the catalog that she helped him to prepare in 1869, before he left Germany to take up his post in Basel. But now Elisabeth no longer had to play second fiddle to Nietzsche: she could make her brother obey *her ideology*, even though he despised it during his lifetime. In this way, she could extract revenge for Nietzsche's hurtful neglect of her, while appearing to herself and others as a selfless and devoted sister.

What is also striking is that Elisabeth wanted Nietzsche *all to herself*, a trait dominant in her reaction to Lou von Salomé and now transferred onto her own mother. Franziska's concern for her son appears levelheaded in contrast, for all her earlier possessiveness toward her offspring. At all events, Elisabeth was by turns calculating and histrionic in her struggle for Nietzsche's copyright, behavior that deeply distressed Franziska and perhaps even hastened her death of cancer of the womb in 1897. To be fair to Elisabeth, she was greatly affected by Franziska's painful illness and tried to provide practical help such as suggesting a woman doctor.

In 1896 Elisabeth became impatient with the fact that Koegel's preparations for volumes 11 and 12 of the collected works (the volumes that contained *Der Wille zur Macht*) were not moving ahead. The chaos of the material and the poor quality of Nietzsche's handwriting in later manuscripts made the problem of editing intractable (Nietzsche had joked to Gast that he himself could scarcely read his own writing), but Elisabeth blamed it all on Koegel, whom she now tried to sack from his position as editor. In December 1896, by intriguing with a reluctant Rudolf Steiner to replace Koegel, she caused a crisis between herself, Koegel, and Gustav Naumann, as Koegel had no intention of going quietly and sought support from the publishing house. By this time, Steiner had lost all respect for Elisabeth, though on principle he would have welcomed the challenge of trying to sort out the notebooks, at that time referred to as the "Umwerthung aller Werte" ("Transvaluation of All Values"). David Marc Hoffmann writes, "Steiner had come to the bitter conclusion that collaboration with Nietzsche's sister, and therefore his role as Nietzsche editor, were both impossible."[6]

Matters were settled when Elisabeth gave Koegel three months in which to prepare *Der Wille zur Macht* for publication, but as this task proved to be impossible, he threw in the towel in 1897. Another factor in Koegel's dismissal was that Elisabeth had taken exception to Koegel's fiancée, Emily Gelzer. Elisabeth objected to the Gelzers' religiosity, but she herself had suggested Emily as a match for Koegel. Peter Gast just thought she was jealous of the younger woman. He wrote to Overbeck on 7 October 1897: "Since he [Koegel] became engaged to Fräulein Gelzer, his star began to wane with Frau Dr. Förster. It appears that Frau Dr. Förster only tolerates bachelors round her, people around whom there floats the slight possibility of a liaison with her."[7]

Elisabeth now appointed Arthur Seidl, who was subsequently replaced by the brothers Ernst and August Horneffer. Elisabeth tersely summed up the situation in a letter to Steiner dated 8–23 September 1898: "Dr. K. [*sic*] lost his position as son and heir of the archive through his bride and his parents-in-law."[8]

In spite of the mutual dislike existing between Gast and Elisabeth, when it finally became clear to Elisabeth that nobody but Gast could read Nietzsche's abominable handwriting, he was summoned to Weimar in the summer of 1900 to resume his task of editing Nietzsche's *Nachlaß*. By this time, most people close to Nietzsche such as his friend Franz Overbeck (who was astonished that Gast could contemplate working with Elisabeth again) and his publisher Naumann were under no illusion about Elisabeth's quest to become *the* exponent of Nietzsche's ideas. To further that end, she had taken instruction from Rudolf Steiner in the rudiments of Nietzsche's philosophy in September 1896, whereupon Steiner had concluded that she was just about the last person to be able to grasp Nietzsche's ideas. As she was a bright and talented child, one must conclude that personality factors rather than a lack of intelligence were the stumbling block. Of course, her motivation in trying to master her brother's philosophy was not a love of learning, but a drive to know every detail of his life and to participate in his work at one remove, by making propaganda for it. Elisabeth's behavior at this point and subsequently can be called shrewd rather than clever.

In order to compile material for the biography of Nietzsche, Elisabeth approached those whom she knew had corresponded with her brother in order to have all his letters returned. Overbeck resolutely refused to cooperate and Cosima Wagner, another main player in this area, declared she could not find any letters written to her by Nietzsche and surmised, perhaps disingenuously, that she must have burned them when she moved from Triebschen to Wahnfried. Cosima and Elisabeth had met at Cosima's hotel in Berlin during Elisabeth's flying visit home in 1891; Elisabeth was at that time on the brink of publishing *Dr. Bernhard Förster's Kolonie Neu-Germania in Paraguay.* In an attempt to maintain their friendship, Cosima invited Elisabeth to Bayreuth that year, but Elisabeth was too busy arranging her second trip to Paraguay to contemplate a trip to Bayreuth—which had once been the summit of her ambition. Another reason for Elisabeth's coldness toward Cosima Wagner soon became manifest when Cosima frankly opposed Elisabeth's whole endeavor to root out Nietzsche's correspondence. "Your brother is still alive, like nearly everyone mentioned in these letters," she pointed out—with masterly tact—in a letter dated 25 August 1894.[9] The next month, in a letter dated 23 September, she asked Elisabeth, "Does publication really matter to you? Whatever your brother had to say of importance, he said, and don't you think, like me, that silence is the only appropriate thing here?"[10] Elisabeth was impervious to Cosima's delicacy and offended by her lack of appreciation of the heroic work she had undertaken. In Elisabeth's support one should also add that Cosima was at that very time establishing a Wagner cult to rival anything Elisabeth was to do; the latter therefore reacted to Cosima with a certain pique.

Although Cosima resolutely refused permission for Elisabeth to print extracts from her own letters to Nietzsche, Elisabeth disregarded her wishes, publishing extracts in the second volume of the biography in 1897, by which time she had settled in Weimar. Forewarned, Cosima wrote a hurt letter in protest dated 20 December 1896: "Why did you not apply to me for permission for this publication?—Or don't you know that I possess the rights to these letters?"[11] She asked for any second edition to leave out any mention of her (which Elisabeth subsequently ignored) and ended on a remarkably conciliatory note, considering their tiff: "Farewell, my dear Elisabeth, and receive the friendliest greetings from your old friend C. Wagner."[12]

As one might expect, the extracts quoted by Elisabeth do not show Cosima in a favorable light. The latter's pompous comments on Nietzsche as the benighted author of *Menschliches, Allzumenschliches* backfire badly, making her appear sententious, which is no doubt why Elisabeth, who herself had trouble with that particular text by her brother, chose to include them. In this way, she obliquely criticized the text with impunity. As we have seen, although Cosima objected to Elisabeth's actions, she resolutely refused to quarrel with her, partly because she had decided to repay in kind by publishing Nietzsche's letters to Wagner in the *Bayreuther Blätter*. She wrote Elisabeth a cordial letter dated 18 February 1901 in which she fully recognized Elisabeth's claim to copyright, but said she was confident that Elisabeth would understand her motives for publication: "The letters which I handed over to the *Bayreuther Blätter* will be the last, and you will, I know, understand the spirit in which I did this."[13]

Although Cosima was paying Elisabeth in her own coin, she still tried to reason with Elisabeth against publication of her own correspondence with Nietzsche, ending her letter thus: "With regard to our letters, I repeat the request that you will not publish them, please. The collected works [of Wagner] are there, the works of your unfortunate brother likewise, they reveal everything and therefore nothing can cloud the truth. Again, I thank you, and ask you to accept my hearty greetings, sent with friendly intent. Yours, C. Wagner."[14]

Cosima had behaved exactly as Elisabeth would have done in publishing Nietzsche's letters to Wagner, but Elisabeth's usual remedy in such cases, the law courts, was not an option: one could not sue the Bayreuth machine. Cosima was in any case much more useful as a friend. Elisabeth went on to publish two extracts from letters written by Cosima to Nietzsche in *Wagner und Nietzsche*. In the first of these extracts, Elisabeth asserts that Cosima had enthused over Nietzsche's two essays "Socrates and Tragedy" and "Greek Music Drama," which Nietzsche had sent to Wagner in January 1870 (actually, Nietzsche had sent only the essay on Socrates). Wagner and Cosima both replied appreciatively on consecutive days (4 and 5 February 1870) and had both told Nietzsche how agitated Cosima had been over what Nietzsche had written: "The Master will have told you how excited I became on reading them,"[15] Cosima began, and she enthused for several pages. Elisabeth's motive in bringing Cosima Wagner into her book on the friendship between Wagner and Nietzsche was to demonstrate how Nietzsche's genius for Greek culture was appreciated by both Richard *and* Cosima, who as Liszt's daughter had an enhanced cultural pedigree and gave her book added *kudos*. Besides that, she could not resist alluding to the letters from Nietzsche, so cruelly destroyed by Cosima: "My brother's answer to the two excited and exciting letters from Wagner and Frau Cosima appears to have been particularly special and out of the ordinary, for Wagner's answer to it is quite gripping. How sad that we do not know what my brother wrote and that this magnificent letter was probably destroyed at Wahnfried."[16]

As it happened, Elisabeth was able to retrieve only *one* letter written by Nietzsche to Cosima from the time of the cordial relations between Nietzsche and the master, though some letters written later are extant. She printed this "unique" letter, dated 19 June 1870, in her late work *Friedrich Nietzsche und die Frauen seiner Zeit* (Friedrich Nietzsche and the Women of His Time, 1935). In this letter, Nietzsche mentions to Cosima that he is including with the letter the fair copies he had promised of the two essays mentioned above ("Greek Music Drama" and "Socrates and Tragedy"). Cosima's reply to Nietzsche on 24 June 1870 incidentally confirms that she had only seen the essay "Socrates and Tragedy" on the earlier occasion:

> Most esteemed Herr Professor,
>   How moved I was by the dedication in the essay which you kindly sent me. Thank you for knowing so surely that it would afford me great pleasure, and for having wanted to provide that pleasure. I read the essay on music drama in the last few days and can only repeat that I view it as an indispensable foyer to the great portal of your Socrates, and that I could have saved myself very extraneous excitement [over the earlier essay] if I had known what a lively, warm description of Greek works of art preceded it.[17]

Cosima's formal tone to Nietzsche, which is characteristic of her excessive politeness in all her letters, was echoed by Nietzsche's own formality in addressing his letter to "Most esteemed Baroness"[18]—Cosima could not adopt Wagner's surname until August 1870.

It was so important to Elisabeth to make capital out of Cosima that she had all Cosima's letters to herself from the time of Nietzsche's friendship with Wagner typed up to help her to prepare *Wagner und Nietzsche*. Though the Goethe-Schiller Archive contains the handwritten correspondence between Elisabeth and Cosima from 1871 to 1901, the typewritten pages stop abruptly at 1879. Ignoring the vagaries of her later correspondence with Cosima, who died in April 1930, Elisabeth wrote a gloriously hypocritical article, "Cosima Wagner," to mark Cosima's ninetieth birthday in 1927, which appeared in *Nord und Süd* that December, as well as the article "Cosima Wagner und Friedrich Nietzsche: Wahrheit und Dichtung" (Cosima Wagner and Friedrich Nietzsche: Truth and Fiction), which appeared in *Der Tag*, 15 May 1930.[19] In the latter, she sought to lay to rest the notion that Nietzsche was Dionysus in the teasing myth set in train by his note to Cosima from Turin, dated 3 January 1889 and headed "To the Princess Ariadne, my beloved,"[20] where he refers to himself as a crucified Dionysus. The classical reference is to the abduction of Ariadne by Dionysus after Theseus had abandoned her on the island of Naxos. Elisabeth insists that in the Wagner circle, Cosima was jocularly referred to as "Ariadne," and that von Bülow was Theseus and Wagner—certainly not Nietzsche—was Dionysus. "Bülow just wanted to express that he was superseded by the God,"[21] she explains. This might be Elisabeth's version of events, and it might even be true, but the myth implicating Nietzsche and suggesting that his admiration for Cosima Wagner was more than just polite friendship will no doubt continue.

The Nietzsche-Archiv, Weimar

One of the friends Elisabeth approached in 1897 in search of biographical material was Meta von Salis, who had already assisted her financially when she wrested control of Nietzshe's literary legacy from Franziska in 1896. After the death of Franziska, Nietzsche was transferred to Weimar so that Elisabeth could care for him and in July 1897, he and Elisabeth moved into Villa Silberblick, then as now number 36 Humboldtstraße, the house that Meta von Salis had specifically purchased to provide a home for Nietzsche as well as premises for the burgeoning archive. That same year, Meta obliged Elisabeth by writing a sensitive account of the time she had spent with Nietzsche in *Philosoph und Edelmensch: Ein Beitrag zur Charakteristik Friedrich Nietzsches* (Philosopher and Gentleman: A Contribution to the Description of Friedrich Nietzsche, 1897). Here, Meta pledges her wholehearted support for Nietzsches's concept of aristocratic values. The short monograph includes a discussion of some of Nietzsche's other key concepts.

Immediately after moving into Villa Silberblick, Elisabeth started work on alterations and coolly sent her patron, Meta von Salis, the bill. The latter was so outraged that she broke off all contact with Elisabeth, to whom she wrote vituperative letters pointing out exactly what she thought of her. Elisabeth ignored these with aplomb. Meta eventually allowed Elisabeth to purchase Villa Silberblick through Adalbert Oehler, as she was no longer prepared to deal with Elisabeth. Meta von Salis was remarkable in that although she was from the Swiss aristocracy, she harbored radical feminist leanings. Circumstances conspired to undermine her activism, and she eventually opted for a quiet retirement on the island of Capri. Though Nietzsche's friendship with such a committed campaigner for women's emancipation as Meta von Salis is even more extraordinary than his friendship with Malwida von Meysenbug, Meta, like Malwida, was a true friend to Nietzsche to the last. It is all the more significant, then, that she broke off relations with Elisabeth, having realized the latter's increasingly reckless arrogance. She and others who cared deeply for Nietzsche were now concerned that both he and his intellectual legacy were in Elisabeth's sole care.

For the three years 1897–1900, Nietzsche vegetated in Villa Silberblick, soon to be renamed Nietzsche-Archiv (and in October 1999 established as the Kolleg Nietzsche-Archiv). He was occasionally put on show by Elisabeth, who allowed people to see him as a grotesque special treat. Finally her brother died on 25 August 1900. He had been ill for eleven years. By this time, and ironically enough, Nietzsche was not only known but already a cult figure. Furthermore, this would have happened even *without* Elisabeth's efforts: a flood of poets, artists, playwrights, novelists, musicians, and (more warily) philosophers of every nationality were beginning to draw their inspiration from his writing. To mark Nietzsche's death, Elisabeth staged a commemorative ceremony at the Nietzsche-Archiv and a large burial ceremony at his birthplace in Röcken. The event at the Nietzsche-Archiv was so oversubscribed that people were crushed against the coffin itself. Nietzsche was buried at the left side of his parents, but when Elisabeth died, her posthumous wishes were carried out, and Nietzsche's grave was moved even further to the left so that her own grave could be placed between those of her parents and that of her brother.

Elisabeth inherited 36,000 marks from Nietzsche on his death, whereupon she was able to repay the loan advanced by the banker Mendelssohn in 1896, already discussed in connection with her tussle with her mother over the rights to Nietzsche's works. Her finances were subsequently routinely precarious, chiefly because of her grandiose lifestyle. In the same year as Nietzsche's death, Elisabeth officially established the Nietzsche-Archiv in the Villa Silberblick as a going concern with a committee consisting of Hans Olde, Elise Koenigs, Hans Rathman, and Harry Graf Kessler. Kessler was an expert in stage design and became director of the Museum für Kunst und Kunstgewerbe (Museum for Art and Arts and Crafts) in Weimar in 1902. He had first approached Elisabeth in 1895 when she still lived in Naumburg, hoping to acquire work by Nietzsche to publish in the periodical *Pan.* Having met Henry van de Velde in 1900, Kessler introduced him to Elisabeth. Van de Velde, after his move to Weimar, undertook the refurbishment of the Nietzsche-Archiv (completed in 1903), and in 1911 he and Kessler drew up plans for a Nietzsche-Memorial, though this project was shelved when Elisabeth objected to the scheme (which included a sports stadium) as too ambitious. Van de Velde left Germany in 1917, but Kessler continued his collaboration with Elisabeth until the 1930s.

The Will to Power

Nietzsche had announced at the end of *Zur Genealogie der Moral* (1887) that his next work would be *Der Wille zur Macht: Versuch einer Umwerthung aller Werthe,* but he never actually *wrote* it, though if he had not suffered a mental collapse he might well have done so, and it would probably have resembled one of his aphoristic texts such as *Menschliches, Allzumenschliches.* All this is speculation. The catchy phrase cloaks a concept rather difficult to define and grasp. Nietzsche first described the will to power in *Also sprach Zarathustra* (1883–85) as a struggle for rank that manifests itself in all things in the natural world: "Wherever I found a living thing, I found the will to power; and further, in the will of the servant, I found the will to be master."[22] At the level of natural phenomena in such a thing as a humble leaf, the will to power seems to have little to separate it from Arthur Schopenhauer's "will to life," and as the driving force in life it can be compared with Darwin's theories. However, Nietzsche remained critical of Darwinism, rejecting the notion that life is a relentless physical struggle of evolutionary significance in favor of his own theory that life entails a straightforward struggle for supremacy: "where there is a struggle, people are struggling for *power*."[23] For Nietzsche, man's *metaphysical* evolution into the "higher man" and ultimately the *Übermensch* was what mattered. Conscious of his need to put clear water between himself and Schopenhauer, Nietzsche also drew a distinction between their doctrines in this area. In contrast to Schopenhauer's nihilism, Zarathustra's yea-saying is a mantra anticipating and warding off the reader's temptation to compare the will to power with Schopenhauer's will to life: "Only where there is life is there also will: but not will to life, but—so I teach you—will to power!"[24]

Nietzsche also forged a link between his abstract concept of the will to power and his even more mystical concept, eternal return, which also receives its debut in *Also sprach Zarathustra*. The important thing is not that the moment of time should recur eternally, but that man should affirm each past moment with his will:

> Every "it was" is a fragment, a puzzle, a nasty accident—until the creating will says to it: "but this is how I wanted it!"
> —Until the creating will says to it: "But I want it to be like this! I shall want it like this!"[25]

Though the will can (indeed for Nietzsche *must*) be creatively active, the will to *power* in *Also sprach Zarathustra* is essentially unconscious. It is perhaps always best described at the abstract level, but Nietzsche gave examples of men of action like Napoleon and Cesare Borgia in whom the will to power was clearly manifested. For Nietzsche, then, the will to power was something that exists in everyone and everything, though the struggle it depicts is not necessarily against others: in the *Übermensch*, the struggle is against petty emotions like envy and resentment (Nietzsche used the nuance-laden French term *ressentiment*) which drags a person down to the all-too-human level. In relation to Nietzsche's sister Elisabeth, who was the complete antithesis of Nietzsche's vision of the *Übermensch,* the will to power, fueled by *ressentiment* at woman's servile role that was probably unconscious, dovetailed with aspects of her megalomaniac propensities to make her a living embodiment of this principle at the personal level. Thus, alas, Elisabeth's will to power dictated that *Der Wille zur Macht* should be published in 1901, though Gast's strategy of highlighting the need for the work in order to ingratiate himself with Elisabeth should not be underestimated.

Nietzsche had written twenty-five outlines for his proposed new work, and Elisabeth decided upon a simple list of four headings as the rubric for the new work:

THE WILL TO POWER.
ATTEMPT AT A TRANSVALUATION OF ALL VALUES.

Book One: European Nihilism
Book Two: Critique of the Highest [in the 1906 version: Former] Values
Third Book: Principle of a New Fixing of Values
Book Four: Upbringing and Breeding.[26]

In *Das Leben Friedrich Nietzsche's* (IIii), Elisabeth stated that Nietzsche had sent her this plan in a letter from Nice dated 17 March 1887. This spurious letter is not found in his correspondence, but the same material is found in the collected works, where Nietzsche's draft, also dated 17 March 1887, is identical except for the fact that he shortens the title to "+++ of all Values." Again we see how simple it was for Elisabeth to pretend that Nietzsche had been in contact with her about his projected work. The problem for Elisabeth's editors was trying to make the erratic jottings fit into this overly tidy formula. William Schaberg, while admitting that "there is some wonderful material in *The Will to Power,*" has expressed grave dissatisfaction with this way of working:

> Elisabeth selected one of the many outlines that Nietzsche had sketched for *The Will to Power* and then raided his notebooks for relevant passages to fit that format. By assembling a collection of unpolished and unrelated jottings, Elisabeth—with the active collaboration of the recently hired Peter Gast—"created" a work that resembled in many respects the aphoristic books that Nietzsche had published between 1878 and 1882. . . . The fiction that the *Will to Power* is one of Nietzsche's books—even his most important book—continues to exist in the public mind and, for that matter, in the minds of many nonphilosophical scholars.[27]

Elisabeth thus gave the impression that *Der Wille zur Macht* was a work that Nietzsche had all but completed, a myth that has gained in strength over the years. She even spread a rumor that she had heard that Nietzsche had completed a manuscript before his collapse and cited rumors that it had been offered for sale for 5,000 marks. She soon persuaded herself that her invention of the missing manuscript was plausible and went on looking for it for three decades. She was still hoping that it would surface when she wrote "Das geheimnisvolle Manuskript" (The Mysterious Manuscript) for the *Naumburger Tageblatt* in 1929.[28] The story helped to substantiate the suspicion that *Der Wille zur Macht* was the rough draft of a coherent work. In fact, as we have seen, it was stitched together in haste under the constantly changing editorship of the archive. For Elisabeth, all delays become intolerable as she moves toward her goal: After so many disappointments, she finally has the opportunity to parade herself as a philosopher in her own right and to present the world with a masterpiece ostensibly by her brother which is really *her* work. She has not just compiled it: She *is* the will to power. At the symbolic level, the book permits her—at last—to seal her partnership with her brother.

Unlike Elisabeth, the editors Gast, Koegel, and their collaborators did not invent passages or stoop to forgery, though they turned a blind eye to many of Elisabeth's practices. On the whole, they were honorable men committed to providing the best possible transcription of what most people would call illegible script. Actually, neither the change in editorship nor the haste with which the work was assembled would have made much difference to the end result: *Nothing* was really going to impose discipline on these jottings until, with the advent of word processing, a proper scholarly method could be devised of transferring an impression of what Nietzsche had actually written onto the printed page. For not only did he scribble sentences and paragraphs virtually at random, he also made so many alterations and corrections that to suggest that these flow as coherent passages, as the current text published as *Der Wille zur Macht* does, is patently ridiculous.

A look at the runic script in Nietzsche's notebooks, in which he sometimes wrote from back to front, or wrong way up—whatever he felt like—clearly shows that the material making up this *Nachlaß* could not be published in 1901 without doing Nietzsche a grave disservice. To what extent is it ethical to print a passage by an author if he has expressly crossed it out? And, moreover, to print it without *saying* that it was crossed out? This systematic double-crossing of both the author and the reader of *Der Wille zur Macht* is what constitutes the scandal of this publication. It is particularly regrettable that this should happen to Nietzsche, the most punctilious editor of his own works. There could be no question of his polished style emerging from these scribbled notes. That said, they are of interest, if only to show us what was going through Nietzsche's mind in the years before he collapsed.

Besides satisfying other unconscious needs for Elisabeth, discussed above,

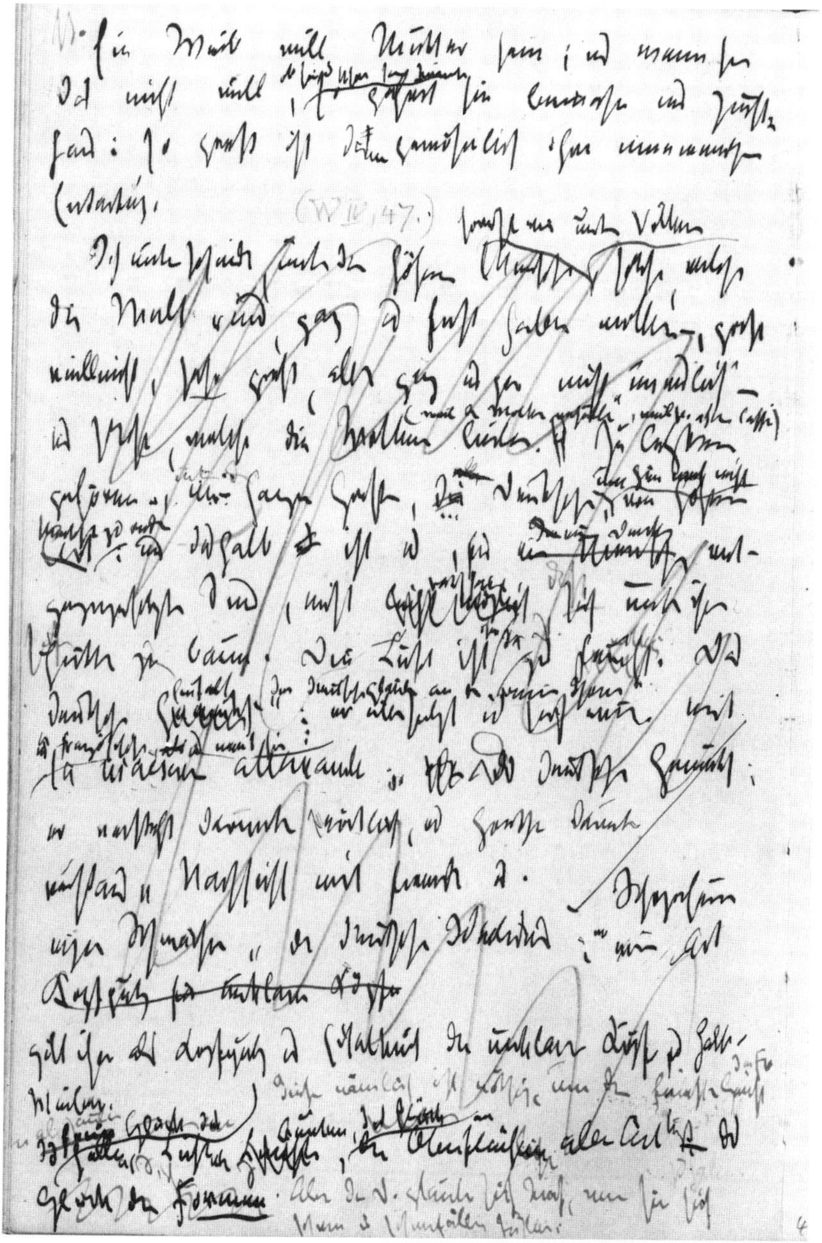

Figure 16. Page from Nietzsche's late notebooks.

Der Wille zur Macht promised to provide much-needed pecuniary help. As indicated already, the text did not enhance Nietzsche's reputation, indeed, on the contrary, some of the shots fired are unworthy. To take one example (top left of figure 16): "A woman wants to be a mother; and if she does not want this, even though she can, she almost belongs in prison, so great is her innermost degeneration as a general rule."[29] True, Nietzsche said some highly misogynic things about women throughout his work, and equally true, he genuinely believed that it was woman's *destiny* to give birth to the next generation, but his dogmatic suggestion that women who do not want to bear children should be sent to *prison* puts him into bed with humorless despots like Bernhard Förster. Only the word *almost* relieves the dogmatic tone somewhat, though this is jeopardized by the ominous last word in the extract, "degeneration." The effect of this passage is offensive, even though it is *interesting*. But Nietzsche did not actually *publish* this sentence, though as can be seen from figure 16, he did not cross it out either; he deleted most of the rest of the page. As we see, Elisabeth did Nietzsche no favors at all by publishing material that her brother had not been able or willing to prepare properly for publication.

When Elisabeth issued *Der Wille zur Macht* in 1901 as volume 15 of the collected works, it contained 483 aphorisms, whereas the expanded version, edited by Elisabeth and Gast and published in 1906, contained 1,067. It is not surprising that Elisabeth preferred the longer version. Moreover, Mazzini Montinari would find, during his investigations in the 1960s that led him to embark on the critical complete edition of Nietzsche's works, closer inspection revealed that some aphorisms in the 1901 version were removed from the 1906 version.

In a chapter entitled "The Will to Power" in *Das Leben Friedrich Nietzsche's* (IIii: 1904), Elisabeth confesses to the shortcomings of the original 1901 version of *Der Wille zur Macht,* knowing full well that a corrective issue was in preparation for publication: "The giant work which the author had in mind remained unfinished. It fell to us as editors at the Nietzsche-Archiv, weak as we were and albeit with insufficient understanding, to conscientiously put together the priceless building blocks in line with such of the author's indications as have survived. In the first edition we did not succeed straight away in giving a general overview, and many things are still missing which the author had expressly intended for this work."[30]

Obviously not happy with the first edition and not yet wishing to reveal the reason—explanation is reserved for *Das Nietzsche-Archiv: Seine Freunde und Feinde* (The Nietzsche-Archiv: Its Friends and Foes, 1907), in which she castigates the editors Fritz Koegel and Ernst Horneffer for their shoddy work

—she fell back on a tactic she used in most of her works: that of quoting extensively from the book in question. Though Elisabeth had quarreled with Peter Gast when she returned to Naumburg from Paraguay, he proved invaluable to the archive in being able to decipher Nietzsche's script, and he is given fulsome praise in *Das Nietzsche-Archiv,* largely, one suspects, in order to bolster confidence for the 1906 edition of *Der Wille zur Macht* that Elisabeth coedited with Gast.

By the time she wrote *Der einsame Nietzsche* in 1913, which also contains a chapter with the title "Der Wille zur Macht," the 1906 and the 1911 versions had come out, the latter with very good notes prepared by Otto Weiss. In *Der einsame Nietzsche,* instead of quoting extensively from *Der Wille zur Macht* in the chapter of that name, which was her usual method of working, Elisabeth attempted to explain the philosophy contained in it, resting much of her argument on quotations from her cousin Richard Oehler. Thus we read that "Nietzsche's transvaluation book is a magnificent prediction of the future development of human culture."[31] This is a pretentious claim for a very dubious text: Oehler's statement, in speaking specifically of the "transvaluation book," refers to the distinction Elisabeth tried to draw between *Der Wille zur Macht,* a huge work which Nietzsche planned to undertake and with which she claims he was occupied from 1882, and *Die Umwerthung aller Werthe* (The Transvaluation of All Values), which she asserts he undertook in September 1888 and had virtually completed when he collapsed. The distinction rests on Nietzsche's letter to Deussen written on 26 November 1888, in which Nietzsche had declared that: "My *Transvaluation of All Values,* with the main title 'The Antichrist,' is finished."[32]

In *Das Nietzsche-Archiv,* Elisabeth divides *Die Umwerthung aller Werthe* into four books:

Book I: The Antichrist; Attempt at a Critique of Christianity
Book II: The Free Spirit; Critique of a Philosophy As a Nihilistic Movement
Book III: The Immoralist; Critique of the Most Disastrous Kind of
    Ignorance, Morality
Book IV: Dionysus; Philosophy of the Eternal Future[33]

Elisabeth's attempt to suggest that *Der Antichrist* was part of a larger work was to a certain extent justified, since Nietzsche himself created this confusion in a series of letters written between September and November 1888. Gloating over the imminent publication of *Der Fall Wagner* (The Case of Wagner), Nietzsche wrote to Gustav Naumann on 15 September to suggest that publication of *Götzen-Dämmerung* (*Twilight of the Idols*), which Naumann had in manuscript, should be delayed so as not to detract from the effect of the vituperative attack on the late Wagner. At this point, Nietzsche was still referring to *Götzen-Dämmerung* as *Der Müssiggang eines Psychologen* (The Idleness of a Psychologist), but he informed Gast of the change of title in a letter dated 17 September 1888. The very next day, having received news from Naumann that the latter had already begun work on *Götzen-Dämmerung*, Nietzsche hurriedly withdrew his suggestion of any delay beyond the one or two months needed for typesetting, and in fact, *Götzen-Dämmerung* appeared in 1889. In the 18 September letter to Naumann, Nietzsche writes that his "incredibly *serious* work" (namely, *Die Umwerthung aller Werthe*) will need to be separated from his other works by at least a year.[34] In a letter to Overbeck dated 14 September 1888, Nietzsche had written "To my own astonishment, I have already finished the final version of up to half the first book of my *Umwerthung aller Werthe*."[35] From these letters we can conclude that Nietzsche viewed half of *Der Antichrist* as finished by mid-September.

Nietzsche worked with feverish haste for the next two months, but what he *actually* wrote from 15 September to 4 November was *Ecce Homo,* as he informed Gast in a comparatively lucid letter of 13 November 1888. The *Dionysos-Dithyramben* and *Nietzsche contra Wagner* also stem from this period. There was simply no time for Nietzsche to write any more of the *Umwerthung aller Werthe* than already existed in the notebooks and that Elisabeth had already published in *Der Wille zur Macht.* Nietzsche reported to Georg Brandes on 20 November 1888 that he had written *Ecce homo,* adding "The whole thing is a prelude to the *Umwerthung aller Werthe,* the work that lies finished in front of me." The next sentence continues "I swear to you that in two years' time we shall have the world in convulsions. I am a destiny."[36] Nietzsche's remark to Paul Deussen on 26 November indicates that in his delusion he had begun to conflate *Der Antichrist* with *Die Umwerthung aller Werthe,* confusing the part with the whole. His remark to Brandes that in two years he would cause turbulence clearly indicates that at a rational level he knew that the *Umwerthung* (alias *Der Wille zur Macht*) would take some time to complete, time that he did not have, as things turned out.

In *Das Nietzsche-Archiv,* Elisabeth clung to the notion that two distinct works were involved. She points out that the first book of the *Umwerthung* had already been published, which is demonstrably true in that *Der Antichrist* had appeared, after Nietzsche's madness, in 1894. The second and third books of the *Umwerthung* clearly overlapped with material already published in *Der Wille zur Macht.* Elisabeth convinced herself, however, that the fourth part of the *Umwerthung* must have been lost, whereas a close reading of Nietzsche's correspondence during the fall of 1888 reveals that even he did not really think that it had been finished. Unable to read Nietzsche's handwriting in the notebooks, Elisabeth was able to speculate that her brother had written more than he had. The point has already been made that Nietzsche's posthumous jottings were too fragmentary to allow a considered structure to be superimposed in this way. Blithely ignoring these considerations, Elisabeth speculated that the spurious "missing manuscript" discussed above might be a version of *Dionysos:* "Perhaps the often-mentioned and sought-after '5,000–mark manuscript' will after all turn out to be a bundle of papers belonging to Dionysus."[37] Again we see that she could not only invent myths aplenty, she could then wholeheartedly believe in them.

It is with amazement that one learns at the end of the polemic *Das Nietzsche-Archiv* that it was Elisabeth's intention to write a history of the archive in this text, for all she does, besides presenting a completely specious methodology for the basis of *Der Wille zur Macht,* is provide an inventory of those against whom she has a grudge and those of whom she approves: We learn that Elisabeth liked Erwin Rohde but hated Overbeck, Koegel, and the Horneffer brothers, and—despite her earlier aversion—thought Peter Gast was wonderful. It is thus astonishing that after her attack on Koegel within the main text, Elisabeth actually includes his 1895 essay on Nietzsche's method of working as part of the appendix at the end. It is as though she scarcely realizes when she is insulting people, let alone speaking ill of the dead (Fritz Koegel and Franz Overbeck had died in 1904 and 1905 respectively).

At all events, the confusion over the text of *Der Wille zur Macht*—which is by its very *nature* confusing—is blamed on the editors of the first edition of *Der Wille zur Macht,* who according to Elisabeth had no respect for dates. Yet Elisabeth's *Nietzsche-Archiv* is itself so confusing that it is impossible to glean any hard facts about Nietzsche or his *Nachlaß* from the text, beyond her assertion that the archive was merely founded to publish Nietzsche's *Nachlaß* and, having done so, will soon disband, something that will make many readers smile in view of her continued attempt to present the world with her version of Nietzsche until the day she died. For example, in both *Das Leben Friedrich Nietzsche's* (IIii) and *Der einsame Nietzsche,* Elisabeth declared that the idea of writing *Der Wille zur Macht* came to Nietzsche when he served for six months in the Franco-Prussian War of 1870. This subtle attempt to link the emergence of the notion of the will to power in Nietzsche's mind with armed conflict is typical of the ploys Elisabeth routinely used.

Martin Heidegger's contribution to the activities of the Nietzsche-Archiv during the 1930s was of crucial importance for the way in which Nietzsche's ideas were manipulated to fit in with National Socialist propaganda. A large part of this manipulation was his insistence that *Der Wille zur Macht* was Nietzsche's definitive text. Heidegger introduced a method of "*Dekonstruk-*

tion" to interpret the text of *Der Wille zur Macht* in his seminal and weighty *Nietzsche* (1961). Many philosophers, especially recently in the English-speaking world, have followed his lead in hailing *Der Wille zur Macht* as Nietzsche's best work. In particular, it has been much quoted in recent postmodern research on Nietzsche, especially in the United States. Following Jacques Derrida's lead in deconstructing Nietzsche, and reading Derrida in translation, scholars have forgotten or not realized the extent to which Derrida was influenced by Heidegger. Furthermore, it is truly astonishing that so many philosophers who claim to be able to interpret Nietzsche cannot actually read him in the original language and do not even see this as a disadvantage.

It was Heidegger's premise that Nietzsche's published works were essays merely leading up to his true philosophy, contained in the notebooks: "What Nietzsche published himself during the period of his productivity is always a foreground. This is also true of his first work *Die Geburt der Tragödie* (1872). The actual philosophy remains behind as *Nachlaß*."[38]

Heidegger goes on to say that we cannot understand Nietzsche's thought "if we have not, in questions on Nietzsche, grasped Nietzsche as the end of western metaphysics and gone over to the quite different question of the truth of being." Heidegger recommends that readers of his lengthy two-volume *Nietzsche* should refer to Alfred Baeumler's paperback edition of the 1911 version of *Der Wille zur Macht.* "It is a faithful reprint of volumes XV and XVI of the collected works, with an intelligent afterword and a brief and good summary of Nietzsche's biography."[39] Having genuflected to Baeumler's accuracy and praised his afterword, Heidegger criticized Baeumler's politicization of Nietzsche's thought and set about demolishing his reliance on a faulty view of Heraclitan flux in *Nietzsche: Der Philosoph und Politiker* (Nietzsche: The Philosopher and Politician), which Baeumler published in 1931. Baeumler provided his own "Nazification" of Nietzsche's thought by stressing the primacy of *Kampf.* Heidegger defines the will to power as follows: "'Will to power' is incontrovertibly a striving toward the possibility of exercising power, a striving toward the possession of power."[40]

Heidegger gave an early warning to his readers of *Nietzsche* that Elisabeth Förster-Nietzsche's biography of her brother, though informative, contained inaccuracies, but he defused his own criticism by saying that this was simply part and parcel of writing a biography: "But like everything biographical, this publication must be approached with great caution."[41] In the same way, he *knew* how chaotic were the notebooks that formed the basis for *Der Wille zur Macht,* but he allowed the pretense to continue that they are a solid body of writing from which sense can be made. A more serious charge one can level at Heidegger is that he made Nietzsche more obscure for readers rather than less so by a plethora of abstract terms, which is precisely the kind of objection Nietzsche held against philosophy. The following example from Heidegger's *Nietzsche,* which purports to be an exposé of the concept of the will to power, is an example of his obfuscation:

> The expression "will to power" designates the fundamental character of that which has being; everything that has being, that is, is, in so far as it is: will to power. By this, the character of that which has being is expressed in its capacity as something which has being. But with that, the first and actual question of philosophy is still not answered, but only the preliminary question. The decisive question for the person who can and must still ask philosophical questions at the end of western philosophy is not just the question as to what fundamental character that which has being shows, how the being of that which has being is characterized, but instead it is the question: what is this being itself?[42]

Heidegger uses ideas from Nietzsche's *Nachlaß* to construct what is virtually a new Nietzschean ontology. Although this is not the place to argue at length on whether a philosopher's political beliefs can be separated from his work, we owe it to Nietzsche to at least raise the query whether he himself would have been as horrified at having his philosophy taken apart and tinkered with by a National Socialist collaborator like Martin Heidegger as he was when the anti-Semites of his day took such liberties. Karl Schlechta (himself a fellow traveler during the Third Reich) in the third volume of his *Nietzsche: Werke in drei Bänden* (*Nietzsche: Works in Three Volumes,* 1954–56), tried to address the issue of the corruption of Nietzsche's *Nachlaß,* but in trying to sort out the dates of the notes which made up the manuscript, he allowed further confusion to creep in. Nevertheless, in *Der Fall Nietzsche* (1958), Schlechta virulently attacked both Elisabeth's falsifications and the more important fraud of pretending that Nietzsche had written a great work entitled *Der Wille zur Macht.* When, in the 1960s, Mazzino Montinari realized the necessity for a new definitive edition of Nietzsche's works, he criticized Heidegger and the team who worked on the *Historisch-Kritische Gesamtausgabe* from 1933 for taking liberties with Nietzsche's literary legacy: "The fact that the epoch-making compilation *Der Wille zur Macht* was not intellectually tenable as Nietzsche's main text was demonstrated in 1906–7 by Ernst and August Horneffer and again 50 years later by Karl Schlechta. . . . Here I merely want to stress once more that this insight—namely that Nietzsche had not written a work of that title nor wanted to write one—was a well-known fact when work was begun on the Nietzsche edition at the beginning of the thirties in the Nietzsche-Archiv itself."[43]

Without Elisabeth's insistence, the material for *Der Wille zur Macht* would

have remained quite innocently as posthumous jottings about which scholarly remarks could be ventured without them being viewed as a true work by
Nietzsche. It is enough to say at this point that Elisabeth's meddling with
Nietzsche's *Nachlaß* was profoundly mischievous, not simply because the text
of *Der Wille zur Macht*, "this gross fabrication" as Schaberg puts it, was "foisted
on the philosophical world"[44] with consummate skill, but because Nietzsche's
reputation subsequently sank or swam with the fortunes of the book. Now
that the circumstances under which it was written are better known, Nietzsche's reputation as a "politically incorrect" author among ordinary citizens
has begun to improve. Given Nietzsche's driven desire for people to understand what he said, and his meticulous care in presenting his thoughts for
future generations, one can see the enormous damage Elisabeth did to Nietzsche and indeed to several generations of earnest scholars. Strangely enough,
though, *Der Wille zur Macht* was not an overnight best seller. Although the
book aroused interest when it was first published, it was not immediately *the*
Nietzschean text one had to have read, for the world of Nietzsche enthusiasts
was at that point still divided into two camps, those who thought *Also sprach
Zarathustra* was his best work and those who preferred *Die Geburt der
Tragödie*. The most popular Nietzschean concepts around the turn of the century and well through the "Expressionist decade" (1910–20) were the emergence of the *Übermensch* (for fans of *Also sprach Zarathustra*) and the culti-
vation of all that was "Dionysian" (for fans of *Die Geburt der Tragödie*).

With the growth of the political right during the Weimar Republic, *Der
Wille zur Macht* came to be highly regarded. Though Hitler loved the sound
of the title, which lent itself so conveniently to National Socialist propaganda, he almost certainly never read a word of it. But ripeness is all. It was easy
for Leni Riefenstahl to cash in on the notion of will in the title of her film of
the 1934 Nuremberg rally, *Triumph of the Will*, in which she idolized Hitler
to the point of deification. Riefenstahl's film, with its obvious resonance with
the central concept of the will to power in its monolithic shots of one col-
umn of soldiers after another, graphically portrayed the might of Hitler's
troops, and indeed, subtly legitimized power per se. Inevitably, Nietzsche's
name became linked with the Fascists through such oblique tactics as well
as through the open welcome of his ideas in the work of leading Fascist ideo-
logues, with Baeumler as a case in point. After the collapse of the Third Reich,
many philosophers, especially in the Soviet bloc during the cold war, chose
to avoid a philosopher whose ideas had been so heartily embraced by the
National Socialists. Hence, Nietzsche scholars are still at work stripping away
the myths with which Elisabeth encased her brother. How to rid him of the
belligerent mantle encapsulated in the slogan "the will to power" is a peren-

Figure 17. Elisabeth Förster-Nietzsche in the garden of the Nietzsche-Archiv, 1904.

nial problem. At some point one has to concede that the two world wars of the twentieth century made Nietzsche's rhetoric on struggle, strength, and mastery hard to defend unless the scholar is prepared to battle out Nietzsche's meaning within the context of his plans for the emergence of a new type of human being.

Friends and Foes

It has been suggested throughout the present work that the will to power manifested itself in Elisabeth though her authoritarian actions and in her virtually megalomaniac self-belief, but this must be seen in conjunction with the very concrete fact that Elisabeth's personality was distorted and at times deluded. If she told a lie, she was able to believe it; it became the truth for her, something Rudolf Steiner had spotted in his dealings with her. Naturally, there were a great many people who knew and admired Elisabeth, and most people, even if they hated her, recognized her charm. But "charm" is hardly a complimentary attribute. Although there are no doubt many sisters whose affection for their brother is disquietingly strong, it is rare for a woman with a mediocre cast of mind to wreak such havoc on a male relative's intellectual legacy (this does not mean that Elisabeth was not clever, rather that she saw no reason to use her cleverness in an intellectually scrupulous way)—and all in the name of love. It brings home to us just how much Elisabeth must have felt thwarted at being sidelined from Nietzsche's life, not just in his attraction for Lou, which must have felt to Elisabeth as though he were being unfaithful, for all her talk about trying to find him a wife, but in his friendships with people like the Overbecks, who came to disapprove of Elisabeth, as she knew. We must now examine Elisabeth's vendetta against her former friend Ida Overbeck, mounted with the same zeal as her fight with Franziska over Nietzsche's copyright but fought more publicly. What made it difficult for Ida Overbeck was that in 1905, the year of Franz Overbeck's death, Elisabeth had made friends with the Swedish banker Ernst Thiel, who now underwrote her legal bills. Elisabeth now could and did sue at will on several occasions.

Elisabeth had tried to retrieve *all* Nietzsche's letters and (*pace* the "missing manuscript") the bulk of his unpublished *Nachlaß* for the archive. She bitterly regretted that some material had gone astray in Sils Maria and Turin, and she blamed the loss on Franz Overbeck, who should have been more careful with documents when escorting Nietzsche back to Germany from Turin. Elisabeth complained that he should have also made sure that Nietzsche's landlord in Sils Maria handed over all papers still in his care. Overbeck's dereliction of duty is not really what made Elisabeth angry, however, but his open contempt for her and, above all, his refusal to hand over Nietzsche's letters to him. As Elisabeth rightly expected, these letters contained highly insulting references to her, especially in the wake of the "Lou Affair." When Elisabeth heard that Overbeck was dying, she asked Ida Overbeck to make him sign a deathbed agreement to hand the letters over to the archive. When Ida refused to do this she, too, was berated as a contemptible enemy of the Nietzsche Archive. In *Das Nietzsche-Archiv*, Elisabeth fired a warning shot to Ida Overbeck that she would sue anyone trying to print Nietzsche's letters; ignoring this warning, Carl Albrecht Bernoulli did precisely that when he published the first volume of *Franz Overbeck und Friedrich Nietzsche: Eine*

Freundschaft (Franz Overbeck and Friedrich Nietzsche: A Friendship) in 1907. Elisabeth immediately obtained a court injunction against Eugen Diederichs to prevent Bernoulli's second volume from appearing, which also contained letters from Nietzsche to Overbeck, which she claimed were the property of the archive. Ultimately she won this battle, but Bernoulli scored a moral victory by having the second volume (which appeared in 1908) printed with large blanks where the letters ought to have been. (Some of the volumes, which had already been printed, had the letters inked out instead.)

Passing over the sheer bad taste of Elisabeth's spiteful comments on the recently deceased Overbeck in her polemic *Das Nietzsche-Archiv,* we can see that much of her anger is really directed at Ida Overbeck, who was very much alive in 1907 and just as stiff-necked about refusing to part with Nietzsche's letters as her husband had been. But there was worse: Elisabeth knew (from Nietzsche) that Ida had made uncomplimentary remarks about her with regard to the "Lou Affair," a period in her life that had been traumatic and that had driven her brother away from her. Ida repeated these allegations in Bernoulli's book. She also openly discussed Nietzsche's putative offer of marriage to Lou in the first volume, asserting that Nietzsche had made it plain to the Overbecks when he visited them in Basel in 1882 that he had only done this for the sake of good form.

Public discussion of whether Nietzsche had offered to marry Lou von Salomé or not was calculated to make Elisabeth see red. Much of her attack on Bernoulli's *Franz Overbeck und Friedrich Nietzsche* was therefore damage limitation to forestall further unsavory revelations. Elisabeth was not really able to attack Ida in *Das Nietzsche-Archiv.* She therefore found Overbeck's weak spot—to which he had admitted—his neglect in making sure all Nietzsche's papers were safely gathered in from his various abodes. The technique of transference was simply another manifestation of her personality disorder, and strictly speaking, one ought to sympathize with her if, as one suspects, she could not help her paranoid excesses. Sympathy is often hard to muster in the light of the damage she did to Nietzsche's name.

The potential damage the Overbeck correspondence could do to Elisabeth was partially averted by litigation, though of course, readers today have access to all Nietzsche's extant letters in the definitive *Briefwechsel: Kritische Gesamtausgabe* (Correspondence: Critical Complete Edition, 1975–). The point is that although Nietzsche had been frank to Overbeck about his sister, he had tried to be direct with Elisabeth as well. Plenty of letters from Nietzsche to his sister contain forthright comments on her behavior, though it is also possible that she destroyed some of his letters if they were too uncomplimentary, just as she removed Nietzsche's bitter references to Franziska and Elisabeth in the first edition of *Ecce Homo*. The following, from a letter dated 31 March 1885, is typical of the kind of comment Nietzsche made to Overbeck: "Dr. Förster has returned from Paraguay, great rejoicing in Naumburg. Perhaps something good for me will emerge from my sister's marriage: She will have her hands full and will possess someone whom she can completely trust and to whom she really *can* be useful: both of which were not always possible with regard to myself."[45] Such comments were obviously potentially highly damaging for Elisabeth, who had set herself up in a role that suggested that she had always been Nietzsche's closest companion.

If the Overbeck correspondence was by no means the *only* potential conduit for insults to Elisabeth, what it also contained, which Elisabeth was trying hard to cover up—since this was the period in her life when she was most dependent on Ernst Thiel's financial support—was Nietzsche's steady barrage of criticism against Bernhard Förster and the anti-Semitic party to which he belonged. For example, Nietzsche, who had not yet met his brother-in-law, wrote to Overbeck on 6 October 1885, "I have not yet set eyes on Dr. Förster, as he is staying in Westphalia, *lecturing* and riding alternately on his two hobbyhorses (Paraguay and anti-Semitism) and will do the same for Saxony in the month of November."[46] Since Elisabeth never did anything by halves, having rendered Bernoulli mute she now drew a veil of silence round her late husband as well, and during her dependence on Thiel's cash she downplayed her husband's characteristics to the point where a contemporary friend and writer, Annie Francé-Harrar, commented: "He was more than buried: he was taboo."[47] When Thiel could no longer subsidize Elisabeth and she had to turn to the National Socialists for financial backing, Förster bounced back into favor. Not only did Elisabeth present Hitler with a copy of Förster's infamous petition to Bismarck, she openly acknowledged what an excellent husband he had been on the first page of *Friedrich Nietzsche und die Frauen*. Elisabeth's Machiavellian principle that expediency was of paramount importance is really only another example of the way the will to power in her personality coincided with a monumental insensitivity toward other people.

After the publication of *Das Nietzsche-Archiv* in 1907, Elisabeth was gratified to find that rather than having to wind up the archive, she was actually able to expand it courtesy of the newly formed Stiftung Nietzsche-Archiv (Nietzsche-Archiv Foundation), founded 6 May 1908. This regularized the existence of the Nietzsche-Archiv as a center for Nietzsche research. With money from Ernst Thiel, who gave financial guarantees for the continuation of the work of the archive, the Nietzsche-Archiv at last seemed launched as a solid academic institution. In theory, the organization should have taken the responsibility for publishing Nietzsche's works out of Elisabeth's hands, since the chair of the committee was Adalbert Oehler, but in practice Elisabeth remained in full control. Other members of the committee of seven constituted in 1909 were Harry Graf Kessler, Raoul Richter, Hans Vaihinger, Max Oehler, Hermann Gocht, and Max Heinze. It cannot be presumed that men like Kessler and Richter knew of the forgeries that were going on under their noses at the archive, but Richard Oehler and Peter Gast were certainly implicated, especially when it came to the question of material published posthumously as *Der Wille zur Macht.* Mazzino Montinari, who had originally merely wanted to know which published texts by Nietzsche could be viewed as definitive so that he could use them as the basis for a translation of Nietzsche's works into Italian, comments

> Our hair stood on end when we came to read, in the shorter Nietzsche-biography by Förster-Nietzsche (1912–1914) [*Der junge Nietzsche/Der einsame Nietzsche*], such comments by Richard Oehler as "apparently [!] not printed in the works" or "cited from the manuscript, not printed in the *Nachlaß*" or "apparently not published in the posthumous works" regarding decisive quotations from Nietzsche cited in the text. Weren't these also texts that we would have wanted to translate? . . . What was still slumbering away in the manuscripts after more than seventy years of which we—in Florenz—would never have been able to learn?[48]

Unbelievably, it is still not possible to state the full extent of Elisabeth's manipulations, for although most of Nietzsche's works and letters have been published in the collected work edited by Mazzino Montinari and Giorgio Colli, his last notebooks still await definitive research, since the *Nachberichte* (supplementary reports) to volumes 6 and 8 of the *Kritische Gesamtausgabe* were never compiled—even though the supplementary report for volume 7 did appear. (The supplementary reports contain Nietzsche's rough drafts and variant manuscripts.) Instead of compiling the relevant supplementary reports to complete their edition numerically, de Gruyter has recently published three volumes of a planned six transcribing the *Nachlaß* of 1885–89 (which is the contents of the last thirteen of Nietzsche's notebooks). These volumes (*KGW* IX i–iii) use a color code to show where and when Nietzsche inserted new comments into his notebooks and provide readers with an accurate impression of the truly chaotic nature of the original material that supplied the text for *Der Wille zur Macht.* When volumes 4–6 have appeared, all Nietzsche's mature work will be available in print. With regard to Elisabeth Förster-Nietzsche, a truly vast amount of material on and by herself still slumbers in the archive.

5 Elisabeth and the Woman Question

Nietzsche and Women

The main platform of the Allgemeiner deutscher Frauenverein (General German Women's Association), founded by Louise Otto-Peters in Leipzig in 1865, was the campaign to increase German women's employment opportunities. In spite of the prevalent view that men should provide for their families, not all women managed to find a marriage partner, and many married women were forced to work. Nietzsche ignored these social factors and instead targeted his attack on the superficiality of better-off women. He often satirized the "*Ewig-Weibliche*" (Eternal-Womanly) as an encapsulation of the deceit involved in a woman's attempt to ensnare a mate, but the term also sums up the caring qualities that Wilhelmine society, including Nietzsche, expected to find in a woman. The leadership of the General German Women's Association certainly did not want to challenge the values enshrined in it, but they did want to improve women's access to education, and this is what put Nietzsche on a collision course with nascent German feminism. It is indeed a paradox that a man so virulently opposed to women's educational betterment should have had so many women friends who were highly educated—often having had to go abroad to achieve this—and who were campaigners for the women's cause, especially as he made jokes about being the *bête noire* of the women's movement when these friendships were at their height. With some exultation he told Elisabeth in a letter of 7 May 1885 that he was now the scourge of Zurich University. Beginning with "My dear, dear Lama" he wrote: "The penny has finally dropped with all those who are mad about 'Women's Emancipation' that I am their *bête noire* [böse Thier]. The female students in Zurich are furious with me. At last!—and how *many* such 'at lasts' do I have to wait for!"[1]

   Although Nietzsche was courteous in his everyday behavior with his women friends, in his writings he castigated women scholars and writers who, he believed, were weakening their sex by denying themselves the breeding role. Nietzsche, the Greek scholar, had convinced himself that the glories of Greek culture had come about only because of the way women in ancient Greece were virtually kept under house arrest. In his quest to rescue German culture, Nietzsche blamed modernity for producing women with new demands about their rights. Underlying much of his hostility was the knowledge that George Sand and a certain proportion of ultra-radical feminists were openly lesbian. Nietzsche's passion for the future could not embrace the thought that such women would ever be tolerated in society: It is as though "Monsieur" George Sand had a contagious disease. Outraged at the "manly" image Sand projected, Nietzsche tarred other women writers like Madame de Staël and Madame Roland with the same brush and declared them anathema: "It betrays a corruption of the instincts—quite apart from the fact that it betrays bad taste—when a woman refers to Madame Roland or Madame de Staël or Monsieur George Sand as if thereby anything were proved to the *advantage* of 'woman as such.' Among men, those mentioned are the three *comical* women as such—nothing more!—and precisely the best unwitting *counterargument* to emancipation and female self-glorification."[2]

   Oblivious to the fact that the three women mentioned above had little in common with each other beyond the fact that they were writers, Nietzsche warned that women surrendered their femininity if they pursued a career: It turned them into *Mannweiber* (manly women). His pronouncement in *Jenseits von Gut und Böse* (1886) really says it all: "When a woman has scholarly leanings, there is usually some malfunction in her sexuality. Even barrenness leads to a certain manliness of taste, man being namely, if you will permit, 'the barren animal.'"[3] For Nietzsche, a woman's sexuality was grounded in her fecundity. If she denied that biological demand, she was unnatural: "The struggle for *equal* rights is, in fact, a symptom of disease: every doctor knows that."[4]

   Nietzsche had already stated in *Also sprach Zarathustra* that woman uses man as a means to her one desire: the child; these remarks are reinforced with a bitterness which verges on hatred in *Ecce Homo*:

> Woman needs children, man is only ever the means: Thus Spoke Zarathustra.— "Woman's Emancipation"—that is the instinctive hatred of the *failure*, that is, the woman who cannot give birth versus the one who is successful,—the struggle against "man" is only ever a means, a pretext, a tactic. In raising *themselves*

up as "woman as such," "higher woman," "woman as idealist," they want to bring the general rank structure of women *down;* no surer method for this than grammar-school education, trousers, and political rights for gullible voters. Emancipated women are fundamentally the *anarchists* of the realm of the "Eternal-Womanly," those who have come off badly and whose underlying instinct is revenge.[5]

Nietzsche's "emancipated" women friends included Malwida von Meysenbug, whose *Memoiren einer Idealistin,* a seminal work for German feminism, had appeared in 1876, the very year that Nietzsche spent the whole winter with her in Sorrento. Malwida's book describes her exile to London after the 1848 revolutions; here she gave German lessons and was for several years housekeeper to the widowed Russian political émigré Alexander Herzen, before turning to writing for an income. Nietzsche's curses upon women who remained single and, worse still, wrote, appeared in print after the friendship with Malwida had cooled slightly, since Malwida was and remained an ardent Wagnerian. We can only wonder whether Nietzsche and Malwida ever actually discussed his views on female emancipation.

Meta von Salis first came into contact with Nietzsche through Malwida, whose book had fired Meta with enthusiasm for the feminist cause. Subsequently, as we have seen, Meta was so devoted to Nietzsche that she made sure he was decently housed in Weimar. Meta von Salis refused to be drawn into an argument over Nietzsche's misogynist remarks. In her tract *Philosoph und Edelmensch: Ein Beitrag zur Charakteristik Friedrich Nietzsches* (Philosopher and Gentleman: A Contribution to the Description of Friedrich Nietzsche), she actually attacked the many vain and superficial women who gave Nietzsche legitimate cause to berate them. Elisabeth, too, found this the best strategy to adopt, as we shall see below. Several students from the University of Zurich, among them Hedwig Kym, Resa von Schirnhofer, and Helene Druskowitz, were also well disposed toward Nietzsche, though they might have paused had they known how Nietzsche spoke about them in his letters (as in his letter to Elisabeth, quoted early in this chapter). Helene Druskowitz took exception to his moral philosophy (as well as his misogyny) and criticized him openly.

Nietzsche's *codex* for women placed Elisabeth in a very difficult position. She had a talent for writing and no talent at all for finding a husband and having babies. Nietzsche had stressed that the emancipated woman seeks her revenge on *other women,* a statement that is absurd if one reflects that the patriarchal system in Germany gave men rights over women, enshrined in law, which extended to women's *bodies:* a husband could insist upon his conjugal rights and could determine when, or indeed if, his wife should breast-feed her baby. Even the civil code of 1900 did little to improve women's status in Wilhelmine German society. Nietzsche displaces the very real grievance women had over their inequality onto the *women* concerned: by stating that those women who have managed to fulfil their biological destiny are the envy of their emancipated sisters, he makes the emancipated woman the repository of *ressentiment.* From being the one with cause for complaint, she becomes the one with a case to answer. His whole argument could be ignored if one did not know how frequently women, even today, insist that they are *not* emancipated for fear of appearing unnaturally manly or "pushy."

If Nietzsche was "dynamite" (in his terms) on many issues, his views on women are not in that category and have dated badly, since even in his day he represented the old guard. This, then, was Elisabeth's dilemma: how to convince her readers that Nietzsche was a friend of women in spite of what he had written in his works and without making it too obvious that she herself had not fulfilled the criteria he had laid down for women. Since attack is always the best form of defense, she followed Nietzsche's lead in criticizing the manliness of the feminists at every juncture, whether or not they actually were "manly" in habit or appearance. As Nietzsche's position on campaigners for women's rights was fundamentally indefensible, even among women who shared his belief that a woman's biology is her destiny, Elisabeth naturally became embroiled in a circular argument whenever she tackled the question of Nietzsche and women. It is all the more interesting to observe how her own views on women's issues emerge through the authorial voice in her novella "Coffee-Party Gossip about Nora," her only surviving sustained attempt to write a novella.

"Coffee-Party Gossip about Nora"

Though "Coffee-Party Gossip about Nora" cannot be dated accurately, it was in all likelihood written in April 1882, during the precise period when Nietzsche was succumbing to Lou von Salomé's charms in Rome. On 23 April 1882 Elisabeth wrote a postcard to Nietzsche to tell him that work was progressing, and on 5 May she wrote a note to tell him that it was complete. From Nietzsche's comment in his letter to Lou von Salomé of 26 June 1882, in which he invited Lou to spend that August with him in Tautenburg, we can see that he viewed his sister's literary attempts with patronizing tolerance at best: "Assuming that you have nothing better to do in the month of August and find it fitting and feasible to live with me here in the forest, my sister would accompany you here from Bayreuth and live with you here in a house. . . . My sister, about whom you might like to ask Rée, would require seclusion for precisely this period in order to hatch out her little novella-eggs."[6]

Leaving aside any further discussion of Elisabeth's disappointment in Lou von Salomé, we can surmise from the above that Elisabeth, who according to the same letter had loyally created an "idyllic little nest" for Nietzsche in Tautenburg, must have felt crushed by his lack of encouragement, informed as it was by his fundamental contempt for women writers, especially since Nietzsche bent his own rules for Lou von Salomé. Perhaps he had some inkling that Elisabeth might become overweeningly egocentric if she took up writing— for this did actually happen when she took up her pen in earnest, ironically enough to spend the next *four decades* writing about Nietzsche. It is a sign of just how close brother and sister still were at this point that Elisabeth bowed to her brother's criticisms and, although "Coffee-Party Gossip about Nora" was finished, she apparently made no attempt to publish the manuscript. Fortunately she did not destroy it, since it is a revealing document. The manuscript does not have a title, so I have given it the provisional title "Coffee-Party Gossip about Nora" because a coffee party is the central event: I also thought it might have been inspired by the pencil drawing of the coffee jug that Elisabeth had laboriously produced (discussed in chapter 2), perhaps after holding a morning coffee party rather like the one she portrays in her novella. The text is given in translation at the back of this volume, and although the story is remarkably witty and well told considering that it was (presumably) Elisabeth's first attempt at a lengthy story, it has very little literary merit. On the other hand, it allows us a glimpse into what lay hidden under the surface of Elisabeth's apparently carefree relationship with her brother.

Wisely locating the story in an environment she knew well, Elisabeth describes Weißenburg (Weißenfels + Naumburg) as a small town where everyone knows everybody else and where a *Kaffeeklatsch* is a major social event. Elisabeth's observation of manners highlights the petit bourgeois behavior of her characters. The village has an eligible bachelor, the philology professor Georg Eichstedt, but he has not yet turned his mind to finding a partner, to the despair of Tante Linchen, who brought him up. The village also harbors several eligible young ladies, one of them the daughter of the "Polish" von Ramstein family (two von Ramstein families inhabit the town), but the only one the reader has any sympathy for is Nora Werner.

In her narrative, Elisabeth draws a clear distinction between women who flatter men—like Julie von Ramstein—and who pretend to be intellectuals when they do not hope to capture a husband and Nora Werner, who simply gets on with reading. She does not read books in order to pursue any particular course of study (a word her mother utters with contempt) but out of a genuine desire for knowledge. Although the novella's heroine promises much by taking the name of Henrik Ibsen's character in *The Doll's House* (1879), which appeared in German in 1880 (substantiating the supposition that the story was written between 1880 and 1882), Nora is not emancipated in any way that ties in neatly with the aspirations of the women's movement: Though hints are dropped, there is no real engagement with the issue of why Nora's education has been so sorely neglected. It is pertinent to recall that Ibsen had to write a revised ending of his play for the German stage because of the resistance in Germany to the idea that a mother could walk out on her children; Nora in the German version *returns home* at the end of the play. By the same token, Elisabeth's Nora is defined by her motherly qualities: She has not remained single in order to pursue a career but in order to look after her motherless nephews.

Nora is at home in Weißenburg for a holiday while her half-brother, for whom she keeps house, visits Japan. Frau Werner hopes that Nora, now relieved of the daily chores of housekeeping, will feel the urge to establish her own household. To her dismay, she discovers that Nora is not interested in receiving the attentions of suitors because she is too wrapped up in trying to understand Immanuel Kant. Like Linchen Eichstedt, Frau Werner despairs of the young generation:

> But the Eichstedt establishment was not the only one this lovely spring morning in the good town of Weißenburg where a parental heart was plagued with worries about the marriage prospects of its offspring, oh no! There were several of them! It appears to be ever harder for the present generation to tie Hymen's knot. Sons are strongly resistant and—would you believe it—daughters too! And these don't just resist for the sake of appearance, as was the fashion in the good old days, no, even the daughters sometimes completely refuse to listen to anything about getting married. A new philosophical generation is growing up which apparently takes as its motto the exact opposite of the biblical saying. "It is a good thing to remain single" these youthful lips inform us.

Nora views herself as too old for romantic attachment, while Georg is so wrapped up in the life of the intellect that he does not actually notice that Nora is pretty until his aunt points it out. Even then, he insists that it is not necessarily a good thing for a woman to be pretty, telling his aunt, "'But you know, I don't consider being pretty a particularly good endowment for a woman. . . . It usually has a weakening effect on what they think and do.'" At this point his father, Colonel Eichstedt—who carries the authorial voice in this scene—strongly disagrees: "'I have always found pretty women more intelligent than ugly women. Being aware of having a pleasing appearance gives women a certain encouragement to develop and show their intellectual potential, while being ugly often has a decidedly depressing and restricting effect.'"

With his pet theory on women, inspired by Schopenhauer (with strong Nietzschean resonance) and hotly contested by his father and aunt, Georg is able to remain impervious to the eligible spinsters of Weißenburg, and it is only when Nora becomes the object of the attentions of the widower, President von Wangenheim, that his theory starts to unravel. Elisabeth debunks Georg's stuffy views on women by showing that the dragon slayer is all talk: When he finally allows his heart to rule his head and declares his love for Nora, we see him emerge as the mighty German oak (Eichstedt), though as an archetypal absent-minded professor he is rather charmingly unversed in the language of love. Even so, since the story depends on wit, the love scene at the close of the story is an anticlimax, and in many ways President von Wangenheim's affection for Nora is much more endearing, middle-aged and disillusioned as he is. His function in the story is to arouse Georg's jealousy so that Georg can become aware of his real feelings for Nora.

The convolutions of the *Kaffeeklatsch* itself, at which the mothers of eligible daughters devise unsuccessful strategies to keep Nora out of Georg's arms, are legion. The event provides Elisabeth with a good opportunity to show that Georg is unwittingly under siege from the mothers of Weißenburg spinsters. But the story also has glaring weaknesses, such as President von Wangenheim's woodland epiphany, a non sequitur, since the music that he finds so inspiring is played by a lonely old lady who is not mentioned again, and he himself soon fades out of the tale. His role is not properly thought through, since the references to his family home as a country seat do not tally with his recollections of the privations of his youth. As already mentioned, the Arcadian ending, with the lovers holding hands in a bower deep in the forest, is pure kitsch, as is the band of students who march past them "singing the song 'If you've found a heart' to introduce the happy end,"[7] written, according to Roswitha Wollkopf's research, by Albert Träger. At all events, the philosopher Georg decides not just to quit his post, but urban life as well, in order to become a bucolic recluse at the end of the novella, and Nora joyfully agrees to a married life in rural solitude. So much for the novella as it stands.

What I would now like to argue is that the novella provides Elisabeth with the perfect opportunity of placing herself in the position of Nietzsche's bride. Roswitha Wollkopf is right to suggest not only that the protagonists Georg and Nora are based on Nietzsche and Elisabeth but that in Georg's former friendship with a girl called Helene, whom he relinquished to his best friend, there could be a veiled reference to Paul Rée, Nietzsche's rival for Lou von Salomé's affections during the course of 1882. This would indicate that the novella might have been finished shortly after the events at Tautenburg. Only this would explain why the portrayal of Julie von Ramstein so neatly matches that of Lou von Salomé. Echoing her friend Bernhard Förster's racism, Elisabeth belabors the point that the Polish von Ramstein establishment is chaotic ("Polish establishment" is a rude reference to a slovenly place)—Lou herself, of course, is a Baltic German who went barefoot in the Tautenburg woods and laughed at convention. It is also important that Julie, apart from having Lou's big-busted sex appeal for men that so aroused Elisabeth's envy at Bayreuth in July 1882, is exactly like her mother: "The same height, the same impossibly thin waist, the same high, rounded bosom (so that at the sight of this upper part of the body one could never say whether the upper or lower part was the most unnatural), the same big mouth with open red lips, the same yellow complexion, the same reddish-brown hair, the same staring eyes, and the same art of attracting men in spite of this somewhat ugly exterior." We recall Nietzsche's letter to Lou's mother, Louise von Salomé, in which he complained of Lou's behavior, the reply to which (dated 10 November 1882) was quoted at the end of chapter 2; what is not known is that Elisabeth wrote to Rée's mother from Rome in the summer of 1883 (probably with Nietzsche's knowledge). Here, after much reluctance ("how often I reach for my pen to try to write to you"), she asks Frau Rée how she could allow herself to be taken in by the "adventuress."[8] What is odd about this exchange of letters is that Fritz and Elisabeth were both still so emotionally attached to their mother that they could not contemplate relationships in which the opinions of the parents were not of paramount importance. It is really bizarre that they should think about Rée and Lou, with their provocatively free lifestyle, in this way.

Elisabeth fulminated at the way Nietzsche was captivated by Lou's intelligence. In real life, she enlisted Franziska's help to drive Lou away, as we have seen; in the story, Georg's father speaks the paternal veto, and since the story tells us certain hidden truths, we can surmise that Nietzsche's dead father is being summoned for assistance against the threat posed by Julie von Ramstein/Lou von Salomé: "But the daughter, affected by the *Zeitgeist,* was more of a philosopher than a writer and was considered an enormous free thinker in Weißenburg. Yes, she was a dangerous woman for Georg, doubly dangerous with her highbrow ugliness, and the colonel watched with displeasure as his son conversed over the water with the ladies in the most amiable manner, helped them into the ferryboat, and then swiftly sat down next to Fräulein Julie von Ramstein."

Colonel Eichstedt projects Elisabeth's model of the sensible father. She uses him to voice her own reservations about Julie's cunning, just as she would enlist the help of her mother, "au nom du père," in driving away Lou von Salomé. In fact, what hurt Nietzsche most in the fracas of the Naumburg in-

quisition was Franziska's declaration that Nietzsche had dishonored his father's memory through his ill-fated liaison. Thus Elisabeth describes Julie/Lou
as not only dangerously intelligent but also ugly, another word for "sexy" in
this context. Georg/Fritz must be rescued at all costs. Yet Nietzsche really *was*
a free thinker (though alas, like Georg, not on the topic of women), something
Elisabeth could not quite grasp, neither in 1882 nor subsequently.

As Wollkopf points out, "In general, sibling relationships play a noticeably
dominant role in all the families described by Elisabeth Nietzsche in her story."[9] Even without Elisabeth's possessiveness toward Nietzsche on one level
the story would be *about* sibling relationships (such as those of Nora and her
brother, Colonel Eichstedt and Aunt Linchen, Frau Werner and her sister).
But chiefly, the story can be interpreted as an expression of Elisabeth's deeply
erotic feelings for Fritz and her blind jealousy at the thought that he might
be stolen—and stolen by somebody with bad habits, to boot—just when the
rift of 1878 had started to heal. Elisabeth's prudishness is all she can hang on
to with emotions like these, and it threads its way through the story, causing
the protagonists many a blush. So Nora is Elisabeth as she would like to be:
a mother before she is a bride, and still a virgin at the end of the tale. Elisabeth's reluctance to allow her fictional lovers to so much as kiss on the lips
shows how deeply she sensed society's taboo against any erotically charged
brother-sister relationship, yet that is what she most deeply desired. She
projects her aspirations onto her heroine: Nora is her sunny side, beautiful,
intelligent, loved—*and* she is past the age of thirty (Elisabeth was presumably thirty-six at the time of writing). Sunny Nora does not experience the
usual dread at being left on the shelf, but Elisabeth communicates to us her
own dark fears about this nevertheless, for she had done very little with her
life since her housekeeping for Fritz had come to an end in 1878. How drab
Naumburg must have seemed in comparison with the excitement of the Basel
years, when she had mixed with the Wagners on intimate terms. Now Niet-
sche's career was over and he would have to live on his meager pension. How
could he support a wife?

Nietzsche's predicament was very similar to that of Georg Eichstedt in the
story: he really did not have much to offer Lou in terms of material security.
In the novella, Nora/Elisabeth smiles to herself at the idea that with their
pooled income, she and Georg/Fritz could really do quite nicely for themselves. This, and not Georg's passionate kiss planted on Nora's *hand,* is the
point where the reader realizes the biographical depths of the story; for Elisabeth's modest fortune was something she cherished. She certainly used it
as an argument when she assured Förster that there was nothing she would
like better than to live with him in a secluded setting, pooling their wealth,

yet this was pure fantasy, and indeed her overestimation of her disposable income constantly bedeviled her in later life. Things were bound to go wrong: Förster was not Nietzsche, and Neu-Germania was not the secluded Arcadian idyll she probably had in mind when she set sail for Paraguay, an idyll that she had conjured up in her novella and that only existed in her head. And she was Elisabeth Nietzsche, not Nora Werner.

Elisabeth and the Women's Movement

After the disaster of the "Lou Affair" in 1882, Elisabeth's rapprochement with Bernhard Förster entailed a strengthening of her right-wing views, though as we have seen, in her novella she teased out the issue of women's education almost against herself. This was really the only area where Elisabeth—despite Nietzsche's views—agreed with the women's movement. The campaign to improve women's education united all factions among the early German feminists, who were otherwise prone to bitter and damaging splits. Helene Lange was the leading "moderate" feminist of her day: the moderates were actually conservative by today's standards. In 1890 Lange founded the Allgemeiner Deutscher Lehrerinnenverein (General German Women Teachers' Association), and made the campaign for an improved structure in women's education her life's aim, proposing far-reaching changes in teacher training. Even so, by the turn of the century little had happened, and grammar schools for girls and access to university education had to wait, in the main, until after World War I for implementation in most parts of Germany. In 1902 Lange took over from Auguste Schmidt as president of the moderate General German Women's Association.

In 1908, the year in which the Nietzsche-Archiv was put on a sound footing by the formation of the Stiftung Nietzsche-Archiv, the women's movement in Germany was thrown into upheaval by the repeal of the Reichsvereinsgesetz (Statute on Association), which had hitherto forbidden women from attending public meetings. This law had traditionally discouraged many conservative women from joining the Bund deutscher Frauenvereine (League of German Women's Associations), as they were nervous about the possibility of contravening the law by attending a feminist gathering. Suffrage societies had great difficulty in attracting members, and eugenically motivated groups such as the Bund für Mutterschutz (League for the Protection of Mothers), founded in 1905 by Ruth Bré but more ably led by Helene Stöcker from 1906 onward, were considered risqué. What happened in 1908 was that conservative women decided in large numbers to join the women's movement, realizing that they now had the power to move it to the right and thus head off the growing influence of socialist feminists such as Lily Braun and Clara Zetkin. The radical leader of the League of German Women's Associations, Marie Stritt, who had almost succeeded in persuading the membership of the league to vote in favor of legalizing abortion in 1908, was unseated in 1910 by Helene Lange's associate, the right-wing Gertrud Bäumer, who led the organization until 1919.

Elisabeth adopted Nietzsche's negative position on the campaign for women's rights at an early stage without necessarily thinking it through; once she had devoted her life to furthering his reputation, her attack on emancipated women became as strident as his own. Only very rarely did she publicly admit that she did not entirely follow Nietzsche's line on the woman question: "It is hard to have to wait for a man on the assumption that only he can give life a goal and purpose," she confessed in an article entitled "Friedrich Nietzsche über Weib, Liebe, und Ehe" (Friedrich Nietzsche on Woman, Love, and Marriage), written in 1899 for the *Neue deutsche Rundschau,* and continued: "in the meantime, it's better to take one's fate into one's own hands." In the rest of the article, however, she defended Nietzsche's low opinion of a woman's education or *Bildung:*[10] "Probably nobody will deny that the present education of our young girls is not very inspiring and every serious-minded man will feel quite properly appalled by it. My brother found their disrespectful prattle about art and artists, great minds and historical events practically unbearable. He thought that serious-minded men should not allow women under thirty to make critical judgments, and gave these pseudo-intellectual daughters of gentlemen the impolite description 'super-clever gabbling geese.'"[11] Elisabeth went on to explain that Nietzsche construed the demand for women's equality as an attempt to usurp man's naturally superior position as thinker. By contrast, she informs us, he valued woman's "health in body and mind, cheerfulness, courage, unassuming nature [*Bescheidenheit*] and aptitude for running a home."[12]

No doubt Elisabeth also felt that these attributes described her personality particularly well. To reinforce the message, she invented yet another letter from Nietzsche for insertion into the article, supposedly dated April 1888; here, Nietzsche purportedly writes to praise her for her fortitude in overcoming the difficulties in Paraguay: "I am proud to have educated you—only a few women would overcome these extraordinary difficulties with such courage, selflessness, and cheerfulness. But please! Try to be a bit less unassuming!"[13] The invented reference to "unassuming" (*Bescheidenheit*) gave Elisabeth a cue to retort that it was impossible to be anything but presumptuous (*unbescheiden*) "with *such* a brother and *such* a husband" [her emphasis]. In this way she made *herself* the center of attention in an article that sold itself as an exposé of Nietzsche's views on women and lamely defended Nietzsche's view that woman's domestic role was hallowed and hallowing. Given Elisabeth's support for women who wanted to improve their minds, like Nora in her novella, we can suppose that she was arguing against her own instincts here. We can also note that Bernhard Förster was still in good odor at this point.

Bourgeois feminists like Gertrud Bäumer agreed with Nietzsche that woman's role was primarily domestic, and like him they viewed the role of motherhood as the goal of marriage, but they mistrusted Nietzsche's other comments on the liberation of the instincts. Right-wing feminists like Ellen Key, who was a passionate Nietzschean, trumpeted the virtues of woman's maternal destiny. In her work *Kvinnrörelsen* (The Woman Movement, 1909), Key lambastes women who seek careers outside the home. Lou von Salomé also held that view, though she, like Elisabeth, remained childless. Lou spoke out on matters concerning women's physiology in essays like "Der Mensch als Weib" (The Human Being As Woman, 1899) in order to draw conclusions about woman's nature very like Nietzsche's own: both were convinced that motherhood was woman's route to bliss. It is ironic that Elisabeth, who did not hold these views on motherhood as woman's sine qua non, was friendly with Ellen Key and invited her to speak at the archive in 1905 (though Key had to break the engagement), but when she learned that Key was also friendly with Lou von Salomé, she promptly allowed their friendship to fizzle out, so strong was her antipathy toward "the Russian" (actually she was a Baltic German of Huguenot extraction).

In *Der einsame Nietzsche,* written, we must recall, more than thirty years after the devastating "Lou Affair," Elisabeth cannot think up a worse insult than to describe Lou von Salomé as a forerunner of women's emancipation. Unwilling to risk libel, she invents a highly respectable elderly gentleman as her ventriloquist to smear Lou as *schamlos* and thus delivers a masterly snub to her old enemy:

> But perhaps Fräulein von Salomé was just a forerunner of one group of modern emancipated women? Not long ago, an elderly gentleman with very fine views came to me and complained bitterly about modern emancipated girls. . . . The word "brazen" (*schamlos*) often occurred in his complaint, but now that I am old, I found words of excuse. "I think these modern women call it being honest with themselves and other people," I said, "and they assume that we old-fashioned ladies with our delicacy must have deceived ourselves and others in those days." If I now think more mildly about the words and views of Frau Salomé which so shocked me then, this never applies to the way she spoke about my brother.[14]

Elisabeth is even able to *patronize* "the Russian" by forgiving her for her misguided rudeness, though not her perfidy toward Nietzsche.

Many radical feminists of varied stamp, such as Hedwig Dohm (for all her reservations about Nietzsche's misogyny), Lily Braun, and Helene Stöcker were firm Nietzscheans. They chose to ignore Nietzsche's objections to women's education and women writers because Nietzsche's philosophy gave them permission to feel free, free to refuse to join the marriage mart, to enjoy their sexuality, and to reject Christianity. Their gratitude easily outweighed their criticism. Elisabeth was aware of the paradox inherent in Nietzsche's simultaneous friendship with and dislike of emancipated women and operated a very similar double standard herself. Part of the problem was that Nietzsche seemed to have something liberating and valuable to offer almost every woman (and indeed every man) from whatever faction. Elisabeth decided to forge her own way through this potential minefield of feminist allegiances. She managed to be friendly with Helene Stöcker and Ellen Key at the same time, which was no mean feat considering their opposed views, though her friendship with both women eventually cooled. Stöcker never lost her respect for Elisabeth, but since she also admired Lou von Salomé, her friendship with Elisabeth was doomed.

Stöcker had come to Elisabeth's notice as an ardent Nietzschean who gave numerous talks on Nietzsche's liberating philosophy. For some time before the turn of the century, Stöcker and Elisabeth corresponded warmly. Helene Stöcker routinely sought to defend Nietzsche from attacks of misogyny. She invariably did this by adumbrating the many instances of Nietzsche's cordial relations with the opposite sex. She had high praise for Elisabeth's affection for her brother, which was no doubt what first endeared her to Elisabeth, and like Meta von Salis had done before her, she blamed women for bringing Nietzsche's antifeminist attack upon themselves.

In the section on local news in the Elberfeld paper, *Täglicher Anzeiger für Berg und Mark,* 19 April 1903, Stöcker's speech on Nietzsche and women is faithfully reported. She began by stating that the only thing most people know about Nietzsche and women is the quotation from *Also sprach Zarathustra:* "Are you going to women? Don't forget the whip!"[15] (Not much has changed in the last hundred years!) After listing the women whom Nietzsche admired (Sophie Ritschl, Cosima Wagner, Marie Baumgärtner—who translated "Schopenhauer als Erzieher" [Schopenhauer As Educator] into French in the 1870s—and Malwida von Meysenbug, all of whom also feature in Elisabeth's book *Friedrich Nietzsche und die Frauen seiner Zeit* [discussed below]), Stöcker asserted that as he grew more ill, Nietzsche's vendetta against women increased: "With the sharpness and bitterness that characterized his last period of creativity, he often turned against famous women, too. Only at this time does one find the bitter animosity toward women that has earned him the name misogynist, and his sister, who is, of course, a representative of the modern women's movement, explains his hard and exaggerated expressions as just a reaction to excesses on the part of women."[16] Stöcker leaves her audience to guess at what these "excesses" were. Presumably what is meant are the wiles of superficial women who are out to attract a mate, like Julie von Ramstein in "Coffee-Party Gossip about Nora," though as the discussion of Elisabeth's single status until the age of thirty-eight has shown, social convention frowned on the spinster, and thus the pressure to find a husband actually induced much of the superficiality Nietzsche abhorred.

When Helene Stöcker visited Weimar in 1911, she tried to contact Elisabeth, writing to her from the Russischer Hof Hotel on 13 January to ask if Elisabeth could see her. As her letter of the next day reveals, she received no reply: "I do not know if you received my message"[17] she writes, dating her note 14 January. Elisabeth did receive the letter but was either too busy to see Stöcker or had started to freeze their friendship. Stöcker had been involved in a court case in 1910 in which she was accused of mishandling the funds of the League for the Protection of Mothers. She was found innocent, but her opponents appealed the decision. Elisabeth moved in reactionary circles where Stöcker's name as a campaigner for sexual reform had become a laughing-stock. Stöcker brought Nietzsche's name into her polemic for sexual reform, in which the liberation of female sexuality under the rubric *neue Ethik* (new morality) was just part of her program for social renewal, with pacifism high on her agenda during World War I. Elisabeth embraced nationalism from the outset of hostilities in 1914 and tried to prove that Nietzsche was a friend of war, while Stöcker, arguing from the opposite camp, became involved with the international pacifist movement. Stöcker nevertheless continued to speak highly of Elisabeth in her publications on Nietzsche, though her reserve broke down in 1938 when, with Elisabeth and Lou both dead, she wrote an article for the *Sonntagsblatt der Basler Nachrichten* entitled "Neues zum Nietzsche-Problem." The article, published on 28 August, was really a review of Podach's *Friedrich Nietzsche und Lou Salomé: Ihre Begegnung 1882* (Friedrich Nietzsche and Lou Salomé: Their Encounter in 1882, 1938), but Stöcker abandoned her reticence to comment: "Certainly the behavior of Elisabeth Förster-Nietzsche in the Lou-Affair, especially her later presentation of these conflicts, demands justified criticism."[18]

Stöcker's apparently wild claim that Elisabeth was a representative of the women's movement needs some explanation. The fact was that the women's movement in Germany was predominantly conservative and would become more so as time progressed. Among conservative women there was almost a competition over who could be most patriotic; in this way, they turned the heat on the radical feminist members of the League of German Women's Associations who, as Roger Chickering points out, "on a range of issues, such as suffrage, legal equality and extending the rights of unwed mothers, found their patriotic credentials challenged."[19] Chickering goes on to describe the way certain women—and Elisabeth fits into the category perfectly—embraced patriotism because it enabled them to pose as national heroines while subverting the conventional role awarded them by society, a role to which they paid lip service.

German colonizing projects were part of this patriotic scheme, with the Deutsche Kolonialgesellschaft, founded in 1887 (as an amalgamation of the Deutscher Kolonialverein and the Gesellschaft für deutsche Kolonisation) acting as "the popular custodian of the symbol of overseas empire."[20] Although the society originally concentrated on sending German colonists to Africa, Bernhard Förster used its good offices to found his colony in Paraguay, and Elisabeth retained her membership in the society until she returned to Germany for good. Chickering argues that there was a very strong racist element within the whole German colonial endeavor, and when the Frauenbund der deutschen Kolonialgesellschaft (Women's League of the German Colonial Society) was founded in 1908, "the literature of their organization was replete with arguments that native Africans, as well as those of racially mixed parentage, were suited only to slavery."[21] Bernhard Förster's colony was the ultimate in racist terms, since it consisted resolutely and exclusively of pure Germans.

Förster's anti-Semitism sprang from a passionate if misguided nationalism. In *Der einsame Nietzsche,* which was written in 1913 at a time when Elisabeth enjoyed the financial banking of Ernst Thiel, who was a Jew, Elisabeth felt constrained to make excuses for her anti-Semitism during her relationship with Förster. She argues that in 1883, with Förster absent to reconnoiter Paraguay, loyalty to the man she loved forced her to argue more vehemently than she would have liked in favor of anti-Semitism: "in this way I developed into a warm defendant of his colonial plans, finally even into a defendant of anti-Semitism, which I actually found unpleasant and for which I had never had the slightest cause."[22] Elisabeth goes on to state that she and Nietzsche came from a conservative family in a part of Germany that was actually represented in the Prussian Landtag at that time by a Jew, one Professor Stahl, pointing out for good measure that Tante Rosalie knew him personally. She adds that she herself had always admired Mendelssohn and his sister and had read Disraeli's novels, and she even voices her regret that Nietzsche was not able to read Disraeli because his English was too poor, especially as "Disraeli is such a wonderful example of the will to power."[23] As children, she and Friedrich never met a single Jew because "in Naumburg, there aren't any."[24]

It does not occur to her to ask why Nietzsche, who shared her childhood, did not *need* to grow up with Jews to be implacably opposed to anti-Semitism.

Finally Elisabeth, grown extravagant in her desire to distance herself from the charge of anti-Semitism, has the nerve to accuse *Nietzsche* of being touchy on the topic. She rewrites the history of her colonizing effort by asserting (truthfully) that it never received the promised backing from the anti-Semites, as though that in any way minimizes Förster's (and her own) anti-Semitic *motives:* "He [Nietzsche] often expressed dissatisfaction and skepticism over the undertaking, which has been wrongly understood from several angles. . . . Partly it was his brotherly concern, on the other hand, its link with anti-Semitism, as already mentioned several times, caused him to judge it so unfavorably. At all events, this link was just imaginary, which I repeatedly tried to set straight, for I must declare in all truth that the anti-Semitic party did nothing at all for my husband's colony."[25] Elisabeth's last point does not wipe away the fact that Neu-Germania was founded as an anti-Semitic piece of *Realpolitik,* even if the anti-Semites failed to come up with the goods to rescue Förster from his own errors and miscalculations.

Elisabeth's colonial endeavors can be viewed as part of a patriotic nationalist movement that allowed certain women from the higher classes to adopt leading roles in society while still mouthing the rhetoric of woman's conventional domestic role. Furthermore, the outbreak of war in 1914 showed just how nationalistic *most* women in the women's movement, now dominated by the conservative faction, really were. In Britain, where the women's movement had a single focus—the suffrage—most leading suffragettes were just as right-wing and during the war were just as patriotic. It might almost be possible to excuse Elisabeth's mistaken adoption of anti-Semitism if she had held to her 1913 stance and blamed everything to do with this part of her life on her husband, but the fact is that she gradually reverted to a position of full approval of all he stood for during the rise of Fascism in the 1920s. Really, all the excuses for Elisabeth run out over the issue of anti-Semitism.

In Elisabeth's late work *Friedrich Nietzsche und die Frauen seiner Zeit,* a book which came out in 1935 only months before she died, she sets out to discuss the women who were important to Nietzsche in his life. Looking back in the chapter "Von der guten alten Zeit" (The Good Old Days) with a certain nostalgia, Elisabeth remarks that life had been more straightforward for girls and less problematic in the good old days, though not necessarily better. She points to the sewing machine as a revolutionary invention that liberated girls from the task of sewing for their trousseaus but that often destroyed the peace of the family, since girls now started to want to do other things, such as pursue their education.

Somewhat disingenuously, to say the least, she states on the very first page that she always saw herself as a helpmeet (*Gehilfin*), subordinate to the men in her life: "I was constantly aware of the superiority of masculine under-standing, as was quite natural with such a magnificent brother and such an excellent husband,"[26] she states, subtly reminding her National Socialist read-ers of her late husband's proto-Fascist credentials. It is interesting that within a few pages she ridicules a book on the conventional role of women that was considered important in her day. The book in question was Joseph Abel's *Historisches Gemälde der Lage und des Zustandes des weiblichen Geschlechts unter allen Völkern der Erde, von den ältesten bis auf die neuesten Zeiten* (His-torical Picture of the Position and Condition of the Female Sex among All Peoples of the World from Antiquity to the Present Day, 1808). Where Elisa-beth takes issue with Abel is his insistence that a woman's existence is worth-less if she does not attract a husband and attract him before she is thirty and loses her bloom. Elisabeth claims that Nietzsche agreed with her when, as a young woman, she contested these views because both she and her brother had a high regard for their maiden aunts Auguste and Rosalie. We must also remember that there was a point in Elisabeth's own life when it looked very much as though she would remain unmarried in spite of the fact that she was not without admirers.

In *Friedrich Nietzsche und die Frauen seiner Zeit* Elisabeth gets into very deep water indeed defending her brother's views on women, primarily be-cause she tries to make them fit in with her other comments on the good old days. She sets out to justify Zarathustra's provocative declaration: "Let woman be a plaything, pure and fine, like a precious stone radiant with the virtues of a world which is not yet there."[27] Her argument seeks to justify Zarathus-tra's words by affirming the young girl's status in the family as indeed that of a petted favorite: "Actually, she was a charming plaything,"[28] she asserts. Elisabeth expands her interpretation of Nietzsche's text by explaining that the young girl held out the promise of the next generation: "She was the adornment of the family, there lay over her the spell of something prescient, of the future; she did not really need to be anything other than good, pure, and innocent to enchant the whole family circle."[29]

There are two things wrong with Elisabeth's interpretation. The first is that Zarathustra is talking about the *Weib*, not sweet little girls. The idea of Zara-thustra being charmed by a naive little girl would be slightly distasteful if that were indeed what Nietzsche had said. Fortunately he did not, though the fact that he was talking about a bullish warlord's need for someone to soothe him and bring out the child in him is not much less controversial. The second thing wrong with Elisabeth's interpretation is the assumption that the magic of an indefinable something awaiting the young girl in the future—sexual maturity and childbirth (which is indeed what Nietzsche endorsed for women)—assumes that the future role for a little girl is to become a wife and mother, precisely the type of judgmental stance Elisabeth had just criticized earlier in the book in relation to Joseph Abel's work. What if these young girls did not *want* this type of magical future—just as she herself had resisted the idea of marriage until she was nearly forty? Elisabeth ties herself in knots because in defending Nietzsche's tunnel vision on woman's domestic role in society—which boiled down to her breeding function—she is fundamentally untrue to her own beliefs. What one can say with certainty is that Elisabeth simplifies the quotation from *Also sprach Zarathustra* into a harmless banality.

Though Elisabeth in *Friedrich Nietzsche und die Frauen seiner Zeit* raised controversial feminist issues, she did not draw the obvious conclusion—that women ought to be able to pursue their education and take up careers if they chose—any more than Nietzsche did. It is a strange blind spot with them both. Thus Elisabeth points out that the women who demanded grammar schools for girls from the 1860s onward tended to smoke cigars and behave in a manly fashion, and they spoke in public about things "which had never before passed the lips of a delicate feminine mouth."[30] In this way, Elisabeth and many other reactionary women (and men) did much to keep alive the cliché of the manly woman, which encapsulated their objection to female emancipation per se. It is very hard for a feminist today to overlook such hypocrisy from a woman whose own "delicate feminine mouth" had recently publicly welcomed Hitler to the Nietzsche-Archiv. In any case, she is factually wrong: Louise Otto-Peters and other early German feminists in the General German Women's Association wanted to preserve the "eternal-womanly" from the deviant encroachments of *Mannweiber* (though actually, Louise Otto-Peters herself very much admired George Sand). The worst pioneers for emancipation were the Russians, Elisabeth tells us darkly—she never forgave Russia for having spawned Lou von Salomé (however indirectly). Thus it was that Frau Elisabeth Förster-Nietzsche, now a dignified doyenne of Weimar high society, held herself aloof from the women's movement and in fact, like Nietzsche, used the phrase "emancipated woman" as a term of abuse.

Ecce Femina

Nietzsche had sent his draft manuscript of *Ecce Homo* to his publisher Naumann from Turin at the end of 1888. As an afterthought, he sent an extra page to Naumann to be inserted in the third section of "Warum ich so weise bin." We can presume that this was not the only piece of bitter invective against his mother and sister to be found in Nietzsche's manuscripts which a horrified Franziska found she had to house; most were destroyed. However, this page led a charmed life. In February 1892, Elisabeth, temporarily in Naumburg between trips to Paraguay, sent Gast to Leipzig to retrieve the page from Naumann, who had informed her of its content. On 9 February, Gast wrote to Elisabeth "I do not think that Naumann has a copy of it. . . . But now it really must be destroyed!"[31] Fortunately for posterity, Gast himself had cheated Elisabeth by making his own copy of the letter before sending it to Weimar for certain destruction. This copy was found among Gast's personal effects after his death in 1918, and in the current definitive edition (*Werke: Kritische Gesamtausgabe*) it has been substituted in its rightful place within *Ecce Homo*, which was originally published in 1908. The most informative passage on the "revised" page is the following comment by Nietzsche on Franziska and Elisabeth:

> When I search for the deepest contrast to myself, the incalculable meanness of the instincts, I always find my mother and sister—it would be to blaspheme against my divinity to believe myself related to such *canaille* [rabble]. The treatment I have received from my mother and sister, up to the present moment, instills an unspeakable horror within me: here, an absolutely infernal instrument is at work to determine with unfailing accuracy the moment when I can be bloodily wounded—in my highest moments, . . . as I have no strength at all to defend myself against poisonous insects. . . . The physiological contiguity makes such a disharmonia praestabilita possible. . . . But I confess that the profoundest objection to the "eternal return," actually my most *abysmal* thought, is always my mother and my sister. (emphasis in the original)[32]

As Gast pointed out in a letter to Ernst Holzer of 23 June 1909: "Here, Nietzsche spoke freely and frankly, finally disgusted by his own polite games, and nothing more devastating has ever been said about anybody than on this piece of paper."[33] Even allowing for a measure of *Schadenfreude* in Gast's remarks to Holzer—he had been relieved of his post as editor of Nietzsche's works in the summer of 1909 and he was at last free to say what he liked about Elisabeth—the "missing link" is certainly of prime importance for the Nietzsche scholar. For although Nietzsche was perilously close to madness when he penned these remarks on Franziska and Elisabeth, there is no indication that he did not mean what he said. In fact, it shows how rational he was, since the section replaced by the missing page was stylistically not really up to Nietzsche's usual standard. The rather flat panegyric on his father in the original version possibly left him ill at ease:

> My father, born 1813, died 1849. Before he took up the position of pastor at Röcken not far from Lützen, he lived for some years at Schloss Altenburg and

instructed the four princesses himself. . . . He was full of piety toward the Prussian king Friedrich Wilhelm the Fourth, from whom he received his living as pastor; the events of 1848 troubled him beyond measure. I myself, born on 15 October, took the Hohenzollern name Friedrich Wilhelm, as was fitting. One advantage the choice of this day had: all through my childhood, my birthday was a public holiday.—I regard it as a great privilege to have had such a father.[34]

Nietzsche's change of mind for this section of *Ecce Homo* might indicate that he was not only tired of hiding his true opinion of his mother and sister from the world but had decided that his clergyman father's devotion to Friedrich Wilhelm IV was not the best recommendation for a free-thinking genius and God-slayer. In the corrective page sent to Naumann, Nietzsche performs the genuflection toward his father by reporting simply that he was a *Prediger* (preacher) of whom it was said "an angel must look like this." He omits the embarrassment of his father's devotion to the Prussian king by swiftly moving on to other matters—the question of his putative Polish descent—until he arrives at the heart of the matter in this section, and the reason for his last-minute missive from Turin: the critique of Franziska and Elisabeth already cited above. Gast took the secret of Nietzsche's late correction to *Ecce Homo* with him to the grave, perhaps because it would have reflected badly on him if Elisabeth had revealed how duplicitous he was to make a copy when he was busy telling her that no copy existed and she should destroy the evidence. Thus, readers of the early editions of *Ecce Homo* were deprived of information about Nietzsche's final contemptuous stance on his mother and sister. Many people since have marveled, as Nietzsche did himself, how it could come about that he should have such a mother as Franziska and, more especially, such a sister as Elisabeth: but there were emotional bonds linking the three that defied rational analysis.

In 1934 Luise Marelle, one of Elisabeth's close friends in Weimar, published an admiring biography of Elisabeth entitled *Die Schwester: Elisabeth Förster-Nietzsche* (The Sister: Elisabeth Förster-Nietzsche) in which no hint can be found that Nietzsche ever found his sister less than perfect. Marelle uses Elisabeth's own method of compiling a biography by giving long quotes from Elisabeth's own works. She provides few dates and very little hard information. Indeed, Marelle was such an unquestioning admirer of Elisabeth that she made numerous factual mistakes; for example, Marelle comments on Elisabeth's enormously strong willpower, which, as she points out, Nietzsche recognized and tried to guide:

He recognized early on, as we must, that the strong and indeed irresistible will in this woman of delicate build is something of a *basic drive:* without deflection, instinctively and unerringly it springs through objections or reservations to the goal, and the otherwise collected and poised figure becomes transformed as though by an elementary force: this will to the deed, to the work, and to *power,* too, this preference to "die rather than leave something in the lurch"—that is Nietzschean, as her brother also said in 1887, in a letter to her in Paraguay.[35]

As we see, Marelle trusts Elisabeth implicitly as a source and quotes the forged letter of 21 May 1887 discussed in chapter 3 as though it were vintage Nietzsche. Furthermore, Marelle complacently refers to Elisabeth's irresistible will as a good thing. We must note that Marelle was writing in Berlin 1933 and was as excited over Hitler's visits to Weimar as was Elisabeth. Nowadays we place the Fascist rhetoric on will within the demagogic context of the Third Reich. The "will to power" is not in itself a gift in a person any more than "will to the deed" or "will to the work" are good in themselves: Hitler possessed all these attributes. What it does mean is that by the 1930s, the term *will* was bandied around with abandon, and Elisabeth's publication of *The Will to Power* in 1901 had played its part in this development.

An article written by Marelle in 1926 reveals how Elisabeth was seen by conservative women in the 1920s. The article appeared in the archconservative journal *Frauenweckruf: Organ des deutschen Frauenbundes* (Women's Reveille: Organ of the German Women's League) on 15 December 1926, and it described the celebrations to commemorate Elisabeth's eightieth birthday, which had been held on 10 July that year:

> Dr. Anselm Ruest hailed her on her eightieth birthday as a "genius at getting things done, of the active deed" and ingeniously described the archive she created as "like a first basin or dam for the gushing waters and fountain of knowledge which poured from F. Nietzsche's own mind. The present trend to control and regulate these treasures leaves one with the impression that there is an eternal flowing and spurting forth anew; an eternally becoming Nietzsche flood, still far from exhausted, continues to cascade its living torrents, the sources of nourishment for a future culture." German women everywhere, the reveille goes out to you to become guardians of the nation's intellectual goods, of the "great German cultural wealth," by becoming members of the "Society of Friends of the Nietzsche-Archiv," one of those "literary archives" which the philosopher Dilthey, amongst others, puts forward as a "general cultural requirement."[36]

What is fascinating in this article is that although Marelle prefaces it with a description of Elisabeth as "this woman who is so physically dainty, yet mentally so strong-willed," the rest of the adulation is reserved for Nietzsche. This brings it home to us more than anything else could that Elisabeth would have been nothing to the genteel residents of Weimar without her trump card, the possession of Nietzsche himself until his death in 1900 and thereafter of his manuscripts, the crown jewels of the Nietzsche-Archiv. That Marelle makes a *virtue* out of Elisabeth's subordinate position to Nietzsche in her capacity of guardian (*Hüterin*) is all of a piece with conservative feminist doctrine that the noblest woman was the one who was content to be man's helpmeet (*Gehilfin*—incidentally and unfortunately, Nietzsche's own position on the matter). Elisabeth, too, used the rhetoric of woman's role as *Gehilfin* to describe her own position in a positive way.

Although it is only too easy to dismiss Elisabeth's publications as unsound in view of her economies with the truth, I have tried to stress throughout this work that she *did* care passionately for her brother. The trouble was that she had no compunction against using underhand methods, provided that the public received an impression of Nietzsche that she herself wished to transmit and control. Thus, in spite of Elisabeth's achievements in creating the archive and stocking it with secondary material on Nietzsche that might never have come to light without her efforts, I would maintain that this is far outweighed by the crushing blow she dealt to Nietzsche's reputation by her complicity with the National Socialists, a topic fully discussed in the next chapter. Ostensibly on her brother's behalf, she worked indefatigably for the second half of her life, passing herself off as the guardian of Nietzsche's legacy by making full use of the masking capacity of the "Eternal-Womanly" that Nietzsche deplored. The mystification of the "Eternal-Womanly" enabled conservative women like Elisabeth as well as her archenemy Lou von Salomé to parade as opponents of emancipation, whereas in truth they *were* emancipated. The secret was to be emancipated, but blame everything wrong with women's lot on "die Emancipierten": which is the exact reversal of Nietzsche's prescription. Thus it was that Elisabeth, independent and resourceful, shied away from radical feminists who wanted to dispel the myth of the "Eternal-Womanly" and expose society's labyrinth of double standards on the woman question.

By the outbreak of World War I, Elisabeth was a famous writer in her own right, in spite of Nietzsche's febrile aversion to women writers. It is even more ironic that she wrote exclusively about her brother. Deeply conservative, she remained aloof from the growth of the women's movement that had taken place in her lifetime and it is perhaps ironic that in spite of her membership in the Deutsche Gesellschaft zur Bekämpfung der Frauenemanzipation (German Society to Combat Women's Emancipation), founded in 1912, she received the suffrage when the Weimar Republic came into being in 1919. Although the kaiser steadfastly refused to read Nietzsche, Elisabeth was on good terms with his wife Hermine and kept in touch with her after the kaiser abdicated and went to live in Holland. Though racked by financial worries during the 1920s, she presided over the frenetic Nietzsche cult with enviable proficiency. In her old age, she liked to think of herself as a very conventional figure, but as we have seen, this was disingenuous on her part. She had not fulfilled the Wilhelmine ideal, which was also the Nietzschean ideal, of motherhood and quiet domesticity, and indeed her whole bearing conflicted with the conventional notion of a woman's subordinate role in society. But she *had* obeyed the dictates of her own brand of the will to power.

6 Frau Dr. Phil. H.C. Elisabeth Förster-Nietzsche

Elisabeth's Library

The books that Elisabeth kept in her private rooms as opposed to placing them on the bookshelves in the public rooms downstairs were recently found in the attic of the Nietzsche-Archiv and are currently shelved in yet another attic in the Schloßbibliothek Anna Amalia in Weimar. Elisabeth's eyesight had deteriorated so drastically by the time she came to Weimar that reading was difficult for her and she became increasingly dependent on secretarial help for her writing. Just when she was able to read less and less, people began to bombard her with books as though they were visiting cards: A large number of them contain a dedication from the donor or from the author (often one and the same). The golden rule to apply is that books dated 1893 or earlier must have been purchased by Elisabeth or given to her; after that date, with Nietzsche's name becoming known and Elisabeth's position as his "keeper" fully recognized, any book subsequently acquired could have been a present, given out of genuine admiration for Elisabeth or out of a desire to be included in the activities of the Nietzsche-Archiv as it rapidly acquired cult status. Her private library is a motley collection of books, pamphlets, and magazines, among which some are gems of their day and others are not worth a second glance. An inspection rapidly reveals that Elisabeth throughout her long life was interested in drama, though to today's reader, many of the plays she had on her bookshelves are obscure. The manuscript of "Coffee-Party Gossip about Nora" is as good as it is chiefly because of Elisabeth's skill with *dialogue*. There are also numerous volumes of collected poems of every type, reminding us that Elisabeth, too, could compose a poem when she felt like it.

What does emerge is that Elisabeth was an inveterate joiner of societies. Her membership card for the Deutsche Graphologische Gesellschaft (German Graphological Association), the brainchild of Ludwig Klages, is dated 1908, and she possessed a copy of the *Graphologische Monatshefte: Archiv für Psychodiagnostik und Charakterologie/Organ der deutschen Graphologischen Gesellen* (Graphological Monthly: Archive for Psychodiagnostics and Characterology/Mouthpiece of the German Graphological Association, 1908). Graphology was in vogue during the first decades of the century, as was the attempt to prove that William Shakespeare was none other than Francis Bacon. Elisabeth's membership card for the Weimarer Bacon-Gesellschaft (Weimar Bacon Society) still exists (GSA 72/938), and she possessed the *American Baconiana* (1923) as well as the *Deutsche Baconiana* (1931). The *Deutsche Baconiana Zeitschrift für Bacon Schakespeare Forschung* (1934) did not just discuss Bacon: volume 10 contains an article on "German Cultural Propaganda Abroad."

Several other books and journals in Elisabeth's private collection show that she retained her interest in colonial matters, having been an active member of the Deutsche Kolonialgesellschaft (German Colonial Society) in the 1880s. She was still a member of the Allgemeiner Deutscher Verband (General German Association) in 1892, though she appears to have let that membership lapse. Nevertheless, America, north and south, still captivated her interest. Not all her books on America were as dryly academic as Karl Knortz's *Nachträge germanischen Glaubens und Brauchs in Amerika* (Supplementary Germanic Beliefs and Customs in America, 1903) or his *Streifzüge auf dem Gebiete amerikanischer Volkskunde* (A Brief Survey of the Field of American Ethnology, 1902), a scholarly work on contemporary history containing the author's dedication to Elisabeth on the frontispiece. She also possessed a book of American folk songs that included "Yankee Doodle" (Professor Karl Knortz's *Poetischer Hausschatz der Nordamerikaner* [Poetical Scrapbook of the North Americans] 1902). Knortz also wrote *Nietzsche's Zarathustra: Eine Einführung* (Nietzsche's Zarathustra: An Introduction, 1906). Herman [*sic*] Georg Scheffauer's *Land Gottes: Das Gesicht des neuen Amerika* (The Land of God: The Face of the New America, 1923) is an academic geographical account, as is Konsul Dr. W. Mann, *Volk und Kultur Lateinamerikas* (People and Culture of Latin America, 1927; the latter also contained the author's dedication). The journal *Süd- und Mittel Amerika* (South and Central America) contains an article by Elisabeth's friend W. Hauff on German schooling arrangements in Argentina, written in 1911. Christian Lassen's *Südamerika: Eine real-politische Studie im Jahre 1925* (South America: A Study in Realpolitik for the Year 1925) is a short pamphlet, one of several dozen on the shelves.

Some of the books are clearly not Elisabeth's: Thomas à Kempis's *Nachfolge Christi* (*The Succession of Christ*), translated by Johannes Gossner (undated), could be her father's book; Josef Schindler's *Erinnerungen von Philo von Walde* (Philo von Walde's Memoirs, 1891) contains the author's dedication to Franziska dated 1893 and Hedwig Kym's *Gedichte* (Poems, 1887) is no doubt Nietzsche's book (Kym, a student at Zurich University, had visited him in Sils Maria in 1887). From the characteristic markings in Jenny Hirsch's translation of John Stuart Mill's *On the Subjection of Women* (German title: *Die Hörigkeit der Frau*, 1872) we can tell that it is Nietzsche's book and not Elisabeth's, who scarcely ever marked a book, not even with her name. Baedecker's *Rheinlande von der Schweiz bis zur holländischen Grenze* (*The Rhine Lands from Switzerland to the Dutch Border*, 1876) could be Nietzsche's too, but given Elisabeth's interest in language I would say that books like Eugène Borel's *Album lyrique de la France moderne* (an anthology of French poems dated 1869) and Otto Fleischmann's *Reisebilder aus Spanien* (Travel Pictures from Spain, 1882) are books that she herself acquired.

Of course, books donated by close friends like Harry Graf Kessler were clearly Elisabeth's private property, for example, the copies of Kessler's travelogue *Notizen über Mexico* (Notes on Mexico, 1898) and its 1921 reprint. Other books were on her shelves because they were donated by close family members, for example, Richard Oehler's *Ernst Baumann: Aus dem Seelenleben eines jungen Deutschen* (Ernst Baumann: From the Spiritual Life of a Young German, 1904), which contains an elaborate dedication. Nietzsche's books, which he had owned or written, were in the archive library (refurbished by van de Velde) for researchers to use. The shelves of Elisabeth's library under discussion house a great many books from Nietzsche worshipers that by rights *ought* to have been housed downstairs in the Nietzsche-Archiv for others to consult. If Elisabeth kept such books on her private shelves it was probably because she did not realize their value. A book like Adolf Wilbrandt's *Osterinsel* (Easter Island, 1894; Elisabeth has the 1896 edition), one of the first German novels to have an outspokenly Nietzschean theme, would in time become a much sought-after classic. This comment applies to many other books on these shelves, spanning many years.

The shelves bulge with complimentary copies of books from Nietzsche admirers too numerous to mention, among them Michael Georg Conrad's autobiographical *Wahl-fahrten* (Chosen Journeys, 1893) and his collection of poems *Salve Regina* (1899), which contains the poem "Zarathustra," Raoul Richter's *Kunst und Philosophie bei Richard Wagner* (Art and Philosophy with Richard Wagner, 1906), and Ernst Bertram's *Rheingenius* (Rhine Genius, 1922). Many of the books were uncut. One such is James Huneker's *Visionaries*

(1905): Huneker was one of the most fervent early American Nietzscheans. His *Book of Dramatists* (1905), a cultural history, was cut but probably not read. One might have expected Adolf Bartels's play *Martin Luther* (1903) to be cut, but one can very well understand that Elisabeth could not be bothered to cut dry academic volumes like *Armin Tille Festschrift zum 60. Geburtstag* (1930). She possessed medical books that might have been of interest to her if she had bothered to have them cut: Dr. Hermann Gocht's *Handbuch der Röntgen-Lehre* (Handbook of X-ray Science, 1903) and H. B. Dresser's *Methoden und Probleme der geistigen Heilbehandlung* (Methods and Problems in Treating Mental Health, 1902) are two such, though it is just as well that she did not cut Elsbeth Friedrichs's *Lernt wieder sehen! Neue Heilwege für kranke Augen* (Learn to See Again! New Healing Methods for Sick Eyes, 1927), as she might have lost what sight remained to her. Friedrichs gives a detailed explanation of how to use a mirror to channel sunlight to shine directly into the eye; her book is thus a highly dangerous blueprint for do-it-yourself laser treatment. After the fuss that attended the 1999 eclipse of the sun, most readers of the present text will be aware of the dangers to the eye of looking directly into the sun.

Other books give clues to Elisabeth's actual taste in reading, though again one must stress that most books were given to her willy-nilly and her eyes were very weak. Elisabeth had a great many literary acquaintances in Weimar, and among these were women writers, though as Weimar is a town that attracts writers and some, like Helene Böhlau, were born there, we might reasonably expect there to be more books by women writers than there are in her library. That said, there are no fewer than fifteen volumes by Friede H. Kraze on her shelves—novels, poems, plays, and children's stories (for example, *Dies war Mariebell* [This Was Mariebell], 1924). Many of Kraze's titles reveal the attitude of a typical middle-class patriot: the collection of poems *Vaterland* (1914) and the novel *Der Kriegspfarrer* (The War Pastor, 1914) being cases in point. Born in Posen in 1870, Kraze was educated in Breslau and was a schoolteacher until, in 1904, she moved to Weimar, where she settled down to write at least three dozen novels and volumes of short stories during the first third of the twentieth century. However, Kraze's dedications in the books she gave to Elisabeth are no proof of friendship any more than a lack of works by any author in the library proves antipathy on Elisabeth's part. The lack of novels by Gabriele Reuter, whose friendship with Elisabeth dated back to 1894 when Reuter traveled from Weimar to visit her in Naumburg, indicates that Elisabeth probably included her own copies of Reuter's books in the consignment sent to Neu-Germania in the early 1930s. Elisabeth's library boasts only two novels by her great friend Gräfin von Bünau, who wrote under the pseudonym Henriette von Meerheimb: *Ich gab mein Leben* (I Gave My Life, 1914) and the deliciously named *Witwenfrühling* (Widow's Spring, 1922), yet Elisabeth wrote a glowing review of Meerheimb's novel *Die Toten Siegen* (The Dead Are Victorious, 1918: GSA 72/95) which is not on the shelves. Likewise, there are only two novels by the prominent writer Helene Böhlau, *Im frischen Wasser* (In the Cool Water, 1891) and *Herzenswahn* (Folly of the Heart, 1888).

Elisabeth behaved with astounding independence during the latter part of her life, though she never confessed to any solidarity with the women's movement for emancipation. Fanny Künstler's *Kulturtat der Frau* (Woman's Cultural Achievement, 1916) is the most radically feminist work on her shelves, which also contain Isolde Kurz's *Meine Mutter* (undated poems). Two novels by the conventional Frieda von Bülow grace the shelves and six by the now-forgotten Elisabeth Gnade. Karl Heinrich Schaible's *Frau im Altertum* (Woman in Ancient Times), with its fulsome dedication to Louise Otto-Peters as the founder of the German feminist movement, would have filled some of the gap in Elisabeth's information on women writers of the past if she had bothered to have it cut. George Eliot's *Middlemarch* volume 3 (1873) is there, but not volumes 1 and 2; the fact that Nietzsche mentioned Elisabeth's reading "a volume" of *Middlemarch* (in a letter to his sister dated 5 June 1887) might indicate that she never did have all three. Books by right-wing feminists who dominated the women's movement in Germany after 1908 include Laura Frost's *Aus unseren vier Wänden* (From Our Four Walls, 1910). Copies of Elisabeth's own works and other significant volumes such as Luise Marelle's biography of Elisabeth (*Die Schwester,* 1934), have long since been siphoned off to the main section in the Schloßbibliothek Weimar, which houses Nietzsche's printed works.

Friedrich Nietzsche, Friend of War

Elisabeth's problem when the war broke out in 1914 was how to make people forget that her brother had made a sustained attack on the cultural wasteland that was Germany. She completely disregarded Nietzsche's repeated declaration that he felt ill when he heard the first line of the German national anthem. In 1889 he wrote, "The Germans are now intellectually bored, the Germans now mistrust the intellect, politics swallows all seriousness for truly intellectual things—'Deutschland Deutschland über Alles,' I'm afraid that was the end of German philosophy."[1] Barely two weeks after the outbreak of World War I in August 1914, Elisabeth rushed into print with an article for the Berlin newspaper *Der Tag* entitled "Nietzsche und der Krieg," exultantly

claiming that Nietzsche would have welcomed this war and would have defended the Fatherland:

> If ever there was a friend of war, who loved warriors and those who struggle,
> and placed his highest hopes on them, then it was Friedrich Nietzsche. "My
> brothers in War! I love you completely, I am and I was one of your kind." That
> is why so many young heroes are marching into enemy territory with *Zarathus-
> tra* in their pocket. My brother could never sufficiently stress the purifying,
> uplifting and sublime effect of war, and as I have already mentioned, he received
> one of his deepest philosophical insights precisely during the period of his war
> experiences.[2]

The same article appeared five days later in the *Hamburgischer Correspondent*. Elisabeth has no compunction about quoting Zarathustra's remarks as
though they are identical with Nietzsche's own opinions—a very common
error among Nietzsche enthusiasts—and she also reminds her readers of a
myth she invented and embellished that Nietzsche thought up the ideal of
the will to power during the Franco-Prussian war of 1870. Her short article
contains a greatly exaggerated account of Nietzsche's brief exposure to war
as a medical auxiliary in that conflict, for though nobody denies that Nietzsche clearly felt he had to do his duty, the fact is that he spent less than a
month in active service (12 August–11 September 1870) before he was invalid-
ed out. Far from firing off letters to his friends glorifying war, he wrote de-
tailing its horrors, as demonstrated in the following extract from a long letter to Carl von Gersdorff dated 20 October 1870:

> I had 6 badly wounded casualties to look after, quite alone, for 3 days and 3
> nights, Mosengel [another medical auxiliary] 5; it was bad weather, our freight
> cars had to be almost shut so that the poor invalids did not get soaked. The
> atmosphere in such a car was dreadful, and in addition, my people had dysen-
> tery, two had diphtheria, in short, I had an unbelievable amount to do, and put
> dressings on for three hours in the morning and the same in the evening. In
> addition, no rest at night on account of the patients' human needs.[3]

Through sheer repetition, Elisabeth elongates Nietzsche's war service in the
reader's mind: we are told he received training as an orderly as though it were
some kind of course, whereas the "training" probably consisted of a demon-
stration of how to wrap a bandage. Then we have a description of Nietzsche
rushing through the battle zone with bullets flying everywhere: "Considerable sums were confided to him and he received a wealth of personal requests,
so that he often had to find his way from one field hospital to another, from
ambulance to ambulance over the battlefields, often in a shower of bullets, only
stopping to give aid to the wounded or dying and to listen to their last mes-

sages."[4] To rally the troops and give them some sense of the war fervor that Elisabeth herself obviously feels—though hanging everything on the hook of "Nietzsche and War"—she allows her imagination to take over as she describes the exhilaration Nietzsche must have felt at watching the troops march into battle: "Finally the infantry came double-time! Their eyes flashed, their regular footsteps sounded like heavy hammer blows on the hard ground."[5]

In 1915 Elisabeth wrote an essay entitled "Nietzsche—Frankreich und Deutschland," which she cannibalized for another essay, "Nietzsche, Frankreich und England." The latter was subsequently published in the *Neue freie Presse* in 1916. In the *original* essay, "Nietzsche—Frankreich und Deutschland," which was never published, Elisabeth declared that Nietzsche would have been proud of Germany's stand in World War I, completing her argument with the ringing words that "Nietzsche is one of the few philosophers who can be seen as prowar."[6] This statement could not be further from the truth. Barely had hostilities ceased when Nietzsche wrote to Gersdorff on 7 November 1870 to express his doubts over Prussian hegemony: "In confidence, I think the Prussia of today is a highly dangerous power for culture."[7] For Nietzsche, the ensuing foundation of the Reich sealed the fate of Germany as a culture in decline. Elisabeth simply failed to grasp what Nietzsche deplored in the Germany of his day, hence her tactic of denial, but not content with suggesting that Nietzsche had not meant what he said about Germany in his late works, she strategically turns the attack on Germany for neglecting its gifted son. In "Nietzsche—Frankreich und Deutschland," Elisabeth was at pains to point out that Nietzsche had not meant his derogatory remarks on Germany that are found in *Ecce Homo* and *The Antichrist*. She adds: "By the way, up to his mental breakdown he did not hear a single word of affection or recognition from Germany,—only bad and ugly things! In all his earlier works he expresses himself much more naturally, and his deep love for Germany caused him to ponder the German character and circumstances repeatedly."[8]

In her article "Nietzsche und Deutschland," which was printed in the *Berliner Tageblatt*, 5 September 1915, Elisabeth reiterated her point: "*Ecce Homo* is not representative of my brother's opinion on the Germans and Germany"[9] and repeated the accusation that Nietzsche had been badly served by Germany: "One should not forget *that my brother, all the time he was intellectually creative, never heard a single word of recognition or acknowledgment from Germany*" (emphasis in the original). This masterly attack had plenty of justification, since Nietzsche *had* been neglected by his fellow countrymen. In "Nietzsche, Frankreich und England," Elisabeth, having described how Nietzsche disliked any French culture after that of the seventeenth century ("Rousseau remained a plebeian"[10]), developed her argument to express

Nietzsche's fear that England's position as a world power would foster the influence of English philosophy "with its plebeianism and its mediocrity."[11]

Though Elisabeth thought the war a wonderful opportunity for Germany to assert itself once more, it is not true that every soldier went to the front with a copy of *Also sprach Zarathustra* in his knapsack—a cheap edition had indeed been rushed into print, but certainly not in sufficient numbers for every soldier to be issued with a copy. Though Nietzsche *had* made comments in *Also sprach Zarathustra* that allowed Elisabeth to stoke up a veritable bloodlust, he did not do so within the context of an *actual* war, but within a discussion of the emergence of the *Übermensch,* for whom most battles will be against himself. This was too subtle for Elisabeth. The damage she did to Nietzsche's longstanding reputation by such irresponsible warmongering was—and still is—incalculable. Nevertheless, Elisabeth dragged Nietzsche's name into war propaganda at every available opportunity so that in Britain at least, where great enthusiasm for Nietzsche had reigned prior to the war, a strong backlash took place in which the war was seen by some as a "Euro-Nietzsche War." Fortunately, by that time *The Complete Works of Friedrich Nietzsche,* edited by Oscar Levy in 18 volumes, had already been published (1909–13). Immediately after the war, Elisabeth joined the ultraconservative Deutschnationale Volkspartei (German National People's Party). Predictably, she had little sympathy with the newly emerged Weimar Republic.

The Nietzsche-Archiv in the 1920s

On 12 June 1921 Jena University awarded Elisabeth a doctorate *honoris causa* in recognition of her major publications in the field of Nietzsche research, but chiefly for her biography of Nietzsche. Elisabeth made full use of her title, signing herself "Dr. phil. h.c. Elisabeth Förster-Nietzsche." Her ambitions had steadily increased from the turn of the century, and she was put forward for the Nobel Prize twice, in 1911 and 1923, but she was unsuccessful on each occasion. In 1923 the prize at least went to a deserving Nietzschean, W. B. Yeats. Meanwhile, Elisabeth continued to surround herself with many clever and several prominent men, and she was fêted and praised at the archive, although questions were now being raised about whether Nietzsche's manuscripts were safe in her hands. It was very easy for her to ignore these dissenting voices in the climate of general adulation. Elisabeth had asserted her will, and this was a period when she could enjoy its fruits. She was truly fortunate in finding men who were prepared to neglect their own interests in order to promote the archive, though without a doubt, most did this out of loyalty to the dead Nietzsche: It is very hard to believe that some of these men found her truly interesting, though the Thiel family were genuinely fond of her, and Kessler, too, had remained faithful, if laconic, up to this point. Hans Vaihinger, a convinced Nietzschean and a genuine admirer of Elisabeth, gave her loyal support over the years. As she aged, Elisabeth received invaluable help from her cousin Adalbert Oehler, now in his sixties, and her other cousins, the brothers Max and Richard Oehler. It is beyond the scope of the present work to provide a comprehensive account of Nietzscheanism during Elisabeth's lifetime; however, the men mentioned in the section below all had a special connection with the activities of the archive during its heyday in the 1920s.

Hans Vaihinger came to Nietzsche through his study of Immanuel Kant when he was professor of philosophy at Halle University. In his immensely influential *Die Philosophie des Als Ob* (The Philosophy of "As If," 1911), Vaihinger raised challenging questions such as whether, in view of Nietzsche's antithetical stance toward the truth of any proposition, one could also suppose that he *might* have posited the existence of God through dialectic reasoning. In his popular *Nietzsche als Philosoph* (Nietzsche As Philosopher, 1902), Vaihinger asserted an affinity between Nietzsche's philosophy and Darwinism. This work explained Nietzsche's attack on moralism, socialism, democracy, humanism, intellectualism, pessimism, and Christianity.

In a specially revised war edition of this much-reprinted brochure with an introduction for soldiers at the front, Vaihinger argued that Nietzsche was a pure philosopher whose ideas ought not to be confused with the aggression of men such as Heinrich von Treitschke or Friedrich von Bernhardi, the Prussian general whose seminal *Deutschland und der nächste Krieg* (Germany and the Next War, 1913) was subsequently hailed as prophetically patriotic (by right-wing German warmongers, who made nationalistic propaganda out of it) or as typically bellicose (by the rest of the world). It is hard to understand how Vaihinger could remain on good terms with Elisabeth, in view of her prowar posturing in Nietzsche's name and her frequent attempts to couple Nietzsche with Treitschke, but Vaihinger remained a strong ally of the archive and, since he was also the mainstay of the Kantgesellschaft (Kant Society), it gave the archive *kudos* to have such a friend. His homage to Elisabeth at her seventy-fifth birthday celebrations in 1921 did not go unnoticed, as Simon-Ritz and Ulbricht point out: "The palpable veneration for the 'philosopher's nurse' from the then most important Kant scholar, Vaihinger, as well as from the equally famous Bruno Bauch, will not have failed to have their effect on the public—chiefly on Elisabeth herself as she celebrated her birthday."[12]

The support of family members was a different matter. Of the three cousins, Adalbert Oehler stood out as the one who devoted his career to the interests of the archive. A lawyer by profession and at one stage the Oberbürgermeister in Weimar (chief mayor of Weimar), he became head of the Stiftung Nietzsche-Archiv when it was founded in 1908. Adalbert had supported Elisabeth against Franziska in the struggle in 1896 over which of them should have the rights to Nietzsche's works. Born in 1860, Adalbert was much older than his cousins Max and Richard and was already elderly by the time Hitler came to power, which does not excuse his adoption of National Socialist rhetoric in his book *Nietzsches Mutter* (Nietzsche's Mother), published in the year of his death, 1940. This work and his slim brochure "Nietzsches Werke und das Nietzsche-Archiv" (Nietzsche's Works and the Nietzsche-Archiv, 1910), which makes propaganda for the Stiftung Nietzsche-Archiv, are the only printed works by Adalbert Oehler of interest to Nietzsche scholars, though one should not overlook his unpublished manuscripts in the Goethe-Schiller Archive, "Das Nietzsche-Archiv in Weimar" (1910), "Zur Geschichte des Nietzsche-Archivs" (On the History of the Nietzsche-Archiv, 1936), and "Die Mutter von Friedrich Nietzsche: Lebensbild einer deutschen Mutter" (Friedrich Nietzsche's Mother: Biographical Portrait of a German Mother). Though undated, the latter's stress on Franziska as a *German* mother in the title indicates that it was written during the Third Reich, and the manuscript was revised for publication as *Nietzsches Mutter*.

Major Max Oehler was a career soldier. He helped in the Nietzsche-Archiv in 1908 while on leave from the army (April–December) and his major work, *Die Geschichte des Deutschen Ritterordens* (The History of the Teutonic Order), was published in two volumes in 1912. After serving in World War I he became archivist at the Nietzsche-Archiv in 1919. He coedited Nietzsche's twenty-three-volume *Gesammelte Werke* (1920–29) with Friedrich Würzbach and his brother Richard Oehler. Max Oehler worked tirelessly beside Elisabeth until her death in 1935, publishing a variety of works on Nietzsche, such as his slim volume *Nietzsches Philosophisches Werden* (Nietzsche's Philosophical Development, 1926), which adulates Nietzsche and which he presented to Elisabeth to mark her eightieth birthday. After Elisabeth's death he became director of the Nietzsche-Archiv. His death at the hands of the Soviet occupying power in 1945 was shrouded in mystery until 1997, when his granddaughters discovered that his grave is in Buchenwald (*Speziallager* 2; not, as presumed by H. F. Peters, in the cellar of a house close to the Nietzsche-Archiv). His daughter is the writer Ursula Sigismund, whose novel *Zarathustras Sippschaft* (Zarathustra's Kith and Kin, 1992) includes her childhood memories, which centered on "Tante Elisabeth" and life at the Nietzsche-Archiv. Her first husband, Ingolf Wachler, pursued plans for theater reform, which merged with the then-popular *völkisch* movement.

Richard Oehler was the more academic of the three cousins and, unlike his brother Max, he had occupied himself with Nietzscheanism from an early age, presenting his Ph.D. thesis in 1903 to the University of Halle-Wittenberg on "Nietzsches Verhältnis zur vorsokratischen Philosophie" (Nietzsche's Relationship toward Presocratic Philosophy), later published as *Friedrich Nietzsche und die Vorsokratiker* (Friedrich Nietzsche and the Pre-Socratics, 1904). Richard Oehler became a librarian, working mainly in Frankfurt, 1903–45 (in the position of director, 1927–45). Nevertheless, he kept a watchful eye on his cousin Elisabeth in Weimar and, with his brother Max, helped negotiate the funding for the Nietzsche-Archiv with Ernst Thiel, thus ensuring the long-term success of the venture.

Richard Oehler was Elisabeth's champion in her quarrel with Carl Albrecht Bernoulli in 1908 over the unpublished Nietzsche-Overbeck correspondence, which led to Elisabeth's court action. In the same year he published his contribution to the polemic, "Zum Kampf gegen das Nietzsche-Archiv" ("On the Fight against the Nietzsche-Archiv") in the *Jenaische Zeitung,* 30 April 1908. During the 1920s he was coeditor of Nietzsche's twenty-three-volume *Gesammelte Werke* (1920–29), and he was a very early National Socialist sympathizer. Oehler's *Friedrich Nietzsche und die deutsche Zukunft* (Friedrich Nietzsche and the Future of Germany), an attempt to Nazify Nietzsche, was published in 1935. In 1938 he gave a talk at the Nietzsche-Archiv that combined an overview of Nietzsche's philosophy—reduced to slogans connected with "Nietzsche-Zarathustra" [*sic*]—with a description of the plan for the memorial hall (Nietzsche-Gedächtnishalle) at that time under construction. The talk was published later that year as *Die Zukunft der Nietzsche-Bewegung* (The Future of the Nietzsche Movement).

During the 1920s, Oswald Spengler was an honored guest at the Nietzsche-Archiv, which he visited for the first time in July 1920. In 1923 he was invited to join the committee of the Stiftung Nietzsche-Archiv, and he joined the committee of the Gesellschaft der Freunde des Nietzsche-Archivs (Society for the Friends of the Nietzsche Society) when it was formed in 1926. Nietzsche is mentioned sporadically throughout volumes 1 and 2 of Spengler's seminal work *Der Untergang des Abendlandes* (vol. 1, 1918; vol. 2, 1923; published in English as *The Decline of the West*), in which Spengler describes socialism itself as a manifestation of the will to power. (According to Spengler, only George Bernard Shaw truly understood socialism and its connection to the eugenics movement.) Spengler's dislike of civilization afforded a clear point of convergence with the views of Thomas Mann, and of course, the two were united in their admiration for Nietzsche. Spengler's hatred of the priesthood exceeded even that of Nietzsche. His rhetoric against the evils of technology found in *Der Untergang des Abendlandes* is amplified in *Der Mensch und die*

Technik (1931; published in English as *Man and Technology*) where, incidentally, the question of diet is reopened: He argues that carnivores seek prey, but vegetarians *are* prey. Man is a beast of prey, but more so in some races (master races) than others. No doubt Elisabeth's late husband would have strongly disagreed with these premises, since he firmly believed that the eating of meat had a weakening effect on man. Elisabeth took a characteristically robust attitude to food, paying lip service to her husband's vegetarian principles only when it suited her.

Ernst Bertram, a scholar, teacher, writer, and member of the circle around Stefan George, was instrumental in causing interest in Nietzsche in Germany to swing to the right from 1918 until the end of the Third Reich. In his acclaimed *Nietzsche: Versuch einer Mythologie* (Nietzsche: Attempt at a Mythology, 1918), which went into seven editions between 1918 and 1927, Bertram systematically claimed Nietzsche as the spiritual incarnation of "Germanness," referring to his *Überdeutschtum* and placing him at the center of a myth about the psychic existence of the German people. Bertram declared that myth had more validity than historical fact. He described Nietzsche as torn by an internal conflict. Like Elisabeth, Bertram explained away Nietzsche's hatred of the Germans, though he characteristically saw it in abstract terms as a manifestation of his asceticism. Though Bertram and Mann found they had much in common, they went their separate ways after World War I, with Mann belatedly diverting his attention to shoring up the ailing Weimar Republic and Bertram turning to the right in politics and at the same time dragging Nietzsche's name more firmly under the *völkisch* rubric.

Thomas Mann, like Spengler, preached "anticivilization" and extolled Nietzsche's Germanness, making political use of Nietzsche's name while at the same time berating "the Latins" for doing just that. It is not surprising that Mann agreed wholeheartedly with the mythical dimension that Ernst Bertram ascribes to Nietzsche. Mann was also—like Bertram—a frequent visitor at the Nietzsche-Archiv during the 1920s and took an active part in the Munich-based Nietzsche-Gesellschaft (resulting in various conflicts of interest, discussed below). The right-wing views expressed in *Betrachtungen eines Unpolitischen* (Reflections of a Nonpolitical Man, 1918), which incidentally deepened the rift between Thomas Mann and his brother Heinrich Mann, coincided with Mann's distrust of democracy, and he was a harsh critic of the Weimar Republic in its early years; however, the murder of Walter Rathenau, the Jewish foreign minister, in 1922 forced Mann to revise his political opinions, and he came to regret not lending his support to Germany's first fragile attempt at democracy. In exile in America, he blamed Nietzsche for much of the chaos of the Third Reich, as in his essay (written in English)

"Nietzsche's Philosophy in the Light of Our Experience" (1947), though he also argued elsewhere that Nietzsche's ideas were taken too superficially by a nation that did not deserve him. This ambivalence is seen in his novel *Doktor Faustus* (1947), where the protagonist, the composer Adrian Leverkuhn, bears many of Nietzsche's traits.

By the end of the 1920s the Nietzsche-Archiv would have three sections that did not necessarily work in harmony. The first was the Stiftung Nietzsche-Archiv, founded in 1908 and discussed in the last chapter. The second was the independent Nietzsche-Gesellschaft (Nietzsche Society), a society founded in Munich in 1919 by Friedrich Würzbach, who was then chair, with a committee consisting of Ernst Bertram, Hugo von Hofmannsthal, Thomas Mann, Richard Oehler, and Heinrich Wölfflin. Würzbach then became coeditor (with Richard and Max Oehler) of the twenty-three-volume *Gesammelte Werke* published in Munich from 1920 to 1929. Because he was responsible for volumes 18 and 19 (1926), which would contain *Der Wille zur Macht,* he asked Elisabeth to see the original manuscripts, only to be told that the volumes of the *Grossoktavausgabe* edited by Otto Weiss in 1911 (15–16), in other words *Der Wille zur Macht,* were definitive. All readers of this present work will realize what a monumental lie that was. The ensuing clash was the first of many between the Nietzsche-Gesellschaft and the Nietzsche-Archiv, or to be more precise, the latter's inner circle, the Stiftung Nietzsche-Archiv. In 1923, conflict arose in the Stiftung Nietzsche-Archiv between Adalbert Oehler and Elisabeth over a dispute with the Kröner Verlag that resulted in Oehler resigning from his position at the head of the Stiftung Nietzsche-Archiv, to be replaced by Elisabeth's old friend Arnold Paulssen, who, however, passed the post on to Richard Leutheußer in the same year. The Gesellschaft der Freunde des Nietzsche-Archivs had been founded to protect the interests of the Nietzsche-Archiv, and it supported the latter in clashes with the Nietzsche-Gesellschaft. Elisabeth, Ernst Thiel, and Adalbert Oehler were made honorary members, as were the international luminaries Karl Joel and Romain Rolland, as well as Anton Kippenberg and Walter Klemm from the Kröner Press. The president was Arnold Paulssen and members included Thomas Mann, Oswald Spengler, and Heinrich Wölfflin. In spite of their disagreements, on 15–16 October 1927 the three separate entities were still on sufficiently cordial terms to celebrate the eighty-third anniversary of Nietzsche's birth by holding a combined three-day conference in Weimar. Papers were read by Oswald Spengler, Max Scheler, Hans Prinzhorn, and Friedrich Würzbach.

Throughout the 1920s the Nietzsche-Archiv struggled financially for survival. In February 1923, Oswald Spengler gave a talk at the Nietzsche-Archiv on the theme "Blut und Geld" (Blood and Money), a topic chosen by Elisabeth with some prescience, since the inflation during that year was halted by the introduction of the *Rentenmark* on 15 November, overnight bankrupting the Stiftung Nietzsche-Archiv. From then until it was "Nazified," the Nietzsche-Archiv was constantly short of funds, and for once, this was not caused by Elisabeth's extravagance. Ernst Thiel could no longer afford to bale her out, and the small grant awarded by General von Hindenburg in 1926 was not sufficient to prevent Elisabeth from ultimately succumbing to the expedient attraction of National Socialism when that seemed the only way to procure sufficient funds. The Nietzsche-Archiv had hoped to capitalize on the honorary doctorate awarded to Elisabeth by forging a scholastic link between the archive and Jena University, but this did not come to fruition and, indeed, caused more of a stir than those at the heart of the Nietzsche-Archiv had intended. Hopes had been set on Hans Leisegang, who became professor of philosophy at Jena University in 1930. In the same year he helped secure official recognition of Elisabeth's authorship of *The Will to Power,* which meant that she was entitled to royalties, but for the rest of Nietzsche's works there was a pressing danger that the copyright would run out at the end of 1930.

To extricate itself from imminent financial collapse, the Nietzsche-Archiv tried to strike a bargain with the Philosophy Department at Jena University to bring out a new collected edition of Nietzsche's works. However, the Nietzsche-Archiv balked at the small print of Leisegang's proposed agreement. Leisegang knew that the university authorities mistrusted the Nietzsche-Archiv's (or rather, Elisabeth's) research methods. As Karl Heussi, the rector of the university, explained to Elisabeth's cousin Adalbert Oehler in a letter dated 3 January 1931: "The scholarly reputation of the Nietzsche-Archiv is not the best."[13] Leisegang therefore insisted that he had to have a free hand with the manuscripts, and that his scholars must be able to work without interference from members of the Nietzsche-Archiv. Elisabeth, in the name of the Nietzsche-Archiv, vigorously opposed this. An article entitled "Warum Jena das Nietzsche-Archiv nicht haben will" (Why Jena does not want the Nietzsche-Archiv), which appeared in the *Vossische Zeitung* on 29 November 1930, placed the blame squarely on Elisabeth:

> As we announced, Jena University has turned down affiliation with the Nietzsche-Archiv in Weimar. The dean of philosophy at Jena, Professor Leisegang, who previously stood close to the Nietzsche-Archiv and was to take on the scholarly direction of the new critical Nietzsche edition, has now published a declaration in which he states that the refusal of Jena University to affiliate with the Nietzsche-Archiv is *final*. . . . In the main, these negotiations collapsed because of the actions of Frau Dr. Elisabeth Förster-Nietzsche, who opposed a purely scholarly procedure and purely scholarly handling of the material.[14]

One has a distinct feeling of déjà vu on reading the article: Leisegang's determination to state publicly that Elisabeth was at fault reminds one of the denunciations from Julius Klingsbeil in 1889. Naturally, Elisabeth could not allow scholars from Jena University to have uncensored access to Nietzsche's original manuscripts, for they would soon discover her fraudulent practices, to which Gast and all three of her cousins had turned an accommodating blind eye. The university's withdrawal of its offer, put in such unequivocal terms, placed the archive in a dilemma, and there were heated discussions over what to do next. The archive itself faced the risk of closure, quite apart from the fact that Elisabeth had been publicly shown in such a bad light. Simon-Ritz and Ulbricht comment: "The same university that, in the year 1921, had awarded an honorary doctorate to the sister of the philosopher for her scholarly services, now distanced itself from her at the end of the 20s to the same degree."[15] The deadlock was broken when Carl August Emge, a philosophy lecturer and convinced National Socialist supporter recently appointed to Jena University, offered to broker a deal; a committee was formed at his instigation specifically to bring out a *Historisch-Kritische Gesamtausgabe* of Nietzsche's works. Constituted in February 1931, the working group included Emge, Richard and Max Oehler, Oswald Spengler, and Walter Jesinghaus. Jesinghaus worked for the Thüringische Ministerium für Volksbildung (Thuringian Ministry of Culture). The committee was joined by Walter Otto in 1933, Karl Schlechta in 1934, and Hans Heyse and Martin Heidegger in December 1935. Other collaborators included Joachim Mette and Günther Lutz, who became chair of the Stiftung Nietzsche-Archiv on Heidegger's departure in 1942. By that date the committee had produced five volumes of Nietzsche's works and four volumes of letters.

That Heidegger had no great admiration for Elisabeth is clear from the fact that he did not join the prestigious committee working on the *Historisch-Kritische Gesamtausgabe* until after her death in 1935, even though he was passionately keen to produce the new collected works. Writing to Schlechta on 13 April 1938, he remarked: "it is becoming ever clearer to me how much our whole work has stood in a bad shadow for the last 40 years."[16] (As I have argued in chapter 4, Heidegger would proceed to throw his own shadow over Nietzsche research for at least four decades.)

On the committee, the only person not comfortable with National Socialist dogma, in spite of his reputation as a right-wing thinker, was Oswald Spengler, though as Simon-Ritz and Ulbricht point out, ironically enough the standard of Nietzsche research at the Nietzsche-Archiv began to improve during this period: "It is noteworthy that under the aegis of Otto and Heidegger and above all, though the activities of Hans Joachim Mette and Karl Schlechta, a more realistic Nietzsche picture began to take shape in an archive that externally continued to be developed as the decisive spiritual home of the 'Third Reich.'"[17] It was, after all, Karl Schlechta who had first discovered Elisabeth's forgeries when he demanded to see the original letters from Nietzsche to herself and her mother. Elisabeth's favorite camouflage was to pretend that a letter to someone else, very often Franziska, was to herself. She was also capable of destroying her own and Franziska's letters, as we have seen. Of Schlechta's confrontation with Elisabeth, Peters writes, "she became furious, uttered a cry of indignation, and threw her heavy oak cane at him."[18]

It was obvious to all those involved with the Nietzsche-Archiv that a sea change had taken place during the 1920s. From being the venue for Nietzscheans of every stamp, the Nietzsche-Archiv had moved to the far right. The situation in Thuringia was unique in that it fell an early prey to virulent National Socialism. Wilhelm Frick, already a zealous National Socialist, had been appointed minister for the interior and education in Thuringia in January 1930 and, ignoring democratic niceties, had already pushed through "measures that bore the traces of folkish-nationalist and racist tenets"[19] before he lost his seat in the 1931 elections and moved temporarily to Bavaria, from where he continued to undermine the Weimar republic. According to Günter Neliba: "Frick was heavily implicated in the destruction of the Weimar Republic's parliamentary system. At the same time, a series of NSDAP measures that would be decisive in the case of a coup d'état were furthermore communicated, strongly or otherwise, in many of Frick's utterances and deeds, in Thuringia and elsewhere, to those who wished to hear and understand."[20]

Matters were exacerbated—for those not persuaded by National Socialism—when the National Socialists under Fritz Sauckel gained power in Thuringia in 1932. On 18 March 1932, Walter Benjamin published an attack on the Nietzsche-Archiv in *Die Literarische Welt* entitled "Nietzsche und das Archiv seiner Schwester" (Nietzsche and the Archive of His Sister). This was simultaneously an appreciation of two works by Ernst Podach, *Nietzsche's Zusammenbruch* (Nietzsche's Collapse, 1930) and *Gestalten um Nietzsche* (People around Nietzsche, 1932) and a bitter attack on the activities of the archive under Elisabeth. The article stated that Nietzsche was worlds apart from the "industrious and philistine spirit"[21] that had become dominant in the Nietzsche-Archiv. Elisabeth was oblivious to criticism of this nature and remained so. She was jubilant that the finances of the archive were buoyant and did not care where the money came from, as we see in her acceptance of Philipp Reemtsma's yearly allowance, from 1928, of 20,000 reichsmarks, though to be fair to Elisabeth, the gift was at first anonymous and Reemtsma's shady dealings with Hermann Göring were only fully revealed after the war.

Although the Gesellschaft der Freunde des Nietzsche-Archivs was at first in the pocket of the Nietzsche-Archiv, its most prominent members now began to drop away as the National Socialist sympathies of the archive became manifest. Once these dissenters had slipped away, the Nietzsche-Archiv was so much in tune with the party machine that it remained untouched by *Gleichschaltung,* or "equalization," as Martha Galindo points out: "The Nietzsche-Archiv did not have to be 'equalized' like other NS [National Socialist] institutions. Its heavily symbolic exchanges with representatives of the NS regime demonstrate that they believed themselves, as guardians of Nietzsche's work, to have a mission in the NS state."[22]

Spengler's resignation from his position on the executive committee in 1935 is an interesting case in point. Although he had coupled Nietzsche's name with that of the German *Volk,* Spengler himself became increasingly ill at ease with the strident tone of nationalism to be found in the Nietzsche-Archiv. He also became disillusioned with Hitler's methods, openly disagreeing with National Socialism in *Jahre der Entscheidung* (*Years of Decision,* 1933). As a result of the views expressed there, Spengler, by now a broken man, provoked a government ban on his name and no doubt escaped a worse fate when he died in 1936. Romain Rolland, having associated with Elisabeth during the 1920s, felt constrained to withdraw his support from the Nietzsche-Archiv when Elisa-

Figure 18. Elisabeth Förster-Nietzsche welcomes Hitler to the Nietzsche-Archiv in 1934. On the far right, Max Oehler.

beth and those close to her openly welcomed Fascism. In a letter to Max Oehler on 4 August 1933, Rolland resigned from the Gesellschaft der Freunde des Nietzsche-Archivs because of what he saw as the group's glorification of Benito Mussolini. Other friends of the Nietzsche-Archiv emigrated, like Thomas Mann, who left Germany in 1933, though he did not express public opposition to the National Socialists until 1936. Throughout the 1920s, Kessler had become increasingly disillusioned with the direction in which the Nietzsche-Archiv was heading, and when the National Socialists came to power, he went into exile in his native France. He recorded in his diary on 7 August 1932: "It is enough to make one weep to see what has become of Nietzsche and the Nietzsche Archives."[23] After the war, trouble awaited those members of the Nietzsche-Archiv who had collaborated with the National Socialists: for example, Ernst Bertram was investigated for his involvement with National Socialism, and Max Oehler, as already discussed, was taken to Buchenwald and probably shot.

Heil Hitler

The fight over the Nietzsche-Archiv with Jena University notwithstanding, Elisabeth continued to enjoy her power as mistress of the archive and remained fully in possession of her faculties. It would be a mistake to believe that the catalog of National Socialist sympathizers mentioned above was taking advantage of her. Tempting though it is to see Elisabeth as a vulnerable old lady responding to political manipulation, her previous history of anti-Semitic tub-thumping indicates that she fundamentally admired right-wing agitators. Her own crudely *völkisch* patriotism, as seen in the articles she wrote during the war, can leave us in little doubt that her coy assurances to Thiel that she had never meant her anti-Semitism were just temporary window dressing. To have dealings with a man like Frick, who had racist views very similar to those of Bernhard Förster, was something of a homecoming for her. On 20 September 1930, Frick replied to a letter from Elisabeth (not extant) thanking her for her congratulations on recent National Socialist electoral success:

> *Most honored lady!*
> *Thank you kindly for your friendly congratulations on the N.S.D.A.P. electoral success. I have not given up hope that you, dear lady, will attach yourself to the freedom movement of the German people, in the spirit of your highly commended brother, the warrior Nietzsche.*
>

*With the highest respect
Your most devoted
Frick. Minister of State.*[24]

The exaggerated politeness in Frick's letter probably expressed his genuine regard for Elisabeth. That December he further endeared himself to her by making efforts to pass a draft regulation, drawn up by himself, which would give authors an extra year of copyright. Since this extra year was 1930–31, and there was no one in the land who would benefit more from it than Elisabeth, Frick's fellow politicians were right to be skeptical, and his draft was rejected, whereafter he continued his efforts to acquire a grant for the Nietzsche-Archiv. Frick accepted several tea invitations to the Nietzsche-Archiv and, after his marriage in March 1934, his wife also viewed Elisabeth as a valued friend. In 1935 Margarete Frick wrote to tell Elisabeth that she was pregnant (and to thank Elisabeth for sending her a complimentary copy of *Friedrich Nietzsche und die Frauen seiner Zeit*). She informed Elisabeth when her daughter was born that September, two months before Elisabeth died.

Elisabeth, who had lost none of her dictatorial propensity, believed categorically in strong leadership. In 1931 Benito Mussolini, the man she most admired at this time, had sent her a birthday telegram for her eightieth birthday, and she reciprocated with a telegram in 1933 to congratulate him on his fiftieth birthday. Mussolini, a convinced Nietzschean, was delighted to discover that the Nietzsche-Archiv was something of a Fascist enclave. Indirectly, Mussolini led Elisabeth to Hitler, as she first met Hitler when he visited Weimar in January 1932 to see Mussolini's play *Campo di Maggio* (which appeared in English as *The Hundred Days*). As it had been Elisabeth who had persuaded the Weimar theater to stage this play in the first place, Hitler paid Elisabeth a surprise visit to her box in the interval. Thus began their bizarre friendship, motivated by expediency and well laced with charm on both sides. Elisabeth next met Hitler in the company of Gauleiter Fritz Sauckel on 2 November 1933 at the Nietzsche-Archiv, when she presented Hitler with Nietzsche's walking stick and a copy of Förster's anti-Semitic petition to Bismarck. In May 1934 Hitler awarded Elisabeth a monthly allowance of 300 reichsmarks from his private purse "for her services in preserving and publicizing Nietzsche's work."[25] On 20 July 1934 Hitler paid Elisabeth a social visit at the Nietzsche-Archiv, and on 2 October of the same year he again visited the Nietzsche-Archiv with his architect Albert Speer to set in motion the building of a memorial hall. It was on this occasion that he was photographed in profile staring at the bust of Nietzsche by the sculptor Fritz Röll. Though she held Hitler in awe, after this visit Elisabeth felt sufficiently confident to write to him on 4 October 1934 inviting him to attend the commemoration of Nietzsche's ninetieth birthday. Her dictated note is the only one extant from Elisabeth to Hitler, though there are several from his office to her:

My most profoundly respected Führer!
Now I will, after all, venture to send you the invitation to the 90th birthday of
my dear brother.[26]

A printed invitation for 15 October 1934 was no doubt attached to this brief but revealing note. Elisabeth obviously had to pluck up courage to write to Hitler, but allowing for her habitual tendency to overegg the pudding when writing to important people, "Most profoundly respected" (*Innigstverehrt*) is obsequious even by *her* standards. There can be no doubt that she thought Frick, Mussolini, and Hitler were all wonderful.

The project for the memorial hall was now set in hand in with a budget of 50,000 reichsmarks, and Paul Schultze-Naumburg was appointed architect. Fritz Sauckel saw the project as a further enhancement of Weimar's cultural reputation, though it was a strain on the Thuringian purse. Building work began in July 1937. Elisabeth did not live to see this grandiose edifice, built beside the archive. She died suddenly on 8 November 1935 after an attack of flu, an unrepentant National Socialist sympathizer. Almost six months before she died, she had sent Hitler a copy of her new book *Friedrich Nietzsche und die Frauen seiner Zeit:* Hitler's letter of thanks is dated 26 July 1935. On Elisabeth's death, the position as director of the archive passed to Max Oehler, whose National Socialist credentials were just as good. When the war broke out, work on the memorial hall slowed down and it was never really finished, even though more money was poured in. And as Simon-Ritz and Ulbricht point out, the National Socialist censorship machine constantly stalled progress on the *Historisch-Kritische Gesamtausgabe* even though Karl Schlechta and Joachim Mette were party men: "Again and again, they had to get through disagreements with individual NS members in charge of literature."[27] If the situation had not been so serious, one could roar with laughter at the thought of a band of National Socialist scribes trying to pick fault with Nietzsche's works: that they found anything at all to let *past* the censor is the joke. In terms of social and cultural events, the war left its mark on the archive as elsewhere, putting an end to most of the talks and other activities. In spite of Alfred Rosenberg's efforts to be upbeat at the modest centenary celebration of Nietzsche's birthday on 15 October 1944, history was about to overtake the archive and its monumental white elephant, the memorial hall.

Elisabeth would probably have made a thoroughgoing attempt to accommodate Nietzsche's ideas to the National Socialist state as she had done in her bellicose rhetoric during World War I, but at her age, her journalistic output was vastly reduced. Nevertheless, in *Friedrich Nietzsche und die Frauen seiner Zeit,* she still managed to make the point that Nietzsche would have approved of the National Socialist insistence on the domestic role of women in the state. Clumsily trying to relate this to Nietzsche, Elisabeth felt that his bachelor status needed to be clarified. She invents a story that Nietzsche had once told a young unmarried man that the status of bachelor within the state was "reprehensible." Next she invents a myth that she once found written evidence of this: "Later the summary of the conversation that he had with the young friend at that time was found in his private notes, and with the greatest astonishment we see that he must have had a presentiment of the legislation of the new Reich in mind, as Nietzsche's views match those of the new laws so wonderfully."[28] This convoluted fib was Elisabeth's method of stating that Nietzsche approved of the family as an institution, which is true, though her point that he would have therefore lent his support to the National Socialists is very wide of the mark. Nietzsche had certainly left himself open to abuse on the woman question by tenaciously pursuing an ultra-conservative position and very much enjoying being the scourge of the campaign for women's emancipation. However, his philosophy constantly stressed that people were individuals and many feminists overlooked his misogynic comments because the rest of his philosophy permitted them to feel *free* and indeed, paradoxically, to feel emancipated.

A parallel dilemma faced National Socialist propagandists when they tried to make Nietzsche's thought fit in with National Socialist collectivism. They soon discovered that their dogma directly conflicted with Nietzsche's uncompromising demand for the freedom of the individual. Here again, though, Nietzsche had provided his enemies with ample rope with which to hang him, in this case in the form of a polemic in favor of strong leaders. He had regularly expressed admiration for Napoleon and Cesare Borgia, and so it is not possible to argue that he wished to see leadership emerge at the cultural level only. Of course, Elisabeth was under some pressure to impress the National Socialists with her political bona fides: not only did she desperately need money, but the climate in Germany after *Gleichschaltung* made it impossible for National Socialist doctrine to be openly challenged. And Galindo is right to say that Elisabeth and the Oehlers were not the only National Socialists at the archive: "The documents show . . . that all the colleagues at the archive collaborated in this process between 1930 and 1945."[29] Nevertheless, it can be stated categorically that Frau Dr. phil. h.c. Elisabeth Förster-Nietzsche and the Oehler cousins certainly set the tone for the Nazification of Nietzsche.

Elisabeth's death gave the National Socialists a chance to put on an elaborate funeral ceremony that echoed the veneration of the mother in the Third Reich; for Hitler had "adopted" her for his own purposes as a mother figure to whom he could show duty and respect. Her memorial service, at which

Hitler and Baldur von Schirach were present, was held at the Nietzsche-Archiv on 11 November; she was buried in Röcken next day. The funeral addresses at the ceremony in the Nietzsche-Archiv reveal just how much a part of the National Socialist state the Nietzsche-Archiv had become by the time of Elisabeth's death. The speeches held on 11 and 12 November are contained in an unpaginated booklet *Ansprachen zum Gedächtnis der Frau Dr. Phil. H.C. Elisabeth Förster-Nietzsche bei den Trauerfeierlichkeiten in Weimar und Röcken am 11. und 12. November 1935.* The program for the formal ceremony at the Nietzsche-Archiv was as follows:

1. String quartet.
2. Address by the president of the Stiftung Nietzsche-Archiv, Staatsminister a.D. Dr. h.c. Leutheußer.
3. Address by Professor Dr. Adalbert Oehler.
4. String quartet.
5. Address by Professor Dr. Meyer-Erlach, rector of Jena University.
6. Address by Gauleiter and state administrator Fritz Sauckel.
7. String quartet.

Elisabeth would have loved this program, especially the tastefully placed intervals of music that, we recall, had been a feature of her early attempt to found an archive in Naumburg, much to Franziska's displeasure. Elisabeth would have liked the speeches even better, though the constant genuflections to Hitler divert much of the focus of the event away from Elisabeth. All those who spoke at the Nietzsche-Archiv prefaced their address with "Mein Führer." At the service at Röcken, much smaller fish such as the local pastor officiated. At the Nietzsche-Archiv, Richard Leutheußer ended his speech with profuse adulation: "Elisabeth Förster-Nietzsche, now at last reunited with your beloved brother in death, your name will be linked with your work for all time! You true guardian of the intellectual output of your great brother, we express our undying devotion and gratitude to you on this solemn ceremonial occasion."[30]

Oberbürgermeister Adalbert Oehler (his official title) gave a thoughtful, albeit tendentious, address. He began by discussing the family tragedy in which Elisabeth and her mother had found themselves caring for Nietzsche, at which point Elisabeth had realized that someone had to take care of Nietzsche's writings as well. He then described the move to Villa Silberblick, the alterations by van de Velde in 1903, and the constant financial problems that Elisabeth had been forced to overcome. All this was true and only mildly contentious, but having reached the topic of finances, Oehler thanked Hitler profusely for his timely financial help to the archive, for which Elisabeth had been so grateful, and proceeded to give the archive over to the Führer lock, stock, and barrel:

> The deceased's great gratitude empowers me, my Führer, to thank you most profoundly and heartily on behalf of the deceased, and at the same time in the name of the Stiftung Nietzsche-Archiv, for the great honor you have shown the dear departed by participating in today's funeral ceremony. She was proud of your repeated visits to the archive. Now, since the archive has lost its founder, its mother, since it is an orphan, I permit myself to express the wish that you, my Führer, will take the orphaned archive under your powerful protection![31]

The above shows just how much the archive would be a National Socialist stronghold during the remainder of the Third Reich, since it really was quite an honor to Elisabeth for Hitler to attend her funeral. That said, the occasion gave him some excellent photo opportunities that sent out the message of a caring son mourning a mother figure: observe Oehler's reference to Elisabeth as the mother of the archive. Fritz Sauckel's address introduced a new twist to the rhetoric by reminding mourners of the close friendship that had existed between Cosima Wagner and Elisabeth (he did not mention that the friendship had been distinctly cool during the four decades prior to Cosima's death in 1930). Elisabeth would have swooned with delight over Sauckel's comments: "Who was not deeply touched by the wonderful personality of this woman who—let us remember Bayreuth—made the liveliest contribution to the struggles and productivity of the greatest German masters, and who was bound in true friendship to Cosima Wagner, likewise a unique woman. I count our German people infinitely fortunate in having been endowed with such noble and magnificent *women* beside greatest statesmen, heroes, generals, and most powerful, culturally creative men."[32]

Rector Meyer-Erlach's speech was the shortest but the worst in terms of hyperbole—from someone of whom one would expect or at least hoped better. It ended: "I salute you, priestess of eternal Germany!"[33] The printed program for the funeral ceremony in Röcken on 12 November 1935 was altogether more low-key, although again there was musical accompaniment, as the brochure notes: "songs by the male choir of the German National Theater, Weimar." Superintendent Förster of Zeitz, Privy Councilor a. D. Professor Dr. Jesinghaus, and Pastor Thörel (first names unrecorded) each gave an address, of which Thörel's was the shortest. Truly, with this address by the local pastor, now the resident in the house where Elisabeth and Nietzsche had been born, the wheel had come full circle for the Nietzsche family, their graves now lying in a neat row that had been *rearranged* by Elisabeth so that she lay between her brother and Franziska. In a way, with Nietzsche on the extreme left and Pastor Nietzsche, father of the family, on the right flank, one could see the men as protecting the women: What could be more fitting, except that Nietzsche's grave had had to be moved to the left to make this possible. It probably did not occur to Elisabeth that this was a desecration, and if it had, she would have had no scruples in pursuing her goal.

As the description of Elisabeth's funeral suggests, the administration at the Nietzsche-Archiv had thrown in its lot with Hitler, and those capable of writing books now did so with the appropriate political slant. Alfred Baeumler's *Nietzsche: Der Philosoph und Politiker* (Nietzsche: The Philosopher and Politician) had appeared in 1931. In this highly influential work, Baeumler argued that Nietzsche's pejorative remarks on the state all referred to Bismarck's Second Reich. He revealed the similarities between the concept of the *Übermensch* and Hitler's *Führerprinzip* (leadership principle) and took the will to power seriously as a philosophical idea with ancient Greek resonance, dubbing it a Heraclitan *Weltkampf* (world struggle). He suggested that Nietzsche's endeavor could be summed up by the phrase "Die Welt als Tat und Gerechtigkeit"[34] (the world as deed and judgment, by analogy with Arthur Schopenhauer's chief work, *Die Welt als Wille und Vorstellung* [The World As Will and Representation], which appeared in 1818), or, even more succinctly, by the phrase "Die Welt als Kampf" (the world as struggle). To reinforce his own agenda of bellicosity, he cleverly reminded his readers of the constant struggles Nietzsche had to overcome in his own life, whereas, of course, Nietzsche had struggled against precisely the type of ideology peddled by Baeumler: "One cannot understand Nietzsche's life or work if one does not take into account what value the experience and concept of struggle and victory have for him."[35]

The references to Heraclitus and Schopenhauer and Baeumler's general scholarly tone gave his text an authority that it did not deserve, since he bent and twisted Nietzsche's thought on every page. He was the first to argue that *The Will to Power* was Nietzsche's most significant text, a position then adopted by Martin Heidegger. It is important to remember that Elisabeth was still alive and compos mentis when Baeumler's book was published with her full approval. Richard Oehler in *Friedrich Nietzsche und die deutsche Zukunft* (1935) argued that Nietzsche's *Herrenmoral* (master morality) found its apotheosis in the German master race. The work consists of excerpts from Nietzsche's writings (a technique much used by Elisabeth herself), with a commentary to show the extent to which Nietzsche's thought could be said to have anticipated Nationalist Socialist doctrine. The book displayed a photograph of Adolf Hitler as its frontispiece. Heidegger, who had been appointed rector of the University of Freiburg in April 1933, accommodated himself to the new regime with apparent ease. It is not so much what Heidegger did, but what he did not do, that is of interest in this discussion. Leaving aside his failure to defend his Jewish colleagues from the long arm of the National Socialist state, his philosophical interpretation of Nietzsche, based primarily on *The Will to Power,* had far-reaching consequences. As a powerful member of the inner circle of the Nietzsche-Archiv, it lay within his power to seek to turn his colleagues away from the course of collaboration with the National Socialists. This he manifestly failed to do.

We come now to the grotesque demise of the Nietzsche-Archiv. The memorial hall by which Hitler had set such store was, despite all setbacks, nearly complete by 1944 in spite of the imminent defeat of the German nation. Himself staring defeat in the face, Mussolini donated a statue of Dionysus to the hall that was expedited from Italy at the very last moment, that is to say while trains were still running. The 15 January 1944 expedition of this useless sculpture at such a time shows just how crazed Mussolini really was. It is also offensive that at the same time as the transport trains delivered human cargo to the extermination camps in anonymous thousands, a dossier of forty-six documents tracked every movement of the statue.[36] But Max Oehler was not much saner. He borrowed a truck and collected the statue from Weimar railway station on 29 January 1944, obediently taking time to sign the receipt while the town was under fire from British bombers. Then the statue turned out not to fit into the designated alcove in the hall. Oehler propped it against the wall in its crate, and rather than escape from Weimar while there was time, he continued to go to work as usual, where he was duly arrested by the Red Army in 1945, by which time Thuringia lay under Soviet occupation. This curious devotion to duty at such a time at least proves that Oehler genuinely believed his own rhetoric. During the Russian occupation, when Nietzsche was viewed as a proto-Fascist thinker in the GDR, the memorial hall eventually became the premises (up to September 2000) of Radio Thüringen, and the Nietzsche-Archiv itself was locked up, but after 1989, with Nietzsche now off the "Index," the Stiftung Weimarer Klassik began to straighten out the situation of the Nietzsche legacy in Weimar and, most important of all, to retrieve Nietzsche's good name. Only now are former residents of the GDR coming to realize that the philosopher who went mad in 1889 had *not* been a proto-Fascist thinker and that instead, it was his sister who implicated Friedrich Nietzsche in National Socialist propaganda.

There has always been a school of thought that pays homage to Elisabeth for her enormous efforts in collecting material for the Nietzsche-Archiv, much of which might have been lost to posterity if Elisabeth had not established an archive for it when she did. Be that as it may, my chief accusation against Elisabeth is that she tarnished her brother's name. I have spent a large part of my career trying to convince the recalcitrant British public that it was Nietzsche's sister Elisabeth, and not Nietzsche himself—long dead—who stood at the door of the Nietzsche-Archiv to welcome Hitler. Few people apart from experts in the field have any inkling that Nietzsche predeceased his sister by some thirty-five years, whereas this fact is generally known in Germany. For all the postmodernist enthusiasm for Nietzsche's ideas, his name in Britain is still widely suspect.

My own opinion on the collecting activities of the Nietzsche-Archiv is that it would often have been better for Nietzsche if Elisabeth had *not* hounded his former friends and associates for mementos. For instance, Elisabeth wrung eight letters from Resa von Schirnhofer in spite of the latter's plaintive comment in a letter to Elisabeth dated 12 February 1903: "I am a nobody and want to remain that way."[37] Resa von Schirnhofer's letters remind us of Nietzsche's vexed attitude toward members of the opposite sex, which was certainly not Elisabeth's intention. (Nietzsche flirted with the idea of flirting with Schirnhofer, but decided that she was too ugly.[38]) Beyond that, the letters add nothing to our understanding of Nietzsche's thought. By the same token, Elisabeth was not able to get her hands on the letters that really would have illuminated Nietzsche's mind: those he wrote to Cosima Wagner. Elisabeth's archivist work thus resulted in too much and too little: There is so much material that one is swamped, and yet the answer to puzzling questions such as Nietzsche's putative syphilis, or what really went on between him and Lou von Salomé behind closed doors, will never be known.

I also believe that the important posthumous manuscripts—*Götzen-Dämmerung, Der Antichrist,* and even *Ecce Homo* (with or without the hurtful comments on Franziska and Elisabeth) would have been published even if Elisabeth had stayed where she was in Paraguay. For in spite of the received opinion that Franziska wanted to burn *Der Antichrist,* she did not do so, although she had plenty of chances before Elisabeth's return to Naumburg. Franziska was not ruthless in matters of Nietzsche's manuscripts, though she was perhaps somewhat careless; crates of paper were less important to her than lugging a couple of dozen buckets of water into Nietzsche's room every other day so that she could bathe him. Nor did she overestimate her capacities: she took the advice of Overbeck and Adalbert Oehler and would probably have been content for Gast to plod away with his deciphering of the *Nachlaß* at his own pace.

It is interesting that in a letter to her nephew of 25 October 1893, Franziska told Adalbert that she had been worried about how the newly returned Elisabeth would react to Gast when they met in Leipzig for a "business meeting":

"thanks be to God that the meeting with good Herr Köselitz went off so well, I had been really anxious about it."[39] A second-rate scholar, Gast was at least sufficiently honorable to do a philological job properly. Unfortunately, he unleashed a whirlwind when he indicated to Elisabeth that money could be made from publishing the *Der Wille zur Macht*. It is probable that Nietzsche's *Nachlaß* would have seen print even if Elisabeth had not lifted a finger and that his name would then have rested solely on his publications—as it ought to do.

The Nietzsche-Archiv founded by Elisabeth, where Nietzsche breathed his last with no inkling that the word *Weimar* would become a central word in German history, is a monument to Elisabeth's vanity just as much as it is and was a place where Nietzsche enthusiasts could (and can) congregate. From its portal, Elisabeth made contact with the men she regarded as the real *Übermenschen* of the twentieth century: Mussolini and Hitler, and under cover of boundless sisterly love, she conducted a vendetta against Nietzsche for having once dared to love Lou by turning Zarathustra into a Fascist ideologue. Within a year of Nietzsche's death she brought into being her master work, which almost had the status of a substitute child, *Der Wille zur Macht,* the monstrous progeny of a philosopher who had agonized over a missing comma in the works he had shepherded into print during his lifetime.

Frau Dr. h.c. Elisabeth Förster-Nietzsche was hailed by the majority of her contemporaries as "the most sisterly of souls" (W. F. Otto's homage to her)[40] in willful ignorance of what she had actually *done* to Nietzsche's name. The respected Vaihinger's praise of her "incomparable sisterly love"[41] (unvergleichliche Schwesterliebe) was the majority verdict. But history has a way of humbling those with hubris. Elisabeth, for all her efforts at collecting material for the Nietzsche-Archiv, was fundamentally a parasite on Nietzsche. The fact that she was made an honorary member of the Kantgesellschaft had much more to do with Nietzsche than with Elisabeth, and there are many more examples of this kind. Rather than see her as a "priestess of an eternal Germany" we should see her as a latter-day Cerberus, though instead of acting as a watchdog jealously guarding Nietzsche's manuscripts, she manipulated and doctored them with impunity. There is something alarming about the way she willfully destroyed the reputation of the man she loved best, her brother. With all her gifts, she refused to acknowledge where her actions were leading; she quarreled with her friends, hurt those she loved, and believed her own lies. The fateful will to power in this novelist *manquée* led her to turn life itself into a dramatic scenario, part tragedy and part farce.

Appendix: Coffee-Party Gossip about Nora by Elisabeth Nietzsche (1882?)

Part One

"You really do have a very good appetite, Georg," said his elderly aunt wistfully, shaking her curly gray locks and staring sadly at her nephew's handsome manly face. From the ivy-clad veranda, the latter stared thoughtfully into the garden, which was in full bloom, while he consumed his elevenses with evident satisfaction.

Georg looked at her agog: Tante Linchen, or rather, Fräulein Caroline Eichstedt, had kept house for her brother, the widower Colonel Eichstedt, for thirty-two years, but nobody during that length of time had ever eaten enough for the good soul, let alone too much. Even the colonel, who made up the third at the table and who, like his son, had been sunk deep in thought, looked up in astonishment at his sister's strange remark.

"Well, well, Caroline," he cried in surprise, "we must be in danger of famine if you're trying to stop your beloved Georg from enjoying home cooking while he's on holiday, and convalescing to boot."

But Tante Linchen shook her gray head again and her pleasant old face puckered into so many painful folds that the colonel finally cried out with a laugh: "Well, out with it, tell us what's on your mind, you really do look wretched!"

"Yes, yes," her learned nephew added, "just tell me why my good-hearted aunt begrudges me my elevenses, with all my learning I can't get to the bottom of it."

"Ah, Georg," she began hesitantly, "I probably shouldn't tell you but I always hoped—and just now actually believed—that you—yes, that you might be a little bit in love." Her nephew burst out laughing—it was a magnificent laugh, one would not have credited the earnest young professor, who must have been already in his mid-thirties, with such a fresh and childlike laugh.

"Oh, Auntie, and now you see by my excellent appetite that I have not yet succumbed to love."

He laughed again, so heartily that the colonel, and even the poor disappointed aunt, were both infected by it. "My good appetite proves nothing, by the way," Georg teased, "it was only fashionable in the good old days for lovers to pine, refuse to eat and drink, and throw themselves on their knees before their beloved. But what in the world could possibly give you this strange idea that I'm in love?"

Georg looked so innocent and genuinely surprised—it really was too much, even Tante Linchen, who had the patience of a saint, could not resist.

"Well, my dear Georg," she replied, annoyed, "it would not be anything so very extraordinary and amazing and surprising for me to conclude that you're in love: every morning at seven on the dot, the moment you've finished your coffee, you shoot off like an arrow to meet a very nice pretty girl for your morning walk, and then you stroll around in never-ending heated debate for two or three hours. Other people in Weißenburg go for walks in the public park as well, and I've heard a lot about it. Frau Fitzner, wife of Privy Councilor Fitzner, came here yesterday and said . . ."

"For heaven's sake, spare me the gossip from your coffee-party cronies," Georg replied, himself now somewhat annoyed, "they make a mountain out of a molehill for want of anything better to talk about. I can't imagine what those silly old women have to gossip about with my innocent strolls."

"Don't be so disrespectful, Georg," his aunt cut in with dignity. "I have a few real friends amongst those 'coffee-party cronies and silly old women.'"

"Of course, Auntie, some of these old Weißenburg ladies are all right," her nephew said soothingly, "but they should leave their fellow men in peace and not spy on them."

"They don't need to 'spy' if you wander round the public park with Fräulein Werner," Tante Linchen said in defense and, changing the subject slightly, she added affectionately, "and what a nice, interesting girl she is."

"Of course she is," her nephew said eagerly, becoming all innocence once more. "Her opinions are so sound that one can have a really sensible conversation with her without a trace of banality; she is natural and upright, a bit like a good chum."

"But Georg," his auntie said mischievously, "she's a very pretty good chum." "Pretty?" The learned professor thought this over. "Hmm, hmm, I must admit that I've never thought about it," he said, almost nonplussed. "But you know, I don't consider being pretty a particularly good endowment for women," he continued animatedly, "it usually has a weakening effect on their disposition to thought and deed, and I would echo the words of a certain philosopher who exclaimed sadly, on making the acquaintance of a clever and beautiful woman, 'Oh, how much cleverer you would be if you were not beautiful!'"

"Well, your philosopher seems to judge the female sex very one-sidedly," the colonel objected with an ironic smile. "I have always found pretty women cleverer than ugly women. Being aware of having a pleasing appearance gives women a certain courage to develop and show their intellectual potential, while being ugly often has a decidedly depressing and restricting effect."

"Oh, father," Georg said heatedly (and one could see he was on his favorite topic), "please give this point your particular attention for once and you will see that the opposite is true: ugliness acts as a spur, women who are of most use to their husbands and also to society are the ugly ones. Women want to shine whatever the circumstances, they achieve this most easily and comfortably with an attractive appearance, but failing that they throw themselves with passion and energy at some other area of excellence: learning, philanthropy, homemaking and so on. Woman's ambitious nature must somehow make itself felt, she loses heart if she is not admired."

"If you had known your mother better you would not be able to put this forward as a generalization," Tante Linchen said softly, and the colonel added seriously: "We have yet another example to disprove this philosophical statement: look at Tante Linchen—has she done everything for us just in order to shine?"

Nothing makes philosophers more uncomfortable than to have their philosophical claims personalized, and it is indeed fatal: none of the nice theories are ever quite right when applied to individuals and facts. Georg wanted to be angry, too, but in his heart he remembered a thousand touching incidents: how his kind aunt had brought him up and cared for him with infinite patience, unflagging love, and cheerfulness, how through long years she had provided him with warm, comforting sympathy, and a willing helping hand through thick and thin, without ever, ever making any fuss! And now she cried, blushing in alarm: "Please, please don't bring me into it, I'm just a poor sinner!"

Tears came to Georg's eyes. "Auntie," he said fervently, "you're an exception."

"No, no, my darling!" Tante Linchen contradicted earnestly, "I'm not an exception, there are much better women than I everywhere. No, I just think that you know too little about women and have only seen their bad side; but if you ever fall properly in love with a really good woman, and ask for her hand on bended knee, and if you clearly feel that your whole life's happiness depends on whether or not she says yes, then, my dear, you might well have other ideas about women."

"Oh, you dear old romantic Auntie," cried Georg, "do you think I would ever go on bended knee to a girl? Me? On bended knee? Me—me?" And again his laugh was so hearty and childlike that the elderly pair joined in, despite themselves.

"Don't bother to give him a romantic impression of getting engaged and married, Linchen," laughed the colonel. "He's an incorrigible rogue in that respect, he doesn't intend to fall in love and marry, and never did." "But father, that isn't quite true," Georg said reproachfully. "You remember eight years ago when I was appointed professor in B, you advised me very strongly to woo and marry the daughter of your friend, Privy Councilor Winter. I wasted half a year attempting to penetrate what pleases women. I studied fashion, read the novels they like, went dancing and skating, and tried to copy other young people in courting Fräulein Winter. It was somewhat boring but I was quite determined to marry Helene Winter."

"Yes, indeed, my dear boy, I remember the case," continued his father cheerfully. "I can picture you now when you told me of your decision; you pulled a face like someone about to make a death-defying dive into water."

"I did feel rather ill at ease," his son agreed pensively.

"True, true," the colonel went on. "I was really worried and concerned. But how different you were when you came running to me at the hotel that same evening to tell me that you could not possibly ask for Helene Winter's hand, as you had just discovered that your best friend was passionately in love with her, and would be desperately unhappy without her. And all the while you radiated happiness as though you wanted to announce the best possible news in the world to me."

"Well, yes," answered Georg with some animation, "I don't deny it, it was like having a weight lifted from my heart to be able to do what I wanted from now on. A veritable flood of happiness swamped my soul and I felt clearly that I would never, ever be fit to marry. I would just find marriage a prison."

"Oh, dear heaven," sighed Tante Linchen, "it would be quite wrong even to advise you to marry if that's what you think."

"It certainly would, dear Auntie," said Georg kindly, adding in earnest, "Besides, I couldn't consider it now for years, even with the best will in the world. How would I keep a wife and child?" Tante Linchen looked at her brother uneasily. Georg stood up and went to his study.

"Ulrich," Linchen asked the colonel, "is it definite, then?"

"Yes," he replied, worried. "Georg wants to give up being a professor of philology; he went to see the university registrar today and wants to start all over again as an unsalaried university professor. Oh! I did not oppose him. I know myself how depressing it can be for a man if he is not fully satisfied with his profession. Georg's studies in philology brought him to philosophy. He's more interested in Greek philosophy and ethics nowadays than in the language. Why should he waste his time and energy on studies and lectures when he could occupy himself with something that really interests him? I know all about doing one's duty in such a joyless fashion, and I want Georg to have an easier time of it."

Tante Linchen sighed. Ah, she well remembered that it had been Ulrich's dearest wish to become a painter, but their father, an enthusiastic soldier, would not hear of it and used every means at his disposal to persuade his son to follow his own profession. Ulrich even enjoyed being an officer for a time, and was very happily married to the most excellent and lovely woman. But after the early death of his beloved Kätchen, his love of painting erupted once more, causing renewed heated battles with his father on account of Ulrich's lack of means at that time. Ulrich's tender love for his two boys decided the matter. If he had resigned his commission against his father's will he would have had to rely on a small pension; how could he have provided his boys with a proper and thorough education? Broken-hearted, Ulrich gave up his heart's desire. He had been a dutiful officer, but Linchen knew ah! only too well how hard, how hard the pressures of life had been for her poor brother.

"And yet," continued the colonel after some time, "I'm not sure I was right to agree with him. Men in their mid thirties often have a sudden urge to leave their wonted career, don't they? It's as though an inner voice keeps calling 'You were born to higher and better things, seize that for which you are best suited!' Is it the voice of truth or is a devil trying to seduce us? I too had a terribly hard struggle then, but the unfavorable circumstances directed me to the path I *had* to take. I found it difficult, and yet after all these long years I think I took the best course; perhaps I was a better officer than I would have been a painter. That saved me from the terrible disappointment a man feels if he finds that he can't achieve perfection in his chosen occupation, in spite of all the sacrifices he has made and his strong inner compulsion. Such periods of discouragement are the worst thing for an honorable man—God preserve Georg from them. If only he had a kind, clever and trusting wife at his side, it's a comfort and relief when things are at their worst, and often even shows us a new direction which we stubborn men would not find by ourselves."

"Yes, but Georg does not have a loving wife and won't find one with his views," Tante Linchen lamented, "he would have to meet a really ugly girl," she added doubtfully.

"Nonsense!" growled the colonel, the artist in him taking offense, but soon a gay and almost mocking smile flickered on his lips. "Linchen," he said, "everything might still be all right, and as far as I'm concerned, if he loves her, then I would welcome the ugliest girl there is as my daughter-in-law!"

Well, well, dear colonel, are you perhaps thinking about the "pretty good chum," hence your Christian humility? But beware, fate usually makes our most secret desires come true in a way we would not wish!

But the Eichstedt establishment was not the only one this lovely spring morning in the good town of Weißenburg where a parental heart was plagued with worries about the marriage prospects of its offspring, oh no! There were several of them! It appears to be ever harder for the younger generation to tie Hymen's knot. Sons are strongly resistant and—would you believe it—daughters too! And these don't just resist for the sake of appearance, as was the fashion in the good old days, no, even the daughters sometimes completely refuse to listen to anything about getting married. A new philosophical generation is growing up which apparently takes as its motto the exact opposite of the biblical saying. "It is a good thing to remain single" these youthful lips inform us.

In the comfortable sitting room belonging to Professor Werner's widow, mother and daughter sat in opposite window seats, and over them, too, hovered the topic of nuptials like a threatening cloud. Poor Frau Werner had already had a great deal of vexation that day. Early that morning she woke with the news that the washerwoman could not come: her children had caught scarlet fever. How annoying when everything has been prepared for a big wash! And worse still, the postman brings her an extremely unpleasant letter. In some families, sisters seem to have the privilege of being able to say the most dreadful things to one another. Thus Frau Werner had recently felt compelled, without any good reason, to speak to her youngest sister about the way the latter was bringing up her daughters, making all sorts of criticisms. Now, of course, the sister, a very courageous woman, delivered a fulminating answer in which the following sentence pierced Frau Werner's heart like an arrow: "I am bringing my daughters up to the best of my ability and, so far as I judge the matter, I am sure that shortly they will both be favorably married off, and won't be left on the shelf, as has happened with your Nora."

Poor disgraced Frau Werner sat there—what is the best certification of a daughter's good education? What determines a girl's worth? Why, certainly, only her marriage at the earliest opportunity to the most favorable match, and Frau Werner lacked this certificate. What use was it when she told her sister again that Nora could have made excellent matches. "But she didn't," the other replied yet again in a highly laconic fashion. Ah, nothing is decisive in this cruel world but true success.

Frau Werner directed an angry glance at her daughter, who in blissful ignorance was immersed in a thick book. She wondered how it had happened that such a pretty daughter had grown so old without being married. Why had she never wanted to? And when Frau Werner glanced again at her daughter, the uncomfortable feeling rose in her simple soul that she actually knew nothing about this daughter and that her daughter's ideas were as remote and foreign to her as if she had lived on another star.

It was correct that Nora had not been home for eight years. Frau Werner had a stepson from Professor Werner's first marriage and this stepson had always been fond of little Nora, especially after the death of their father. Out of this fondness, a true friendship had gradually developed, especially after he had married Nora's best friend, a charming Englishwoman, a complete orphan. Nora's emotions and interests were completely taken up by these two dearly loved people: Her heart was quite fulfilled by keeping house for them and, later, looking after their children, and in fact, she completely forgot about herself in the process.

When a lover whom Nora had gently rejected asked her angrily: "Don't you ever want to fall in love?" she looked at him with big, astonished eyes and replied thoughtfully, "Oh yes, of course, but I've never had the time."

But the moment was fast approaching!

Nora's friend was weak and often ill after the birth of her second child. The doctor sent her to Badenweiler in the spring, and Nora went with her to look after her. There they lived in the same house as an elderly scholar, a most kindly man with the finest mind. He chivalrously looked after the two young women and, from the first, Nora was the object of his devoted admiration. Her lively and well-informed mind, and not least, her sweet nature, delighted him; he forgot his age and delicate health—he was filled with a deep yearning to spend the rest of his life in the radiance of Nora's wonderfully dark starry eyes—these beautiful eyes which looked up at him so adoringly and joyfully! Yes, it was a blissful spring of love, their hearts found one another.

The betrothal was to be kept secret for a while until the groom's health had improved; he wanted to be in full possession of his strength before he went to ask his mother-in-law for the hand of his treasure. He returned to the university town to request extended leave and to prepare everything for a winter in Italy. He died of a heart attack in the night after he arrived.

Poor, unhappy Nora, how could you possibly bear it? Especially as the news of the death reached you just when the doctor had told you that there was no hope for your sister-in-law, your best friend? Ah, year upon year has passed since then, but you will never be able to speak about that terrible autumn, which followed such a rapturous summer.

Frau Werner had never properly discovered what had actually happened at that time. She found her child so altered after the death of her daughter-in-law that she told her women friends in strictest confidence that she felt at the time that her daughter had been swapped for another. Naturally the sad love story could not be concealed from her, nor that the lover had made "Fräulein Nora Werner, the most adorable of women" his heiress, in a strange presentiment of his own early death. He had been so alone in the world that, even before he made sure of her love, he was gratified to think that this charming woman would at some point have dominion over everything he possessed.

Frau Werner did think that a short period of mourning was in order—but she asked herself, "How could anyone be so devastated over the 'old gentleman'—no, she could not understand it!"

Her solemn, silent daughter with her strangely unhappy eyes thoroughly unnerved her and therefore when her bereaved stepson asked if Nora could be allowed to bring up his two motherless boys, she gave her consent fairly promptly.

Nora was a splendid mother to her two nephews and slowly, slowly the deep sorrow was banished from her young face by the happiness of keeping house and looking after the children. Her red mouth laughed again, her eyes shone and now, ten years after the storm had wrecked her chance of happiness in life, the pain over her loss had receded into the blessed realm of memory, and Nora again surveyed life around her, happy and carefree.

Now my young readers will say: "Well, at thirty she's already old and ugly." Certainly, thirty is a respectable age but nobody needs to look ugly. No, Nora was now lovelier than ever! To be sure, fulfilling household tasks, and thoughts both great and good, keep one looking young better than balls, social gatherings, and speculations about marriage.

Frau Werner had had her daughter home for a visit for some time. Her stepson, the director of an observatory, had joined an expedition to Japan and, during his absence, at Frau Werner's urgent request, the two boys were sent to an excellent boarding school so that Nora could spend some time at home with her mother, unencumbered.

Frau Werner had her own secret agenda in particularly wanting her daughter to be with her. Now, she felt, the time had come to finally marry Nora off.

Surely the latter would experience a certain vacuum without her nephews and her own house to keep, and would this vacuum not be best filled by a suitable engagement? And did not Nora still have two admirers, both still quietly hoping for her hand?

And now imagine poor Frau Werner's quiet despair as Nora seemed not to find any vacuum at all, but instead with a kind of bliss threw herself into "studying," as her mother called it. Nora told her mother she wanted to use the free time to fill up some gaps in her scant knowledge, and now she sat so happy and content with her books and publications that Frau Werner directed a veritable loathing at the whole "scholarly caboodle."

Just when she looked up from her work, she saw Nora fetch yet another hateful book and sit at the writing desk.

"You have another scholarly book," Frau Werner said in an irritated tone. "Please don't take offense at my writing just now," her daughter replied in a friendly manner. "I would just like to take a few notes before I give the book back to Professor Eichstedt."

Her mother's anger subsided: "When did he give you the book?" she asked with curiosity. "Early yesterday; I sometimes meet him on my morning walk."

If the mother could have seen her daughter's face, which was turned away, she would have noticed that she was blushing slightly. Not on account of Professor Eichstedt, oh no! but Nora did not like the fact that the meeting had been mentioned, because she knew that her mother would pin all sorts of hopes to it.

True, Frau Werner's countenance brightened considerably."Ah, now what is he doing here for so long?" she asked with animation, "the universities are not on holiday?"

"No, he was forced to stay here: during the Whitsuntide holiday, Colonel Eichstedt, with his passion for fruit growing, had climbed up a rather high tree to examine a graft, and would have had a very nasty fall if his son had not caught hold of him. He hurt himself in the process, spraining his arm. The colonel won't let him go again until he is quite better."

"That's true, I remember he had his arm in a sling recently. But he seems to me to be quite well again now? Listen Nora, he's staying here on your account!"

"Unlikely," laughed Nora, "or if it were the case, my powers of attraction are now at an end. He's going away the day after tomorrow." "Well, he has not gone yet— heavens! Fancy my not thinking of it till now! That's the suitor the barrister's wife told me about so secretively on her way home."

"Nonsense," said Nora angrily, "typical coffee party gossip. Professor Eichstedt has not the remotest intention of marrying, and is not even in a position to do so. He wants to stop being a professor of philology and start his career again as an unsalaried university lecturer in philosophy."

"Good God, how stupid young people are," said Frau Werner, shaking her head, "he could so easily marry now and be happy."

"But he might find, as other people have, that marrying brings no particular happiness," Nora joked.

That was too much—to hear Nora today making jokes on the topic of marriage, *that* was what Frau Werner could not stand.

"Well yes, as other people have!" she burst out angrily. "Those who don't have a care about whether they bring joy or sorrow to their mother, who reject the best offers in silly pride, showing their poor mother up in front of relatives and friends as though she had brought her daughter up badly!"

"But, for heaven's sake, who is going to want to marry me now, nobody gives it a thought, I'm too old for it!"

"Oh, don't talk like that! Your cousin Eberhard and Captain Langer would both be ready to marry you any day if you gave them a little encouragement."

"It's true my good cousin would take me *faute de mieux* as there is no suitable girl within ten hours of his remote estate, but the captain is a holiday acquaintance. He thinks I'm younger and in particular that I'm richer than I am. Just tell him I'm nearly thirty-one and only have a private disposable fortune of ten thousand Thalers, and his 'unchangeable love and respect' will be cured forever."

"Well, you find something wrong with each one, but I predict that I shall live to see you a dissatisfied, lonely, embittered old maid!" grumbled her mother.

"I also think I'll probably be an old maid," Nora said with a smile before adding seriously, "and is that not a thousand times better than to sell oneself and marry without love? Is solitude so terrible? Can't it be peopled with objects of one's affection and good books? And why does a single person have to be dissatisfied and bitter? Isn't the world full of opportunities to make oneself useful? Isn't the life of the mind so rich, so endlessly rich in ideas and goals that are interesting and worth striving for?"

Beautiful in her enthusiasm, she stood tall and slender in the middle of the room, her charming oval-shaped face, crowned with dark curly hair, was raised a little, her cheeks were slightly flushed and a noble fire shone in her big dark eyes. It was a charming sight! Even Frau Professor Werner could not resist the magic.

"You still look rather good!" she said in surprise, and shook her head.

It was not quite a reply to Nora's heated speech, but the latter made do with it.

"I'm pleased to hear it, dear old mother!" Nora laughed as she kissed her.

"What a lot of nice-smelling flowers you have," Professor Eichstedt complimented his father as they wandered through the latter's well kept garden in the afternoon.

"Oh, yes," the colonel replied agreeably, "and yet man is never content. Recently the gardener at Schloß Balzeneck told me about a new type of Japanese lily which is supposed to have a particularly gorgeous scent, and ever since then I've been longing to get hold of it. He did promise to send me some bulbs, but he seems to have forgotten; it's so annoying!"

"Do you want me to go to Balzeneck to remind him?" his dutiful son asked. "Walking is the best way of carrying out the doctor's orders."

"Yes, I would be most grateful. It's too much for me, but a three to four hours' walk in the morning is easy for you. Would you mind doing it tomorrow morning?"

"I can't very well go tomorrow morning," his son told him rather sheepishly, without going into the reasons. "But I could go at once, it's such a beautiful afternoon."

"All right," the colonel said, smiling. "Dinner can be a bit later this evening, and I shall come to meet you at half past seven at the ferry."

The Balzeneck ferry was a wonderful place, and one of Colonel Eichstedt's favorite spots. He arrived a little before the agreed time and looked contentedly through the arbor overgrown with pumpkin foliage at the pleasing spectacle before him: the river in the foreground, on the other side a deep green valley enclosed by steep rock walls and Schloß Balzeneck on its high plateau in the far distance.

Suddenly a familiar peal of laughter reached him from the other side.

"Right enough, it's Georg—and again in feminine company," the colonel said to himself in astonishment, busily peering over the water. Suddenly his face darkened. "Confound it, it's the Polish von Ramsteins, the stupid boy!" he growled angrily. For the good colonel also had his likes and dislikes and the "Polish" von Ramsteins belonged in the latter category.

In Weißenburg there were two retired Major von Ramsteins: the "Polish" von Ramstein and the "Other" von Ramstein. The first had acquired his attribute because he had served in a Polish garrison town for many years and had married the daughter of a Polish nobleman. As a consequence of this marriage he lived in disorderly circumstances, which the colonel, who had served for a time in the same regiment, had had ample opportunity to observe. The Other von Ramstein had moved to Weißenburg a little later than his brother and was therefore given the epithet "Other." Things were completely *different* for these von Ramsteins, and the home of the Other von Ramsteins," who were childless and extremely rich through the wife's inheritance, was held up as a model. The Other Frau von Ramstein, otherwise a kindhearted woman, could never think about the Polish establishment of her sister-in-law without a sigh.

As far as intelligence, cunning, and stubborn egoism were concerned, well, here the "Polish" Frau von Ramstein was far superior to the "Other," and therefore she occupied a much more dominant role in Weißenburg, and if ever a person had to choose between the two Frau von Ramsteins, then the choice fell on the Polish one, as her sharp tongue was a dangerous enemy.

In her youth, the Polish Frau von Ramstein had also been a writer, but to the particular annoyance of Colonel Eichstedt, she did not restrict her imagination to stories, essays, and the like, but transferred this to the realm of everyday life, so that one had to be extremely cautious about believing anything she said. The good colonel, with his respect for truth, had often been duped in years gone by, and that is not so easy to forgive.

Besides having two sons who caused them much worry and trouble, the Polish von Ramsteins had an adult daughter who had blossomed in the last few years into the exact replica of her mother. The same height, the same impossibly thin waist, the same high, rounded bosom (so that at the sight of this upper part of the body one could never say whether the upper or lower part was the most unnatural), the same big mouth with open red lips, the same yellow complexion, the same reddish-brown hair, the same staring eyes, and the same art of attracting men in spite of this somewhat ugly exterior.

But the daughter, affected by the *Zeitgeist,* was more of a philosopher than a writer and was considered an enormous free thinker in Weißenburg. Yes, she was a dangerous woman, doubly dangerous for Georg with her highbrow ugliness, and the colonel watched with displeasure as his son conversed over the water with the ladies in the most amiable manner, helped them into the ferryboat, and then swiftly sat down next to Fräulein Julie von Ramstein.

"What the devil do they have to talk about?" growled the colonel crossly.

Yes, yes, my dear Herr Colonel, if a crafty woman *wants* to captivate a man, then she does. Heaven knows who shows her the weak flank of a man's heart, but she recognizes it on the spot: Fräulein Julie von Ramstein spoke to Professor Eichstedt about his latest philosophical book.

But the mother was no less skilled in the art, for as the colonel stepped out of the pumpkin arbor with profound reluctance, Frau von Ramstein knew just how to please and flatter by remarking that one would always meet the colonel like the true painter he was, at the most poetic spots, and what an admirable talent he had in discovering a picturesque corner, even in places with no charm. She would never forget how, as quite a young woman, she had come to D. and been almost depressed by the cheerless surroundings. Then one evening she went for a walk with her husband and had seen him, Colonel Eichstedt, walking ahead at some distance. "Please let's follow him, he might take us to a reasonable spot," she had said to her husband. "And do you still remember, dearest colonel, how we suddenly emerged from behind the old shed by the mill [Rautenmühle] and were delighted by the unexpectedly lovely view? Ah, we were happy then!" "Yes, it was a very merry evening!" laughed the colonel heartily, immersed in cheerful memories.

"And how Löwenfeld then suddenly appeared?"

"And insisted on making a punch!"

"And the only ingredients he had at first were water and sugar!"

And "do you remember this" and "do you recall that" went back and forth, and Colonel Eichstedt was soon in the liveliest and jolliest discussion with the Polish Frau von Ramstein, and in the colonel's heart the amazing idea arose that actually the Polish woman was a charming lady.

Yes, indeed: flies are caught with sugar; the whole world is caught with adroit compliments, but old people with happy memories of their youth in particular!

In the meantime it had grown dark, and when the two pairs reached the deep shadows of the promenade, still in lively discussion, it was just dark enough for Fräulein Julie to empty her heart to Professor Eichstedt: how lonely and misunderstood she felt in the vulgar town of Weißenburg, how her mind longed for truth and especially for strong masculine guidance which could provide her philosophy with a goal and direction: how the professor's latest book had seemed like a revelation to her in her need, and how today's discussion had been of inestimable value. It was touching to listen to—especially for someone who believed it, and had no idea that Fräulein Julie had often rehearsed this nice speech and not without success, and that she already believed she had actually found the strong masculine guidance of a grammar school teacher with whom she carried on a correspondence, vacillating between love and philosophy.

But Professor Eichstedt, in his serious and genuine quest for knowledge, suspected nothing of all this and really believed in Julie's earnest striving, and where is the man who would not be dazzled by such words, who would not willingly stand by a soul in quest, a striving mind? He was about to ardently offer himself as Julie's teacher and friend—but the heavens showed no favor to the Polish von Ramsteins.

Up till then the moon had stood behind thin clouds, but now it suddenly shone clearly and—leaving the promenade in darkness—brightly illuminated Frau Professor Werner's house, the tidy front garden, the pure and lovely countenance of Fräulein Nora, who was standing at the garden gate saying to a tall masculine figure: "I am so grateful to you for accompanying me such a long way." And then the said tall figure answered forcefully, with a strangely agitated voice,

"*You* should not be thanking me; no, *I* must thank you for allowing me to accompany you, as I have not had such an idyllically heart-cheering walk for many, many years."

At that point, the moon again disappeared behind a thick cloud, and left everything in darkness and twilight.

All of a sudden, all Professor Eichstedt's ideas had vanished, and when Fräulein Julie, who had turned her back on the moonlit scene and, ending her account of the needs of her mind and soul, looked up to see if it had had the desired effect, she found an extremely distracted listener who finally, it is true, manfully said a few polite words, but these sounded so remote and cool, however, that something inside Julie cried out: "boring clod!"

It was strange that as soon as the colonel had left the beguiling presence of the Polish Frau von Ramstein, his usual antipathy gradually returned, and when he noticed how peculiarly absent-minded his dear son Georg seemed, it returned fully and completely.

And it was truly astonishing what the good lad got up to that evening, distracted as he was. He did not hear when asked something, and if he was eventually made aware of this, another long period of time elapsed before he collected his thoughts, and then the answer was still invariably as though he found himself on a distant planet.

The colonel became impatient and growled something about the "damned Polish von Ramsteins" to himself. Finally, however, his anger erupted. Tante Linchen had already asked for water three times in her soft voice, and Georg had first given her the ham, then the salt, and finally the teapot. Then the colonel yelled out,

"Water! Tante Linchen wants water!" At which Georg really did take the water jug, which was just near him, and hurried to pour some water for his good aunt, but unfortunately into her woven key basket and not into her glass.

There was a splash! Water flowed onto the table and Linchen's dress, everyone had to stand up. The colonel swore—even though Linchen tried to pacify him by saying that the basket needed a wash in any case.

They parted in a fairly unpleasant mood. What was Georg thinking of? He himself hardly knew, but lots of things—lots of things! But in between, he kept hearing the hasty, vibrating words:

"*You* should not be thanking me; no, *I* must thank you for allowing me to accompany you, as I have not had such an idyllically heart-cheering walk for many, many years."

Yes, it is always unpleasant and difficult to understand when "nice good chums" converse and go for walks with other people, when one believes oneself to have exclusive rights over their pleasant and idyllic companionship. One can always allow oneself some leeway, but it is always a nasty surprise when this happens with the other party.

So Georg lay restless in bed, and every time the vibrating words returned in his memory, he wondered irritably: "Who was that masculine figure?" Well, we know!

The bright spring sunshine had also enticed President [of the superior provincial court] von Wangenheim abroad on this lovely afternoon, and as he wandered round the town gate, he suddenly came upon a horribly stony passage. He very much wanted to be alone and was not bothered by the frequent polite greetings which, as the town's most respected inhabitant, he constantly received. Stiffly genteel, he strode down the stony highway, so deeply sunk in thought that he paid no attention to the uncomfortable path.

Life had not been easy for him in his youth, and he had not made it easy for himself, but now, advanced in years, he possessed everything the heart can desire: high office and a splendid fortune, yet in spite of this it did not occur to him to enjoy these privileges in comfort. A life of leisure cannot simply be learned late in life: the ascetically inclined president lived as rigidly as in his youth and it never occurred to the excellent man that he could have a much nicer life.

Or had it occurred to him today, perhaps?

Earlier during his walk round the town, he had seen a mean little house with a narrow strip of garden, in which a man and two children were busy planting vegetables. It seemed to be very amusing work because happy laughter, bass and soprano, accompanied the endeavor. The man looked up for a moment, and at once rose to greet the president respectfully. He was a messenger for the superior provincial court, and up to a few months ago he had been a truly morose fellow—a typical grumbling bachelor. At that time, he had worriedly confided to the president that his brother-in-law had died, and he would now have to take in his sister and her two children. And how the man had altered since then! He had lost at least a dozen wrinkles and looked so happy that the young articled clerks declared he must have been courting. And yet the whole transformation came about because he had a woman to care for him, and his empty old house was now filled with the sound of children playing and laughing.

The president sighed.

In general, President von Wangenheim was somewhat indifferent and skeptical toward women; he had felt a warm and deep inclination to only three women in the whole of his life: his mother, his sister, and his wife. The only one of these three still alive was his sister, who was very unhappily married to a spendthrift officer who gambled and drank. As a keen lawyer, the president felt strongly that everyone ought to respect the public and private well-being of others and nobody had the right to interfere in these matters, but that did not stop him from harboring desires deep within him which were highly prejudicial to the public, private, and indeed eternal, well-being of his brother-in-law. "Let him go to the devil," he muttered gruffly to himself. Then it would be so nice if his sister and her three children came to live with him: how differently he would raise the children than at present, when their father's bad example wiped out their mother's best attempts to bring them up! He himself had had such a difficult youth that he would have liked to make life easier for other children, especially the children of his sister, who had been such a dear and true companion to him in his youth. Even as a little girl, she had always tried to pacify her irascible father, who, impecunious as ever, sometimes nearly went crazy over his shy, scholarly son's request for books. In her harmlessly well-intentioned way, she had greatly comforted her brother at that time. Oh, if only she had never married, and a care-worn president thought back to the most eventful year of his life.

It must have been about fifteen years ago (the president was now fifty) when his father died on New Year's Day. Four weeks later, his mother inherited a large fortune of several hundred thousand Thalers, a country house, and art treasures from an odd and very old uncle. Unfortunately, the president's wife fell ill with a lung disease at the same time. He rushed to Italy with her and stayed there until the summer, but she grew more ill, and at last, all he could do was bring the corpse of his loved one home. Meanwhile, his sister had married a former playmate of her youth, the latter having swiftly presented himself as suitor after the grand inheritance. The president reproached himself mercilessly for not having made sufficient inquiries about the groom's life, since the first thing the president had to do after the marriage was to pay off a 30,000 Thaler debt. Oh, what trouble this brother-in-law had caused the upright president!

The president sighed again, turned off the rough street, and took a side path that led to the forest. Suddenly he felt the desire to visit an old couple, former retainers, who had a little farm on the other side of the forest and who were still attached to "her dear late ladyship," that was his mother, "his young lordship," that was himself, and the "merry young ladyship," that was his sister.

The farm was situated very close to the forest, and when the president stepped out from the trees, he immediately heard old Christine call out: "Josef, Josef, the young lordship is here!"

And then she herself appeared, after she had quickly put on a clean pinafore, and was overjoyed at the honor of the visit, inquired after his health and how he was in general with real concern, and had lots of things to tell him herself; how she had recently visited Eckenstedt (the name of the old seat of the Wangenheims) and how the burial place of the dear late ladyship was a veritable rose garden, and how there were still as many nightingales in the park, that nowhere in the world could boast oak trees comparable to the ones at Eckenstedt, and that the little table which the young lordship himself had carpentered still stood under the tallest oak, and one could still read the initials which he had carved into it, F.v.W.& L. v. W. "And the tenant farmers still call the servants through the same megaphone," she ended, "which reminded me of the dear young ladyship, who was always so full of fun; if the young lordship had hidden himself in the grounds with his books, she would quickly fetch the old megaphone and shout into the trees with a deep voice: 'Friedrich, what are you up to? Friedrich, where are you hiding?'"

The president felt rejuvenated and quite at home.

And now Josef joined them and his first concern was to show the Herr Präsident what he had just made: a table and bench under a magnificent beech tree adjacent to the forest, and the honored guest had to try it out at once, and he really did find it very nice and comfortable. "Now get on with your work, dear people, I would like to sit here alone for a while," the president said at last.

"The Herr Präsident will do us the honor of taking some refreshment, I have such nice buttermilk and such tender ham," said Christine.

"And we already have radishes, too," Josef added.

"Well," said the president, "it's impossible to refuse such a good offer."

Christine and Josef beamed, and were about to disappear to prepare the repast, when a few chords of an old piano resounded from the house.

"Do you have a piano, and who is playing?" the president asked in astonishment.

"We have a paying guest for the summer," Christine whispered mysteriously, "the top room where the old teacher used to live was empty; after his death, we bought his few pieces of furniture, and the piano was among them. His heirs didn't think the things were worth the transport. Not long ago, an old spinster came and asked me if we would rent the room to her; she has had some tragic experiences and wants to be alone. We like her, she's such a good lady."

"I see," said the president, and the retainers disappeared. The president fell to reverie. What Christine had told him had transported him back to his youth; how lovely it had been in spite of all the battles, how innocently cheerful, although they were poor and had to do without things!

Was he any happier now that he was rich? His heart contracted.

It was such a lovely afternoon, the warm, golden sunshine lay pure and clear over the spring-green valley, not a breath of air, not a leaf twitched in the dark foliage of the treetops, everything around him so still and remote from the world; only the bees and the grasshoppers softly, softly sang their monotonous song. In the distance he could hear the sound of children shouting, jolly laborers laughing, dogs barking, and cattle lowing. There was life out there, joyful life—here, nothing but silent solitude. Oh how alone, how lonely the poor man felt.

"How silly I am today," said the president, pulling himself together and trying to concentrate on an interesting judicial case in the last session.

Learning, ambition, high office, dusty books, and dusty files can weave such a thick shield around a person's heart that its possessor feels it can no longer be moved, and is even proud to go through life so well-protected and well-established.

But if a person trusts his heart, it can be disobedient, and will sometimes cast the shield aside and refuse further constriction.

Today, the heart of the president was behaving in just such an unusual manner; he wanted to ignore it and desperately tried to think of the case of *Köhler v. Grün*, but today his heart was on vacation—with fate on its side. The sounds of a few chords on an old spinet emerged from the open farmhouse window, and then a soft soprano voice began to sing a little song:

> Trusty home of dearest loved ones,
> Memories of you I find,
> Silent thoughts both glad and sad,
> Tears of longing fill my mind.

It was an old-fashioned, old-fashioned little song, a . . .

Part Two

A spring morning had arrived of such bewitching beauty that poetic young things, who live in expectation of something new and wonderful, ecstatically viewed the gorgeous flowers, the roses in bloom, and the deep blue sky and happily told themselves: "Happiness is on its way, today's the day."

Even Privy Councilor Fitzner's wife, who was usually rather moody, could not deny that today was a pleasant day. She wandered round her long stretch of garden, and by early morning she was equipped with her spectacles, lorgnette, and opera glasses. Well, well, what was she up to?

As in many large towns, the western part of Weißenburg was the most genteel, and had been for a generation. Anyone in search of a nice apartment looked in the region of the Kreuzgasse, since that was where the best and most imposing houses stood. Beside and behind these were found the most magnificent old gardens, surrounded by old-fashioned ivy-clad stone walls, which usually gave the charming impression of romantic isolation. In the olden days, people liked to enjoy their gardens in privacy, though from their own domain they also liked to steal a glimpse at unsuspecting passersby, and this was particularly tempting in the case of this row of gardens, with their furthest walls backing onto the so-called Lindengang [Linden Walk], Weißenburg's main promenade. These good people knew what to do: all these gardens had a sort of mound by the far wall, with comfortable seats; hidden from view, they had a wonderful opportunity to see and hear the passersby through the overgrown railings that crowned the wall. Imaginative souls had christened these mounds with many a nice name, for example, "*colline de la rêverie*" [dream hill], "rose promontory," "the lookout," "solitude" and so on, but the good burghers of Weißenburg called these mounds by the plain and simple name "spyhole." Anyone who had once lived in the Kreuzgasse and was initiated into the secrets of the gardens there avoided taking a walk in the Lindengang all his life if the weather was anything like decent—he felt safe from observation only in 10 degrees of frost.

Like other curious people, Privy Councilor Fitzner's wife had her spy hole and now, well armed and keen, betook herself thither on this spring morning. She drew up a garden chair, leaned her arms on the wall, and pushed the leaves a little to one side; now part of the Lindengang was comfortably open to view, and the spectacle could begin.

The Lindengang was a twin-track boulevard lined with particularly beautiful shady trees, but at this early hour it was quite empty and deserted. Frau Fitzner became restless. "It's well past seven; why has nobody turned up?" she thought, and was about to rise, when footsteps were heard: the hero in the drama appeared, a very handsome hero in the form of Professor Eichstedt, tall and slim with curly blond hair, a blond beard, and big, intelligent eyes. "What a fine figure of a man, what a noble head," thought Frau Fitzner in admiration; she nearly swooned: the hero was irresistible, nobody would turn down the offer of his hand!

The hero, having looked all round searchingly, disappeared along one of the hidden paths of the public park, which abuts the Lindengang.

Frau Fitzner treated herself to a little rest, put the opera glasses to one side and surrendered to a sanguine train of thoughts: but heavens! The heroine had floated by! Frau Fitzner could have easily missed her, but luckily the heroine seemed to be weighed down by two heavy books, she put them down on a bench opposite and paced up and down, providing Frau Fitzner with ample opportunity to observe Fräulein Nora Werner. Yes, she was pretty, very pretty, the eavesdropper could not deny it, and looked very distinguished, too, even though she was wearing only a plain pale blue cotton morning dress. If this woman was a rival to her Mariechen, Frau Fitzner reflected, her Mariechen would lose out. She felt most uncomfortable and looked round worriedly for the conquering hero. And there he was, hurrying up to the young lady in delight. How joyfully he greeted her, but Nora, calm and collected, just said in a friendly manner that she was pleased to have this final chance of returning the books to him in person and of commenting on what she had read.

As the books still lay on the bench, and even Professor Eichstedt seemed to find them rather heavy, both now walked up and down in front of the bench. Frau Fitzner strained her ears, overjoyed at the opportunity, but it was most odd: however much she strained, and she could clearly make out every word, she understood not a thing of what the two were talking about.

Lord above, what foolish stuff: "origin of language," "wau-wau theory," "pah-pah theory," "phonetic sounds," Frau Fitzner had never heard the like; she shook her head. Was this serious or a joke?

Meanwhile, the pair seemed to have grown tired of walking up and down—Professor Eichstedt seemed to make a suggestion, Nora hesitated, finally she seemed to agree. Both approached the bench, and Frau Fitzner heard Professor Eichstedt say: "We'll give the books to the park attendant to look after," whereupon they both disappeared along the nearest path.

The eavesdropper relinquished her strenuous position and sighed. If she thought about it, she had not actually found out anything, except that the pair certainly did not talk about love. She returned to the house, disappointed.

The sun climbed higher and higher, and smiled affectionately on the blossom-covered earth. There was not a single dark or desolate spot that did not boast its cover of flowers or beautiful greenery. Today, even the gloomy Weißenburg cemetery looked beautiful, although it usually made an almost uncanny impression with its ancient, south-facing boundary walls and the thick cover of tall trees. For this reason, the residents of Weißenburg marveled that it should have ever occurred to an eccentric old man to build himself a house and plant a large garden right next to the cemetery. The house stood bang in the middle of the garden, so that the front of the house looked straight at the graveyard, and as the people of Weißenburg were cheerful folk, and did not wish to have their good mood spoiled by a *memento mori,* the eccentric's house stood empty for several years after his death.

Then the venerated Oberpfarrer [pastor] died, and his widow, who had laid to rest everything she loved out in the graveyard, decided to buy the eccentric's house, even though her loyal old servant Hanne harbored serious misgivings in her breast.

"I want to be close to my loved ones, and be able to glance at their graves if I feel too lonely," the longsuffering woman had said, and Hanne had no argument against that because she, too, had held none more dear in her life than the pastor and the three young gentlemen, who all rested out there.

The old pastor's widow had now lived with her servant in the eccentric's house for many a year, and as both were kind and friendly, the house, too, had acquired a friendly feel, and friends of the old lady, formerly of the opinion that they would never be able to take coffee or tea in the house in full view of the cemetery, had long ago accustomed themselves to it and did not find it the least bit eerie. But the same topic came up every time the pastor's widow held a coffee party: why had the old eccentric only put a single window at the gable end, which had the prettiest view toward the forest, and it was the window of the storeroom to boot, a room in which one is not usually inclined to enjoy the beauty of the landscape.

But today, it was so lovely outside that at eleven o'clock, when the pastor's widow and Hanne were taking stock of their preserves and wondering what they should consume or give away, as there would soon be new fruit, neither could resist casting a few admiring glances at the old horse chestnut trees with their red and white umbels of blossom, and beyond them, along the path that led into the forest.

"Frau Oberpfarrer, Frau Oberpfarrer," Hanne cried out, quite excited: "Look! A pair of lovers!" quickly closing the curtains so that they could both watch the lovers unobserved.

"How pleased the dear colonel will be," exclaimed the worthy dame in delight, "only recently he was complaining of how distressing he found it that his eldest son had absolutely no intention of finding a wife."

"Yes, and he could not find a better or prettier Fräulein than Fräulein Nora," Hanne rejoined triumphantly, Nora having for ever won Hanne's heart not long since with an excellent dressing for a bad finger.

"Just look at the professor, happiness personified, carefully helping her over the ditch—now he doesn't want to let go of her hand—he wants to lead the way, but she refuses—I expect they don't want to announce the engagement yet," Hanne continued. "Now Fräulein Nora wants to go the quickest way home along the green alley— they're saying goodbye—he's staring at her, can't tear himself away, ah, now he has to go—but he wants to have her posy—oh, Lord, now he's kissing the posy—just like Herr Emil kissing Fräulein Helene's blue ribbon," she finished softly and brushed her sleeve over her damp eyes.

But Hanne's were not the only eyes full of tears; the sight of the happy pair had awakened deeply painful memories in the kind old lady.

"Hanne, we'll check the preserves tomorrow," she said with a trembling voice, and went quietly into the front room, glancing over to the four white crosses where her loved ones lay in peace, and tear after tear rolled down the kind old furrowed face. Ah, over there was where she had once had to lay to rest in the cold earth her youngest son Emil, still in the midst of his youthful joy and beauty. His wedding day had already been fixed when a violent nervous fever suddenly carried off the flourishing youth. And her thoughts flew to another green mound in a country graveyard where, under roses and weeping willows, Helene, the fair daughter of the pastor, had lain sleeping many a year. She, the pride and joy of the village, had lain down her tired head to eternal rest, so young and yet so willingly. The happiness of youth, the roses in bloom, how quickly they pass!"

"Hanne," the old pastor's widow called that afternoon, standing on the stairs in her finery, ready to proceed to a big coffee party given by the Other Frau von Ramstein. Hanne appeared. "Yes, Frau Pastor?" "Hanne, you won't forget that we are not going to mention what we saw this morning," the good pastor's widow said earnestly. She had taken her late husband's sermons about the sins of the tongue to heart. Hanne considered for a moment, disappointed at having to keep such a juicy piece of news to herself, but knowing full well that her mistress, who was otherwise so kindly, had no tolerance in this connection. So she answered resolutely: "Certainly, I won't say a word to a soul."

"Well, don't forget," the pastor's wife warned her urgently one last time.

The Other Frau von Ramstein was holding a big coffee party; at least twenty ladies had gathered to honor the brown liquid, and as it was a long time since the last coffee party, today's was particularly lively. In the intervening period, the ladies' own joys and sorrows or those of their nearest and dearest had accumulated, and all these events awaited general discussion and judgment.

Those assembled formed two circles: one consisting of the worthy, elderly married ladies who set the tone, the other of old maids and younger women, but the same liveliness reigned at both tables. Where the circles touched, the hostess presided with great satisfaction: the party had got off to such a good start, she happily listened to all the compliments on her beautiful apartment, splendid coffee, delicious baking, etc.

Her neighbor Frau Euler, the doctor's wife, asked, "My dear, where did you get this excellent cream?"

The Other Frau von Ramstein named her source, adding with a sigh, "It's always this good, and I like a lot of cream in my coffee, but oh God, I'm getting so fat I don't dare to take it any more." The doctor's wife eyed her up and down: "My dear, it's true, you really have noticeably put on weight recently. Ask my husband to put you on a proper diet."

"Oh, Lord," complained the Other Frau von Ramstein, "it would be so awful for me to have to cut out everything nice. My husband does so like a good table, and it wouldn't be very pleasant for him to make him eat all the best dishes by himself, he wouldn't enjoy it."

"Well, at least take a little more exercise," advised the doctor's wife, who was judged to be something of a medical expert on account of her husband.

"I had already considered it," answered the Other Frau von Ramstein; "the weather is so glorious." "But you must get up early and go for an early morning walk," continued the doctor's wife, "that's the most effective thing. By the way," she continued with a smile, raising her voice, "as my husband says, it's quite fun walking in the Lindengang and seeing the new lovers."

"The new lovers?" the Other Frau von Ramstein asked curiously.

The general conversation came to a halt. Frau Fitzner had just given her neighbor an excellent recipe for preparing potato dumplings so that they came to the table all of a quiver. The president's widow, who enjoyed an elevated position from her wealth and former position, had just praised the new orthodox preacher; the little lawyer's wife was telling a few anecdotes about her new housemaid, a country innocent; the Polish Frau von Ramstein and the wife of war councilor Willmann, both aesthetes and the two sharpest-tongued ladies in the company, were conversing quietly over a French novel which did not distinguish itself for its morality, but all these conversations were suddenly interrupted by the magic words "new lovers": "Lovers! Who, then?" they shouted as though in unison.

"Professor Eichstedt and Nora Werner," said the doctor's wife, pleased at being the center of attention. In the ensuing mêlée could be heard "What! Who would have thought! Neither wanted to get married! I've known that for ages, it's an old story! I wonder if it's true?"

The pastor's widow said nothing and smiled quietly to herself.

Frau Fitzner also remained silent, listening attentively to what the others were saying.

The fat little lawyer's wife also remained silent, but threw her head back mockingly as though to say: "How can anybody be so stupid as to believe that?" "Is the engagement official yet?" asked the Polish Frau von Ramstein with an apparently nonchalant air, although the news had been like a dagger's thrust to her. Surprisingly she, who usually knew everything, had heard nothing about it.

"No, I know nothing about an engagement," said the older Fräulein von Lingen, "but they meet for a walk in the Lindengang every day and hold the most heated conversations." She added, with a sentimental expression on her face, "It's so romantic!"

"Romantic!" cried the late president's widow with deeply condescending disapproval. "Romantic? I find it quite simply unseemly!" "No, one can't call it unseemly," the other Fräulein von Lingen said in defense. "Just a bit strange, as they discuss things about which no good Christian understands a syllable."

"What do they talk about? What do they discuss? Is it in Latin?" everyone shouted at once.

"No, no," laughed Ernestinchen von Lingen, "they speak German, but such a terribly scholarly German: can there be anyone among us who understands when they speak of 'critique of pure reason,' 'substance,' 'empiricism,' 'causality,' 'categories,' and such like?"

War councilor Willmann's wife laughed mockingly. "Oh, yes," she said laconically.

"But as I said earlier, I find it completely unseemly when a young man and a young girl go for walks without being engaged. And when they talk about things other people do not understand, that is even worse," said the former president's widow unctuously.

"Good heavens, one can't call Nora Werner young," Frau Fitzner interjected morosely.

"But she's still one of the prettiest girls in the whole town," said the lawyer's wife, proud of her young friend.

"What is there that age can ruin in such a face?" stated the war councilor's wife. Having no daughters, she could judge beauty objectively. "She has a perfect oval face, a small mouth, big, expressive eyes, anyway, brunettes last longer than blondes, whose beauty wanes with the first flush of youth. And furthermore, Nora Werner possesses something which has always been a great rarity here—namely, a brain," war councilor Willmann's wife concluded, and looked at the president's widow—not accidentally.

A slight antagonism had reigned between the two women since days of old, when the late president had noticeably paid court to the war councilor's wife—at that time still single—only to marry his present wife for her wealth. The president's wife had certainly brought a good deal of money but a very small dose of intelligence into the marriage, and the late president, a clever but ruthless and unkind man, had not been able to resist making jokes on the matter. People said that he privately joked to a friend, who had congratulated him when both his daughters became engaged at the same time: "Dear friend, don't get too excited with your congratulations. The girls are like my wife, rich and stupid, which produces only a certain measure of happiness in marriage and an awful lot of boredom."

The late president's widow felt dimly that the last remark made by the war councilor's wife was directed at her. She broke in irritably: "And this cleverness, so rare a commodity here, relieves the bearer of the duty to behave and converse in a seemly manner?"

"My God, I don't know what *you* understand by seemly conversation," replied the war councilor's wife with malicious stress. "If a woman discusses intellectual things with a man instead of clothes, amusement, and her own charms: I call that seemly and attractive. And most men think so too, even if they only do so once they have married, and are bored by an incompatible marriage partner."

The late president's widow blushed scarlet, and a bitter feud was about to break out, but the fat little lawyer's wife, who liked peace and quiet for all her liveliness, held the warriors at bay with the words "I don't know why the ladies are getting so excited about Nora Werner's innocent walks, if only you knew *how* innocent, with no further consequences. The doctor prescribed Nora's walks and she is just obeying orders."

"Of course," said the doctor's wife, "that's just what I wanted to say, but nobody let me get a word in edgewise. Fräulein Werner was so exhausted by looking after her two young nephews with scarlet fever this winter that my husband had to prescribe a tonic water and morning walks."

"But not with Professor Eichstedt," Ernestinchen von Lingen interjected mischievously.

"No," the lawyer's wife laughed, "the doctor does not do things like that, and if he knew the true nature of the matter, he would certainly recommend someone else as her companion."

"Someone else?" several voices cried in astonishment. "Does Nora Werner have another admirer here?" The lawyer's wife smiled secretively. "Come on, come on, out with the news," pleaded the Other Frau von Ramstein.

The cheerful little woman smiled even more craftily but shook her head.

"Hey, the lawyer's wife is just teasing us," said the Polish von Ramstein provocatively, longing to know who the "other" admirer was.

"No, no, no," said the lawyer's wife, who felt her decision to say nothing was now somewhat under threat.

"Or the 'other' is someone of no interest to us all," the Polish von Ramstein continued.

"Of no interest to us all!" shouted the lawyer's wife, hurt. "Well, ladies, is President von Wangenheim of no interest to us all, or not?" She surveyed the circle in triumph. "President von Wangenheim!" everyone shouted at once, followed by a pause of breathless astonishment.

Had there been any man in the good town of Weißenburg who had set more hearts a-flutter in the last three years than President von Wangenheim? Was he not the object of the strongest desire for every mother with an unmarried daughter? Was he not the object of hopeful longing for every genteel widowed or still-unmarried female between seventeen and forty-five? Naturally we won't go into whether this longing was really directed at his stiff personality. But what woman's heart in these unromantic times, when love in a hovel is out of fashion, would not be susceptible to a house fitted with every luxury and with the most wonderful artistic treasures, with magical greenhouses and gardens with rarest blooms, an elegant coach and horses of enviable beauty? Ah, what woman's heart would not swell with ambition and desire at the thought of being the town's unchallenged principal lady of tone, held in reverence by all?

And Nora Werner, who lived apart from social life, had quietly taken possession of this object of general hope and desire? It was unbelievable, it was extremely annoying! A veritable uproar arose among the ladies, even the late president's widow, who had up till then stared ahead in vengeful silence, forgot her grudge and shouted emphatically:

"My dear lady, Fräulein Werner is such a favorite of yours that you're blind, where in the world are these two supposed to have met, they don't know each other!"

"The lawyer's wife must have introduced them," the Polish von Ramstein said, smiling sweetly. She had taken real pleasure in the news. "The lawyer's wife was the president's best friend when they were both young."

"No, I had nothing to do with it," the little woman defended herself. "No, they met quite by chance, but I'll happily tell you about it."

"Tell us, tell us," everyone demanded.

"Three weeks ago," the lawyer's wife began, "the wife of Regional High Court Justice von Hausen expected a visit from her uncle, Privy Councilor von Wülfing. Wülfing, Wangenheim, and I were all boarders at my uncle Professor Friedrich's as children. Nobody made a fuss over mixed boarders then, especially as I was six months older than the two boys. We were the best of friends and playmates for years. A while ago, Frau von Hausen said that if her uncle came to see her, Anton and I, together with President von Wangenheim, must have lunch with her. It so happened that on the day of Wülfing's arrival, it was his birthday. The von Hausens decided to celebrate in style, as the poor man has a miserable home life. His wife is prone to depression and had to go to a clinic again this spring. Wülfing was expected at eleven, and we were invited to a formal luncheon at two o'clock. But poor Frau von Hausen had woken up with such a terrible migraine that she couldn't do anything. Von Hausen was so worried, poor soul, that he was completely distraught. He always did hate giving parties and couldn't contemplate doing it without his wife. At ten o'clock, along comes Nora Werner, who is a good friend of Frau von Hausen's from earlier times, to collect Frau von Hausen's children for the day, as agreed. Suddenly poor Frau von Hausen had the brilliant idea of asking Nora to take her role as hostess and sending the children to the servants, who would be pleased to look after them. Von Hausen was delighted to be relieved of the sole burden of entertaining, and I must say," the lawyer's wife continued, raising her voice, "you could not wish for a more charming, kinder deputy for a sick hostess and anxious host than Nora Werner was that day. She was so attentive, so full of fun and tactful, that we had a splendid time. Frau von Hausen said she was going to take to her bed every time she had visitors, as her husband had burst in on her three times, shrieking in delight: 'It's going fine! Nora Werner is an angel, an angel,' and disappearing again. And von Hausen was not the *only* one who thought Nora was an angel, all four [actually, three!] men were firmly convinced of it. Wangenheim took us home, and the only thing that interested him was what Anton and I thought of Nora."

The Other Frau von Ramstein's serving girls had long since appeared at the door with a second serving of desert, but Frau von Ramstein waved them away. The sight of the marvelously successful charlotte russe would have been wasted on the ladies while they were still breathless with excitement at what the lawyer's wife related. But now that the well-fed little lady had come to an end, quite heated by her account, in came the delicious food, a highly beneficial *Intermezzo,* and conflicting emotions had a chance to settle down. But oddly enough, once the dish had been passed around and everyone had taken a taste, nobody wanted to return to the topic previously discussed so heatedly; perhaps there were several ladies who feared to reveal too lively an interest in it. True, Ernestinchen von Lingen made a diffident attempt, saying to the lawyer's wife: "So there's nothing between Professor Eichstedt and Fräulein Werner, or rather, it's a scholarly friendship?"

The lawyer's wife replied with gusto: "Definitely nothing but a scholarly friendship!" but even she broke off abruptly and spoke about something else, her conscience quietly warning her that she had already said too much.

The good pastor's widow felt most discomfited: She had seen a lot of things in this world, but it had never yet occurred to her that two people with a scholarly friendship could look at each other with such happy blushes.

The doctor's wife had been very absent-minded since Nora Werner's second suitor had emerged. We wish to explain this phenomenon by simply observing that the worthy woman had two marriageable daughters and that the president, her husband's patient, often came to their home. She also left the coffee party remarkably early, followed by Frau Fitzner. The Polish Frau von Ramstein looked quizzically at the two ladies taking their early leave and then rose shortly afterward herself and, turning to her sister-in-law, said, "Excuse me, Caroline dear, I must leave your charming and interesting coffee party, too, I have just remembered I have an appointment with the dressmaker to try something on."

With graceful farewells, she disappeared from the circle of chattering ladies and swiftly rushed home on foot, making straight for her husband's study.

"Philipp," she burst out somewhat breathlessly, "isn't today the day you regularly play whist in the Harmony with President von Wangenheim, the doctor, and Fitzner?"

The Polish von Ramstein nodded and looked at his wife inquiringly.

"Well, just listen to this carefully," she continued. "This evening, the doctor and good Herr Fitzner, if he can, will try to turn Wangenheim against Nora Werner, they will conjure up a relationship between her and Professor Eichstedt with unseemly walks, intimate conversations, and so on. Naturally, I don't really care a fig about what people say about Nora Werner, but I have reason to believe that it would be advisable for Nora Werner to be married as soon as possible, and *not* to Professor Eichstedt. I noticed yesterday that our Julie had made an impression on Georg Eichstedt, and it would have been a decisive impression if he had not looked otherwise preoccupied. Georg Eichstedt is the right man for our Julie. If Nora Werner can be betrothed and married off by the university holidays, he would naturally look round for another female friend who understands his work. The coast is then clear for our Julie. Do you see? So be Nora Werner's champion today, you clever man," she finished with an encouraging smile.

The Polish von Ramstein was no fool, and with a sly smile he thoughtfully twiddled the ends of his gray moustache: "All right, I know what to do. I'd like to get one over that smart doctor," he said finally.

An hour later the four whist players sat in the Harmony's brightly lit rooms earnestly engaged in their game. President von Wangenheim had to deal. Before he took the cards, he closed his eyes for a moment as though he were tired.

"Aren't you feeling well, Herr Präsident?" asked the doctor in concern. "You don't seem to be quite as fresh and lively with the game as you usually are."

Wangenheim almost reddened, as it was indeed remarkably difficult for him to keep his mind on whist today. It kept wanting to wander off in a romantic direction of its own.

"I did not sleep well at all last night," he answered quickly, by way of apology.

"You ought to take more exercise and take advantage of the nice weather for long walks. I must prescribe a tonic for you to force you to go out regularly," the doctor said with the dignity of a family doctor, half in jest and half in earnest.

"I don't like morning walks," the president answered, once more half submerged in thought.

At the mention of the words "morning walk" it was as though the absent-minded Privy Councilor Fitzner had received his cue.

"Well, well, why doesn't the Herr Präsident like morning walks?" he said, childishly gratified that he was able to bring everything up, just as his wife had coached. "Morning walks are the height of fashion. You can have all sorts of experiences and observe all sorts of things, like the new lovers Professor Eichstedt and Nora Werner."

Meanwhile Wangenheim had started to deal the cards, but at those last words, he suddenly started, then forced himself to be calm, even though the hand holding the cards trembled a little, and he directed a piercing look at Fitzner. He asked himself inwardly· "Is this man a malicious rascal?"

But good Herr Fitzner sat there like innocence itself, yes, he positively beamed: had he not done this for his Mariechen? Yes, he was a good father. What would his wife have to say!

The doctor was amazed that the shy privy councilor had suddenly seized the initiative like that, and it was now up to him to provide support.

"Ha, ha, ha," he laughed, almost naturally. "The whole of Weißenburg is getting agitated about this new pair of lovers. I gave Fräulein Werner a prescription for a tonic and she obediently goes for walks, but every day a kind young gentleman joins the lady on her walk, which is not quite what I ordered. Well, but why not, if the young people are in love, but they ought to make the engagement public, otherwise these daily rendezvous are rather unseemly."

"Nonsense, my dear doctor, don't talk like one of Weißenburg's old gossips," the Polish von Ramstein interjected suddenly in a mocking, nasal tone, "anyone would think we were at a ladies' coffee party, where innocent events are interpreted in the most stupid fashion. The simple facts are as follows: Fräulein Werner takes her prescribed morning walks and occasionally meets a close friend of my brother (the close friendship was von Ramstein's invention). Why should the two not hold a conversation? Does a girl have to fall immediately in love with a man if she speaks to him on occasion, especially about truly abstruse, learned things?"

The president was no friend of officers in debt, but at that point he felt the most avid goodwill toward von Ramstein percolating through his soul.

But the doctor was again amazed, set his spectacles straight, and said to himself, "Heavens, what's the Polish von Ramstein up to?"

"Yes, of course," said Fitzner, whose love of truth now made him forget his cunning plan, and all he remembered was his wife's distress at lunch that neither Professor Eichstedt nor Nora Werner had spoken of love in the slightest. "Yes, of course, they discuss things like we men discuss, which have absolutely nothing to do with themselves."

The president's good opinion of Fitzner was restored.

"What a silly ass to have as ally," the doctor continued to himself, but he was a skillful man and said out loud with a cheery laugh: "You see, Herr Präsident, this new betrothal or nonbetrothal is a much-discussed topic, it almost lights the torch of discord. There's nothing for it but for you, as senior representative of the goddess of justice, to judge the case with your own eyes. No, joking aside, you ought to take a day off in the fresh air tomorrow," he finished in the tone of a concerned medical adviser. "You have been working too hard and you really look under a strain."

The president dealt the rest of the cards.

"Well," he said curtly and with assumed indifference, "tomorrow I can do some gardening."

The game of whist continued, but the president had never played so badly and soon rose under the pretext of tiredness, and he went home early harboring the firm intention to take a stroll in the Lindengang next morning. Such are the long-distance effects of a ladies' coffee party.

The splendid pastor's widow went home from the coffee party privately alarmed; she disliked it when people of whom she had a particularly good opinion behaved in such a manner that one did not know what to think about them.

"Hanne," she said, when she took her spectacles off after evening prayers: "You didn't tell anyone about Professor Eichstedt and Fräulein Nora Werner, did you?"

"Certainly not," replied Hanne vehemently, having wavered for a moment when she went to fetch the milk, to emerge triumphant.

"Well, Hanne, we must have made a mistake," the pastor's widow continued, avoiding Hanne's gaze. "They aren't lovers."

Hanne was an excellent servant, but her strong and domineering temperament was not the sweetest on this earth. In her affection for her employer, these qualities were rarely seen, though elsewhere she felt justified in making her views known; her mistress was much too good and much too gullible in her opinion, she would be a puppet in the hands of others if she, Hanne, did not stick up for them both.

"Not lovers?" asked Hanne with her hand on her hip, which with her was always an indication of a belligerent mood. "Not lovers?" she repeated with scarcely disguised contempt, "if you please, Frau Oberpfarrer. . . ."

"Hanne," warned her mistress.

Hanne had been on the point of saying "Don't let yourself be taken in." She suppressed the disrespectful remark, coughed, and began again: "I only wanted to say, I think they really are lovers."

"No," said the good pastor's widow, "they only have a scholarly friendship." "Is that something newfangled?" asked Hanne mockingly.

"At any rate it is something you don't understand!" replied her mistress with dignity. Hanne could no longer contain herself:

"Of course Hanne cannot understand newfangled scholastic stuff, but my eyes see what they see, and if this is not a pair of lovers then the world is bewitched and everything is turned upside down!" Hanne shot out and rummaged round in the kitchen, holding an angry conversation with herself.

"Not lovers! They can take my mistress in, but they're not going to tell Hanne that black is white: let's see who's right—not lovers!" she laughed angrily, and thumped the copper kettle, so that it rang out. That, too, was the long-distance effect of a ladies' coffee party.

But Hanne, clear-sighted Hanne, don't be so hasty; the world is not yet turned upside down, and if a man and woman look at each other as happily as your eyes have witnessed, the pair are most certainly not just scholarly friends and good chums, but—lovers. It has always been thus and nothing has changed. Sometimes, I admit, it looks different, and therefore I sound a warning to everyone, men and women, who want to have nothing to do with love and marriage: Beware! Many things which look like cold, dead stone have an unseen hot fire. Only a slight knock is needed to break the stony exterior: and beaming bright, the flame of love gushes forth. Above all, you enemies of marriage who will definitely, absolutely definitely *never* marry, take care that you don't go for a blissful forest walk in springtime, on a wonderful spring morning, at least not with a charming member of the opposite sex. The magic of the forest in spring has a peculiarly overpowering influence. The most confirmed bachelor, for whom refined cuisine is *de rigueur* and who would not deem life possible without caviar, strong wine, truffles, pâté de foie gras, theater, travel, complete independence, and absolute comfort, the very same will experience an unfamiliar hesitancy of soul when once surrounded by the magical weave of the forest. He reviews his whole life and can't help asking himself: "Is that happiness? This egotistic selfishness, this egocentric whirl?" He sees a bird's nest: The fledglings twitter and stick their heads up out of the nest to demand food, and their parents fly back and forth filling the open beaks, and suddenly his friend does not seem so pitiable, no, he even almost envies him. At midday yesterday they had returned from court together; at his friend's door, two children greeted their father.

"Daddy," said the little boy, without much enthusiasm, "today we're having beef and diced potatoes." "But" added the little girl eagerly, "mummy is making a lovely big pancake and then she'll fill it with a thick, thick layer of plum jam. Isn't that lovely?"

His friend had laughed happily and said, "Well, yes, that's really lovely."

The bachelor found that incomprehensible. "Good heavens, what a lunch," he sighed, and added mockingly: "My poor friend." And afterward, when he looked at the menu for his haute cuisine hotel dinner he had again thought: "Poor friend." Why did he suddenly feel quite different? Yes, it's the magic of the forest in spring—And you strong, high-minded single women who, perhaps because one particular person did not love you, or because you are separated from someone by cruel chance, are you going to go through life alone? Or those of you who have dedicated your lives to art, or science, or altruistic care of the sick, beware of the spring breeze. Oh, all these brave decisions and reflections will vacillate, you will be seized by an insuperable longing to lay your head on a strong, manly breast and no longer struggle for existence so alone, so reliant on yourself. And even if you have high-flying plans, if you want to help the poor and the sick, you sometimes suddenly feel weak and in need of succor, as though you can do nothing without the firm support of a man. Ah, perhaps all these plans, even those you want to put into effect for the good of your fellow men, will suddenly seem like froth, a dream! Perhaps you will suddenly decide that your highest ideal, the height of happiness, is life in a domestic sphere, making just three or four people happy? What is it that suddenly makes strong women so timid and feminine? The magic of the forest in spring!

Now all you enemies of marriage, listen to what happens to the two people I will tell you about. Early in the morning they were nothing but cool, scholarly friends and a few hours later—well, just what keen-eyed Hanne saw, to wit: lovers. Beware, don't copy them, or—take them as your example.

It occurred to Professor Eichstedt, as he was walking with Nora in the Lindengang, how lovely it would be at the witches' well on this beautiful spring morning, and he suggested to Nora that they should walk there. Nora hesitated a little, but this enticing spring sunshine overcame all her small reservations. She so loved to go for walks in the charmingly varied surroundings of Weißenburg, but her mother was bad on her feet, and all Nora's former friends had married and gone to other parts during her long absence. So she had nobody to accompany her and her mother would never have permitted her to go alone. Nora scarcely considered that it was not fitting to go for a walk with a young man. For years she had been no longer accustomed to thinking of herself as a young girl. She had such a dignified position in bringing up her nephews and keeping house for her brother that she had quite forgotten that the social rules laid down in Germany for young girls, as is quite proper, are extended to older women in small places. Nora had the cheerful confidence and lack of inhibition of a married lady; another reason was that she thought her life was finished after the painful experience of her youthful love, and never even dreamed that she would still marry. And now Nora was thirty and all my female readers, even those who are thirty, will agree with my statement that at thirty, one is definitely no longer young, and one has no need, at this age, to look out every day and hour for the danger of setting a man's heart alight.

And yet, and yet, I warn you thirty-year-old spinsters to beware! Don't think that your age buys you a dispensation from the heated emotions of youth. Oh no, even thirty years are no protection from love, and more remarkable still, from being loved.

Professor Eichstedt and Nora Werner left the public park with its broad, well-kept paths and strolled toward the forest. They were having a lively conversation and were considering the different ways in which incomparable works like *The Iliad* and *The Odyssey* by Homer could have been created, and reviewed several different theories. Now they entered the solemn forest shade. "How beautiful" they both cried in delight, with lowered voice, as though they feared to disturb the somnolent hush. Suddenly they both forgot what they had just been talking about. Homer—scholarship—antiquity—times past—everything disappeared, all they were aware of was the present. The woodland led uphill to allow a view of a pretty hamlet, sweetly nestled in the green valley, with its friendly houses and red roofs.

"How I would love to live in a house like that," Nora said dreamily.

"And how many houses in town do you see before you feel this, before this desire wells up in your soul?" Georg added.

Nora nodded in agreement.

"Yes, the simplest things in life, solitude and nature, are still the object of desire for more refined human beings," Georg continued.

"Yes, everyone in the city hubbub would long to go back to nature," Nora said softly.

"And the bigger the town, the greater the disgust with the hubbub. All those characterless houses with a myriad of unnecessary windows staring out so stupidly provoke outright disgust," Georg went on, becoming more animated, "from this autumn, I shall be living in the country, too."

"How are you going to combine that with your new course of philosophy lectures?" Nora asked in astonishment.

"The village is only half an hour away from town," Georg told her. "I had to buy the house because I already had a large claim on it."

The good, noble-spirited Georg did not say that he had paid almost double the necessary amount, *en amateur* as it were, and all to rescue some poor, good people, whom he had come to know by chance, from the hands of the villainous usurers. He went on to say how pretty the house was, how remarkably airy and roomy for a farmhouse, that it had a sweet front garden and an extensive orchard and vegetable garden, and how he was having the house and garden nicely restored, and then how the aged widow of the former owner, who was a clean and sensible old soul, was to stay in the house and run his household in a simple fashion.

"How beautiful it will be for you," said Nora in delight, looking at him happily with her big, radiant eyes.

"Oh yes," said Georg, looking down, slightly confused by the enchanting expression in Nora's pure countenance. "Oh yes, beautiful," he repeated in an oddly heartfelt and dreamy manner. It almost seemed as though he were referring to his delightful companion and not to his house and his well-ordered future.

They were both silent.

"But, well—rather lonely," Georg continued hesitantly after a little while.

"Yes, rather lonely," said Nora hastily, and she suddenly felt quite strange; a blush stole over her, too.

And now neither could say a single word. They had nothing more to say, nothing, absolutely nothing.

There was a restlessness in Nora's heart, she was overcome by a quite unfamiliar feeling of embarrassment, which made her angry with herself. She ought not to have come on this long walk, her companion was not a close friend—or was not sufficiently distant, she thought in the midst of these indistinct emotions. Why on earth had Professor Eichstedt embarked on this walk? And having once suggested it, why didn't he stay the same as usual: cool and friendly, at least in his behavior? They had known each other formerly, and when Nora was traveling to see her mother, they had met by chance *en route,* they had struck up such an interesting conversation about a book which had just appeared and which they had both read, that both had wanted to continue the conversation. By chance, they had met again on their morning walks, exchanging views and books, but until today they had *never* talked about personal matters. "Why was Professor Eichstedt so different today?" Nora wondered, feeling increasingly self-conscious and cross. She gave her companion a furious look, as though he were a heinous enemy. But when she looked at him, so handsome, noble, and manly, walking along dreamily, Nora was truly shocked.

No, the enemy she had to fear was not strolling beside her, but in her own breast. Nora felt like crying.

Even nature had turned restless: here and there, light clouds obstructed the sun, the shafts of light in the forest trembled restlessly up and down between the trees, the flowers and bushes swayed back and forth, the tall trees bowed to each other, shaking their branches; dead leaves and needles trickled softly to the ground. It was as though the firs were groaning, a whispering, a question full of longing seemed to ripple though the forest. As though in a dream, Nora listened to all this longing astir in the forest; to her mind, she and the forest were both asking the same question, but she didn't know what that question was.

Suddenly a fair note rang out: in sweet lament, a nightingale began to sing its rapturous song; it sang and sang; the sound swirled up, leaving behind all doubt, lament, and fear, and it rejoiced in highest bliss, in most blissful certainty. That was the answer.

And now the forest had understood the answer. A rapturous murmur whirled through the treetops with great force; a thousand birds sang for sheer joy and blissful pleasure: the anemones had tears of happiness in their pure, floral eyes.

But Nora, too, now understood both question and answer; her heart and the forest had both asked yearningly: "What is happiness?" And now the air was filled with a roar of joy that echoed blissfully in her heart: "To love! Love! And be loved!"

Nora put her hand over her beating heart.

Meanwhile the forest path had narrowed. Nora went ahead of Professor Eichstedt for a few steps; she stared remotely at the narrow blue strips of deep blue sky visible between the foliage, as though paradise were revealed to her up there. Suddenly she stepped back with a half-smothered scream, and clutched Professor Eichstedt's arm in fright. A man was lying across the narrow forest path with his head propped on the raised bank of the path: was he dead? But no, it was someone who had been peacefully asleep, and was now awake, thanks to Nora's little scream. The man stared into Nora's frightened face in amazement:

"Did I alarm the gentlefolk?" he said with a good-natured smile and in rustic accents; "I'm sorry. I set off from my home village in the middle of the night to take my strawberries to town, and rested a bit here, and then I fell asleep. The lovely lady needn't be afraid."

He looked at Nora admiringly while he slowly rose and smiled again in a friendly manner. Nora looked indescribably enchanting with her tousled hair.

"Well, well, sir!" he continued, "how lucky you are. Such a lovely sweetheart. Eyes like two stars and a mouth as red as my strawberries."

Eichstedt and Nora both blushed.

Nora bent over the man's basket. "Do you have any strawberries for sale?" she asked.

"Yes, yes, my lovely Fräulein," said the man happily. "You want to buy some? Money from such a lovely lady will bring me good luck."

Nora bought a little basket of the choicest wild strawberries. She did not bargain; she paid what the man demanded and even a bit extra, and now they were both able to negotiate the narrow spot on the path.

"All happiness to you both, you handsome pair!" called out the man with the strawberries. Eichstedt had already placed Nora's hand in the crook of his arm when she was alarmed and now held the little hand a prisoner.

They were still bereft of words, could not even look at each other, and yet they were so close to one another that each could almost hear the other's heartbeat. "If only he would let go of my hand," Nora thought, petrified.

"I think I've lost a letter," said Nora hastily, and slipped her hand from Eichstedt's arm. She rummaged in her bag. Naturally, the letter was there; her hands were trembling, so that she dropped it.

Eichstedt picked it up quickly, his sharp eye reading the signature, stiff from lack of practice: "Your ever loving Georg."

"Who is *this* ever-loving Georg?" asked Eichstedt, with special emphasis.

"My nephew," said Nora softy.

"That makes two of us!" said Georg with a deep sigh.

Nora was overwhelmed by strange feelings.

At last they reached the witches' well. One could well see why the spring had acquired its name, as there was a hint of mystery in this remote corner of the forest. The bright silver jet spurted from gray-brown rocks into a weathered, strangely shaped basin; ancient trees with deep shadows allowed scarcely a ray of sunlight to penetrate, and the rustle of the wind and the song of the birds had fallen silent here. Opposite the spring, encircling a tree, was a little bench. Eichstedt and Nora sat down to rest, slightly turned away from each other because of the shape of the seat. They were relieved at not having to look at each other.

Nora found the oppressive silence between them embarrassing and put the little basket of strawberries between them. "Won't you try the strawberries?" she asked, just to say something.

Eichstedt woke from his reverie, a painful one to all appearances, and quickly turned to Nora to catch a glance from her. Her big hat hid her eyes from him, however, and he could see only her chin, a little of her flushed cheek and her mouth. Strange—twenty-four hours ago he had solemnly declared that being ugly was a woman's greatest piece of fortune, and that being pretty was a terribly damaging luxury; but now he would not wish for this enchanting mouth to be less pretty for anything in the world, just so that Nora could thereby become a more useful member of human society. He wanted to accept the invitation to eat the strawberries, but forgot again, and was suddenly suffused with the thought of how much more inviting this red mouth was than the red strawberries.

Never had such terribly immoral thoughts entered the philosophical head of the learned professor. With a deep sigh, he leaned back against the tree. A song rang out from afar; apparently a band of students was walking along the broad path overhead which skirted this hidden corner of the valley. They sang a song in parts, and the melancholy tune echoed longingly down to the pair in the depths:

> If you've found a heart
> That is good and true.
> Come what may in life
> Hold her close to you.

You've a right to claim
Happiness today.
Will you learn too late,
That she's gone away?

Gradually the sounds dispersed in the distance, but one final time, the wind carried the last words of the refrain down to them:

Will you learn too late,
That she's gone away?

"We usually recognize what happiness is when it's too late," said Georg with a faltering voice. The notes of the song seemed to have opened the portal to his heart. "Just a few days ago I knew of no higher goal more worth striving for than to live in the solitude of learning and to satisfy my thirst for knowledge. I thought it would be true paradise to follow my studies in my lonely farmhouse, and yet today I know that I shall feel miserably unhappy, consumed with longing for my 'lovely lady.'"

Unwittingly he used the rustic strawberry man's expression. Georg, so inexperienced in love, did not have a wealth of terms of endearment to hand.

Nora had lowered her head and folded her hands.

"And now I have wrecked my own happiness by acting too hastily," Georg continued, his voice faltering with passion. "I've resigned my professorship, and could never presume to lead the woman I love into meager poverty."

His words sounded like a cry of pain.

"Perhaps she would look on this meager poverty as the height of happiness," Nora said in a scarcely audible whisper.

Georg's first sensation was to throw himself at the feet of this wonderful girl, but before a man as stubborn and proud as Georg can really humble himself, a few more things have to happen!

"No, no," he cried with bleak passion, "it would be dishonorable and cowardly to take advantage of the magnanimity of an admirable woman and not provide for her properly. It would break my heart to see her suffer and have to struggle to make ends meet."

It had not occurred to noble, heartbroken Georg that in the real world of today, the beloved comes complete with fortune and dowry, and that if he reckoned Nora's income with his own, they could both live a simple life on a farm without starving or having to do without. Idealists often have a difficult time on account of their insufficient knowledge of mundane matters.

"His pride is stronger than his love, or else he himself is scared of having to make sacrifices," Nora told herself sadly. She stood up and went to the spring for a drink. She was an enchanting spectacle standing there, not at all suited to lightening poor Georg's heart.

Her hat had sunk to the nape of her neck, her charming head stood out against the brown rockface, her upper body was bent gracefully forward, and her pink hand cupped the silver jet of water.

"Let me drink too!" asked Georg, suddenly standing close to her. Georg's voice had that deep, sonorous tone which turns a request to a woman into a command.

She held her hand again under the jet of water, but by the time it reached Georg's lips, it had shaken so much that the water had spilled, but if the hand could no longer serve as a drinking vessel, it was nevertheless seized with ardor and covered with hotly passionate kisses.

"Nora . . . ," Eichstedt began with the most tender, pained expression.

"Don't say anything! Don't say anything!" cried Nora, tearing her hand away, "we don't know what we're saying and doing today! We are changed, under a spell! Yesterday we were so sensible," she complained with tears in her lovely eyes. "I don't want you to say anything today which you might regret tomorrow."

Georg wanted to protest passionately.

"No, no, don't say any more," she pleaded again, "let's go home the quickest way, let's go back to reality. We're under a spell here."

She hurried away, Georg following with inner delight, since her inclusion of the little word *we* in her lament had filled him with a kind of rapturous intoxication. They spoke little on the way home, but their eyes told one another of the most marvelous things.

Yes, sharp-eyed Hanne, they *were* lovers.

On the bench by the witches' well, the little basket of strawberries stood alone and forgotten. A bird flew round it, looked around cautiously, then approached it, picked at the strawberries, turned its little head with its clever, tiny little eyes from side to side, and twittered mockingly: "those stupid humans!"

Notes

Abbreviations

GSA   Goethe-Schiller Archive, Weimar
KGB   *Briefwechsel: Kritische Gesamtausgabe*
KGW   *Werke: Kritische Gesamtausgabe*
KSA   *Sämtliche Werke: Kritische Studienausgabe*
Za   *Thus Spoke Zarathustra*

Chapter 1: Lieschen-Lisbeth-Lama

1. Oehler, "Die Mutter von Friedrich Nietzsche," 6.
2. Lacan, *Écrits*, 218.
3. Förster-Nietzsche, *Der junge Nietzsche*, 67.
4. Matt. 18:3 (King James).
5. Oehler, "Die Mutter von Friedrich Nietzsche," 6.
6. Förster-Nietzsche, *Friedrich Nietzsche und die Frauen*, 27.
7. Oeynhausen, *Worte mütterlicher Liebe*, 261.
8. Ibid., 137.
9. Förster-Nietzsche, *Das Leben Friedrich Nietzsche's*, 1:65.
10. Welch, *Protestant Thought*, 1:29.
11. Franziska Nietzsche, quoted in Gabel and Jagenberg, *Der entmündigte Philosoph*, 34.
12. Oehler, "Die Mutter von Friedrich Nietzsche," 109–10.
13. Oehler, *Nietzsches Mutter*, 139–40.
14. Förster-Nietzsche, *Das Leben Friedrich Nietzsche's*, 1:5.
15. Förster-Nietzsche, *Der junge Nietzsche*, 7.
16. Ibid., 10.
17. Ibid., 17.
18. Förster-Nietzsche, *Friedrich Nietzsche und die Frauen*, 29.

19. Ibid., 28.

20. Förster-Nietzsche, *Das Leben Friedrich Nietzsche's*, 1:26.

21. Förster-Nietzsche, *Der junge Nietzsche*, 32.

22. Förster-Nietzsche, *Das Leben Friedrich Nietzsche's*, 1:70.

23. Förster-Nietzsche, *Der junge Nietzsche*, 66.

24. Förster-Nietzsche, *Friedrich Nietzsche und die Frauen*, 30.

25. Raumer, *Die Erziehung der Mädchen*, 108.

26. Ibid., 98.

27. Kreyenberg, *Mädchenerziehung und Frauenleben*, 259.

28. Gleim, *Erziehung und Unterricht*, 129.

29. Ibid., 87.

30. Herloßsohn, *Damen-Conversations-Lexikon*, 87–88.

31. Elisabeth Nietzsche, "May This Year," MS 72/1035a, and "My Methods of Saving Time," MS 72/1035c, both in GSA.

32. Elisabeth Nietzsche, Volkschule report, 1854, MS 72/1034, GSA.

33. Elisabeth Nietzsche, exercise book, 1861, MS 72/1035i, GSA.

34. Elisabeth Nietzsche, diary entry, 27 Dec. 1860, MS 72/854, GSA.

35. Elisabeth Nietzsche, diary entry, 11 Apr. 1861, MS 72/854, GSA.

36. Elisabeth Nietzsche, exercise book, 1862, MS 72/1036f, GSA.

37. Elisabeth Nietzsche, exercise book, 1862, MS 72/1036b, GSA.

38. Nietzsche, *KGB*, Ii, 198.

39. Förster-Nietzsche, *Das Leben Friedrich Nietzsche's*, 1:92.

40. Förster-Nietzsche, *Der junge Nietzsche*, 44.

41. Goch, "Elisabeth Förster-Nietzsche," 411n.128.

42. Schoedler, *Das Buch der Natur*, 2:453. Europeans in the nineteenth century confused the llama with the camel.

43. Lenz, *Kleine Naturgeschichte*, 43.

44. Nietzsche, *KGB*, Ii, 248.

45. Förster-Nietzsche, *Das Leben Friedrich Nietzsche's*, 1:164.

46. Friedrich Nietzsche to Elisabeth Nietzsche, 4 Aug. 1863, MS BW 271, 1, GSA. Elisabeth renders this with four dots in *Das Leben Friedrich Nietzsche's*, 1:162.

47. Nietzsche, *KGB*, IIi, 80.

48. Ibid., IIv, 180.

49. Ibid., IIv, 184.

50. Ibid., IIv, 394.

51. Förster-Nietzsche, *Das Leben Friedrich Nietzsche's*, 1:35.

Chapter 2: *Fräulein Nietzsche*

1. In E. T. A. Hoffmann's story *Ritter Glück* (Sir Gluck, 1809) the arias from *Iphigenie en Aulide* are discussed. "Ritter Gluck" was also Nietzsche's nickname in the Franconia *Verbindung* (students' society) in Bonn.

2. Elisabeth Nietzsche, poem for Friedrich Nietzsche, 20 Dec. 1864, MS 72/98, GSA.

3. Nietzsche, *KGB*, Iiii, 62.

4. Elisabeth Nietzsche, diary entry, 1 May 1862, MS 72/854, GSA.

5. Franziska Nietzsche's introductory sentence to Elisabeth Nietzsche's diary, which Elisabeth transcribed around 1885; MS 72/855, GSA.

6. Nietzsche, *KGB*, Iiii, 44.

7. Ibid., Iiii, 45.

8. Ibid., Iiii, 46.

9. Ibid., Iii, 61.

10. Ibid., IIi, 185.

11. Ibid., IIv, 216.

12. Ibid., IIvi/i, 443.

13. Ibid., IIv, 70.

14. Ibid., IIv, 216.

15. Ibid., IIvi/i, 16. Emphasis in original.

16. Ibid., IIv, 9.

17. Ibid., IIi, 125–26; reprinted in Förster-Nietzsche, *Friedrich Nietzsche und die Frauen*, 182–83.

18. Nietzsche, *KGB*, IIvi/i, 43.

19. Cosima Wagner to Elisabeth Nietzsche, 2 Apr. 1875, MS 72/BW 57, 19, 1, GSA.

20. Förster-Nietzsche, *Der junge Nietzsche*, 371.

21. Cosima Wagner to Elisabeth Nietzsche, 17 Feb. 1877, MS 72/BW 57, 19, 1, GSA.

22. Peters, *Zarathustra's Sister*, 48.

23. Nietzsche, *Menschliches, Allzumenschliches*, III, 135: "The Religious Life," in *KGW*, IVii, 129.

24. Nietzsche, *Die Fröhliche Wissenschaft*, 125: "The Madman," in *KGW*, Vii, 159.

25. Cosima Wagner to Elisabeth Nietzsche, 20 Feb. 1878, MS 72/BW 57, 19, 1, GSA.

26. Elisabeth Nietzsche to Franziska Nietzsche, 26 July 1882, MS 100/532, 1, GSA.

27. Nietzsche, *KGB*, IIIi, 256. Emphasis in original.

28. Ibid., IIIii, 303.

29. Ibid., IIIi, 277.

30. Ibid., IIIi, 267.

31. Ibid., IIIii, 301.

32. Ibid., IIIii, 304.

33. Ibid., IIIi, 338–39.

34. Ibid., IIIi, 468.

35. Ibid., IIIi, 509.

36. Förster-Nietzsche, *Das Leben Friedrich Nietzsche's*, vol. 2, part 2, p. 417.

37. Ibid., 418–19.

38. Förster-Nietzsche, *Der einsame Nietzsche*, 197.

39. Salomé, *Nietzsche*, 49.

40. Förster-Nietzsche, *Das Leben Friedrich Nietzsche's*, vol. 2, part 2, p. 408.

41. Förster-Nietzsche, *Der einsame Nietzsche*, 177.

42. Nietzsche, *KGB*, IIIi, 405–6.

43. Förster-Nietzsche, *Der einsame Nietzsche*, 242.

44. Förster-Nietzsche, *Friedrich Nietzsche und die Frauen*, 120.

45. Nietzsche, *KGB*, IIIi, 408. Emphasis in original.

46. Bernhard Förster to Elisabeth Nietzsche, Easter Sunday 1883, MS 72/BW 1400, GSA.

47. Nietzsche, *KGB*, IIIiii, 24–25.

Chapter 3: *Frau Eli Förster*

1. Elisabeth Nietzsche to Bernhard Förster, April–June 1883, MS 72/1158a, GSA.

2. Bernhard Förster to Elisabeth Nietzsche, 30 Nov.–1 Dec. 1883, MS 72/BW 1400, GSA. Goethe's sonnet "Die Liebende abermals" is written from the perspective of a woman to her lover. Förster adapted the first stanza by altering several key words.

3. Ibid.

4. Bernhard Förster to Elisabeth Nietzsche, 15 May 1884, MS 72/BW 1400, GSA. Emphasis in original.

5. Bernhard Förster to Elisabeth Nietzsche, 14 Oct. 1884, MS 72/BW 1400, GSA.

6. Peters, *Zarathustra's Sister*, 77.

7. Bernhard Förster to Elisabeth Nietzsche, 24 Mar. 1885, MS 72/BW 1400, GSA. Emphasis in original.

8. Podach, *Gestalten um Nietzsche*, 126.

9. Ibid., 127.

10. Nietzsche, *KGB*, IIIiii, 64. Emphasis in original.

11. Ibid., IIIiii, 148–49. Emphasis in original.

12. Förster-Nietzsche, *Friedrich Nietzsches Briefe an Mutter und Schwester*, 2:663n.

13. Ibid., 2:721.

14. Förster, *Über nationale Erziehung*, 20.

15. Ibid., 34.

16. Ibid., 40.

17. Ibid., 41.

18. Förster, *Zur Frage der "nationalen Erziehung*," 25.

19. Förster, *Der deutsche Prosastil in unseren Tagen*, 122.

20. Förster, *Die Frage der Vivisektion*, 8.

21. The Deutschkatholiken, not to be confused with Roman Catholic Germans, were a popular radical group of the 1840s led by the dissenting Catholic priest Johannes Ronge. Ronge advocated allowing priests to marry and castigated the hypocrisy of the church of Rome. He was excommunicated in 1844. By 1859, the sect had merged with the Lichtfreunde.

22. Petition to Otto von Bismarck, 13 Apr. 1881, MS 72/BW 1400, GSA.

23. Förster, *Das Verhältnis des modernen Judenthums*, 33.

24. Ibid., 51. Emphasis in original.

25. Förster, *Deutsche Colonien*, 42. The author's original copy in the Anna Amalie Schloßbibliothek, Weimar, is rather quaintly dedicated "To the author's truest colleague and dear little wife."

26. Elisabeth Förster-Nietzsche to Bernhard Förster, 18 Sept. 1885, MS 72/1158c, GSA.

27. Ibid.

28. Elisabeth Förster-Nietzsche to Franziska Nietzsche, 18–28 Mar. 1888, MS 100/533, 1, GSA.

29. Förster-Nietzsche, *Friedrich Nietzsches Briefe an Mutter und Schwester*, 2:726.

30. Nietzsche, *KGB*, IIIv, 83.

31. Ibid., 166.

32. Ibid., IIIv, 194.

33. Ibid., IIIv, 427.

34. Ibid., IIIv, 320–21.

35. Elisabeth Förster-Nietzsche to Bernhard Förster, 10 May 1887, MS 72/1158d, GSA.

36. Elisabeth Förster-Nietzsche to Bernhard Förster, 11 June 1888, MS 72/1158e, GSA.

37. Elisabeth Förster-Nietzsche to Bernhard Förster, 24 Oct. 1888, MS 72/1158e, GSA.

38. Elisabeth Förster-Nietzsche to Bernhard Förster, Feb. 1889?, MS 72/1158g, GSA.

39. Elisabeth Förster-Nietzsche to Bernhard Förster, undated note, MS 72/1158g, GSA.

40. Bernhard Förster to Elisabeth Förster-Nietzsche, 22 Feb. 1889, MS 72/BW 1400, GSA.

41. Elisabeth Förster-Nietzsche to Franziska Nietzsche, 9 Apr. 1889, MS 100/533, 2, GSA.

42. Bernhard Förster to Elisabeth Förster-Nietzsche, 2 June 1889, MS 72/BW 1400, GSA.

43. Elisabeth Förster-Nietzsche to Bernhard Förster, undated letter (presumably spring 1888), MS 72/1158g, GSA.

44. Oehler, *Nietzsches Mutter,* 142.

45. Peters, *Zarathustra's Sister,* 112.

46. Elisabeth Förster-Nietzsche to Franziska Nietzsche, 2 July 1889, MS 100/533, 2, GSA. Emphasis in original.

47. Förster-Nietzsche, "Ein Sonntag in Nueva-Germania," 7.

48. Ibid., 15.

49. Ibid., 17–18.

50. Förster-Nietzsche, "Ein Sonntag in Nueva-Germania," in *Dr. Bernhard Försters Kolonie,* 45–46.

51. Ibid., 46. Emphasis in original.

52. Ibid., 48.

53. Ibid.

Chapter 4: The Will to Power

1. Cited in Podach, *Gestalten um Nietzsche,* 171.

2. Peter Gast to Elisabeth Förster-Nietzsche, 6 Oct. 1893, MS 102/302, GSA. I am greatly indebted to Ralf Rosmiarek for drawing this to my attention.

3. Goch, *Franziska Nietzsche,* 326–27.

4. Letter quoted in Gabel and Jagenberg, *Der entmündigte Philosoph,* 47.

5. Ibid., 33.

6. Hoffmann, *Zur Geschichte des Nietzsche-Archivs,* 282.

7. Letter quoted in Hoffmann, *Zur Geschichte des Nietzsche-Archivs,* 270.

8. Letter quoted in Hoffmann, *Zur Geschichte des Nietzsche-Archivs,* 283.

9. Cosima Wagner to Elisabeth Förster-Nietzsche, 25 Aug. 1894, MS 72/BW 57, 19, 1, GSA.

10. Cosima Wagner to Elisabeth Förster-Nietzsche, 23 Sept. 1894, MS 72/BW 57, 19, 1, GSA.

11. Cosima Wagner to Elisabeth Förster-Nietzsche, 20 Dec. 1896, MS 72/BW 57, 19, 1, GSA.

12. Ibid.

13. Cosima Wagner to Elisabeth Förster-Nietzsche, 18 Feb. 1901, MS 72/BW 57, 19, 1, GSA.

14. Ibid.

15. Nietzsche, *KGB,* IIii, 138.

16. Förster-Nietzsche, *Wagner und Nietzsche,* 35.

17. Nietzsche, *KGB,* IIii, 223.

18. Nietzsche, *KGB*, IIi, 125–26; reprinted in Förster-Nietzsche, *Friedrich Nietzsche und die Frauen*, 182–83.

19. Elisabeth Förster-Nietzsche, "Cosima Wagner," *Nord und Süd*, 8 Dec. 1927; Elisabeth Förster-Nietzsche, "Cosima Wagner und Friedrich Nietzsche: Wahrheit und Dichtung" (Cosima Wagner and Friedrich Nietzsche: Truth and Fiction), *Der Tag*, 15 May 1930.

20. Nietzsche, *KGB*, IIIv, 572.

21. Förster-Nietzsche, "Cosima Wagner und Friedrich Nietzsche."

22. Nietzsche, *Za*, II, "Von der Selbst-Überwindung" (On Self-Overcoming), in *KGW*, VIi, 143–44.

23. Nietzsche, *Götzen-Dämmerung*, "Streifzüge eines Unzeitgemässen" (Expeditions of an Untimely Man), 14 (Subtitled "Anti-Darwin"), in *KGW*, VIiii, 114.

24. Nietzsche, *Za*, II, "Von der Selbst-Überwindung," in *KGW*, VIi, 145.

25. Nietzsche, *Za*, II, "Von der Erlösung" (On Deliverance), in *KGW*, VIi, 177.

26. Förster-Nietzsche, *Das Leben Friedrich Nietzsche's*, vol. 2, part 2, 691; see also Nietzsche, *KGW*, VIIIi, 326.

27. Schaberg, *Nietzsche Canon*, 189.

28. Elisabeth Förster-Nietzsche, "Das geheimnisvolle Manuskript" (The Mysterious Manuscript), *Naumburger Tageblatt*, 20 Dec. 1929.

29. Nietzsche, *KGW*, VIIiii, 192; for the original text see MS 71/209, GSA.

30. Förster-Nietzsche, *Das Leben Friedrich Nietzsche's*, vol. 2, part 2, p. 694.

31. Richard Oehler quoted in Förster-Nietzsche, *Der einsame Nietzsche*, 446–47.

32. Nietzsche, *KGB*, IIIv, 492.

33. Förster-Nietzsche, *Das Nietzsche-Archiv*, 55. This is identical to the division in Nietzsche, *KGW*, VIIIi, 347.

34. Nietzsche, *KGB*, IIIv, 441.

35. Nietzsche, *KGB*, IIIv, 434.

36. Nietzsche, *KGB*, IIIv, 482.

37. Förster-Nietzsche, *Das Nietzsche-Archiv*, 55.

38. Heidegger, *Nietzsche*, I:8.

39. Ibid.

40. Ibid., II:263.

41. Ibid., I:19.

42. Ibid., I:15.

43. Nietzsche, *KSA*, vol. 14, foreword, pp. 11–12.

44. Schaberg, *Nietzsche Canon*, 186.

45. Nietzsche, *KGB*, IIIiii, 33.

46. Ibid., IIIiii, 96. Emphasis in original.

47. Francé-Harrar, "Nietzsche—gesehen durch die Familienbrille," 188.

48. Nietzsche, *KSA*, vol. 14, foreword, p. 14.

Chapter 5: Elisabeth and the Woman Question

1. Nietzsche, *KGB*, IIIiii, 49. Emphasis in original.

2. Nietzsche, *Jenseits von Gut und Böse*, VII, "Unsere Tugenden" (Our Virtues), 233, in *KGW*, VIii, 178. Emphasis in original.

3. Nietzsche, *Jenseits von Gut und Böse,* IV, "Sprüche und Zwischenspiele" (Sayings and Interludes), 145, in *KGW,* VIii, 98.

4. Nietzsche, *Ecce Homo,* "Warum ich so gute Bücher schreibe" (Why I Write Such Good Books), 5, in *KGW,* VIiii, 304.

5. Ibid. Emphasis in original.

6. Nietzsche, *KGB,* IIIi, 210–11.

7. Wollkopf, "Elisabeth Nietzsche," 266. I am indebted to Wollkopf, not just for the insights in this article but for her cooperation in allowing me to publish this story.

8. Elisabeth Förster-Nietzsche to Frau Rée, summer 1883, MS 72/823, GSA.

9. Wollkopf, "Elisabeth Nietzsche," 266.

10. Elisabeth Förster-Nietzsche, "Friedrich Nietzsche über Weib, Liebe, und Ehe" (Friedrich Nietzsche on Woman, Love, and Marriage) *Neue deutsche Rundschau* 10 (1899): 1062.

11. Ibid., 1067.

12. Ibid.

13. Ibid., 1068.

14. Förster-Nietzsche, *Der einsame Nietzsche,* 182–83.

15. Nietzsche, *Za,* I, "Von alten und jungen Weiblein" (Of Old and Young Women), in *KGW,* VIi, 82.

16. Helene Stöcker, *Täglicher Anzeiger für Berg und Mark,* 19 Apr. 1903.

17. Helene Stöcker to Elisabeth Förster-Nietzsche, 14 Jan. 1911, MS 72/BW 5336, GSA.

18. Helene Stöcker, "Neues zum Nietzsche-Problem," *Sonntagsblatt der Basler Nachrichten,* 28 Aug. 1938, 139.

19. Chickering, "Women's Patriotic Activity," 159.

20. Ibid., 174.

21. Ibid., 179.

22. Förster-Nietzsche, *Der einsame Nietzsche,* 259.

23. Ibid., 349.

24. Ibid.

25. Ibid., 347.

26. Förster-Nietzsche, *Friedrich Nietzsche und die Frauen,* 5–6.

27. Nietzsche, *Za,* I, "Von alten und jungen Weiblein," in *KGW,* VIi, 81.

28. Förster-Nietzsche, *Friedrich Nietzsche und die Frauen,* 19.

29. Ibid.

30. Ibid., 18.

31. Letter quoted in editorial commentary in Nietzsche, *KSA,* 14:461.

32. Nietzsche, *Ecce Homo,* "Warum ich so weise bin" (Why I Am So Wise), 3, in *KGW,* VIiii, 266.

33. Letter quoted in editorial commentary in Nietzsche, *KSA,* 14:462.

34. Nietzsche's original version of this paragraph was first published in *Friedrich Nietzsches Werke* (Leipzig: Kröner, 1908), 184.

35. Marelle, *Die Schwester,* 8–9. Emphasis in original.

36. Marelle, "Elisabeth Förster-Nietzsche," 184.

Chapter 6: Frau Dr. Phil. H.C. Elisabeth Förster-Nietzsche

1. Nietzsche, *Götzen-Dämmerung*, "Was den Deutschen abgeht" (What the Germans Do Not Have), in *KGW*, VIiii, 97–98.

2. Elisabeth Förster-Nietzsche, "Nietzsche und der Krieg" (Nietzsche and War), *Der Tag*, 10 Sept. 1914, 9, also published in *Hamburgischer Correspondent*, 15 Sept. 1914, 2.

3. Nietzsche, *KGB*, IIi, 148–49.

4. Förster-Nietzsche, "Nietzsche und der Krieg."

5. Ibid.

6. Förster-Nietzsche, "Nietzsche—Frankreich und Deutschland," TS 72/17, GSA, 17.

7. Nietzsche, *KGB*, IIi, 155.

8. Förster-Nietzsche, "Nietzsche—Frankreich und Deutschland," TS 72/17, GSA, 14.

9. Elisabeth Förster-Nietzsche, "Nietzsche und Deutschland," *Berliner Tageblatt*, 5 Sept. 1915, supp.

10. Förster-Nietzsche, "Nietzsche, Frankreich, und England," *Neue Freie Presse*, 11 June 1916. (Originally published in TS 72/17, GSA.)

11. Ibid.

12. Simon-Ritz and Ulbricht, "'Heimstätte des Zarathustrawerkes,'" 162.

13. Karl Heussi to Adalbert Oehler, 3 Jan. 1931, MS 72/2015, GSA.

14. "Warum Jena University das Nietzsche-Archiv nicht haben will" (Why Jena University Does Not Want the Nietzsche-Archiv), *Vossische Zeitung*, 29 Nov. 1930. Emphasis in original.

15. Simon-Ritz and Ulbricht, "'Heimstätte des Zarathustrawerkes,'" 166.

16. Galindo, *Triumph des Willens zur Macht*, 201.

17. Simon-Ritz and Ulbricht, "'Heimstätte des Zarathustrawerkes,'" 170.

18. Peters, *Zarathustra's Sister*, 218.

19. Neliba, *Der Legalist des Unrechtsstaates Wilhelm Frick*, 58.

20. Ibid., 69.

21. Benjamin, "Nietzsche und das Archiv seiner Schwester," 1–2.

22. Galindo, *Triumph des Willens zur Macht*, 186.

23. Kessler, *Diaries of a Cosmopolitan*, 426.

24. Wilhelm Frick to Elisabeth Förster-Nietzsche, 20 Sept. 1930, MS 72/BW 1496, GSA.

25. Galindo, *Triumph des Willens zur Macht*, 183.

26. Elisabeth Förster-Nietzsche to Adolf Hitler, 4 Oct. 1934, MS 72/792, GSA.

27. Simon-Ritz and Ulbricht, "'Heimstätte des Zarathustrawerkes,'" 173.

28. Förster-Nietzsche, *Friedrich Nietzsche und die Frauen*, 169.

29. Galindo, *Triumph des Willens zur Macht*, 182.

30. Richard Leutheußer address, *Ansprachen zum Gedächtnis*.

31. Adalbert Oehler address, *Ansprachen zum Gedächtnis*.

32. Fritz Sauckel address, *Ansprachen zum Gedächtnis*.

33. Meyer-Erlach address, *Ansprachen zum Gedächtnis*.

34. Baeumler, *Nietzsche: Der Philosoph und Politiker*, 68.

35. Ibid., 65.

36. The dossier is in TS 72/2611, GSA.

37. Resa von Schirnhofer to Elisabeth Förster-Nietzsche, 12 Feb. 1903, MS 72/588, GSA.

38. See Diethe, *Nietzsche's Women,* 91–92.

39. Letter quoted in Gabel and Jagenberg, *Der entmündigte Philosoph,* 22.

40. Otto, afterword.

41. Vaihinger, "Johanna Schopenhauer und andere Philosophenmütter," 245.

Selected Bibliography

Ansprachen zum Gedächtnis der Frau Dr. Phil. H.C. Elisabeth Förster-Nietzsche bei den Trauerfeierlichkeiten in Weimar und Röcken am 11. und 12. November 1935 (Funeral Orations in Memory of Frau Dr. Phil. H.C. Elisabeth Förster-Nietzsche at the Ceremonies in Weimar and Röcken on 11 and 12 November 1935). Weimar: Wagner Verlag, 1935.

Baeumler, Alfred. *Nietzsche: Der Philosoph und Politiker* (Nietzsche: The Philosopher and Politician). Leipzig: Reclam, 1931.

Benjamin, Walter. "Nietzsche und das Archiv seiner Schwester" (Nietzsche and His Sister's Archive). *Die literarische Welt* 8, no. 12 (1932), 1–2.

Bernoulli, Carl Albrecht, ed. *Franz Overbeck und Friedrich Nietzsche: Eine Freundschaft* (Franz Overbeck and Friedrich Nietzsche: A Friendship). 2 vols. Jena, Ger.: Diederichs, 1907–8.

Chickering, Roger. "Women's Patriotic Activity in Imperial Germany." *Past and Present* 118 (Feb. 1988): 156–85.

Cohn, Paul. *Um Nietzsches Untergang: Beiträge zum Verständnis des Genies* (On Nietzsche's Downfall: Contributions toward an Understanding of Genius). Hannover: Morris, 1931.

Diethe, Carol. *Nietzsche's Women: Beyond the Whip.* Berlin: de Gruyter, 1996.

Förster, Bernhard. *Deutsche Colonien im oberen Laplata-Gebiete mit besonderer Berücksichtigung von Paraguay: Ergebnisse eingehender Prüfungen, praktischer Arbeiten und Reisen 1883–1885* (German Colonies in the Upper La Plata Region with Particular Regard to Paraguay: Results of Thorough Research, Practical Work, and Travels, 1883–1885). Naumburg, Ger.: Förster, 1886.

———. *Der deutsche Prosastil in unseren Tagen* (German Prose Style in Our Time). *Preußischer Jahrbücher* 46 (1880): 109–25.

———. *Die Frage der Vivisektion im Deutschen Reichstage: Ein Stück Kulturkampf* (The Question of Vivisection in the German Reichstag: A Piece of Kulturkampf). Bayreuth: Burger, 1882.

———. *Olympia: Ein Blick auf den allgemeinen Kunst- und Kultur- historischen Werth der Grabungen am Alpheios* (Olympia: A Look at the Artistic and Cultural-Historical Value of the Excavations at Alpheios). Halle, Ger.: Hendel, 1886.

———. *Parsifal-Nachklänge: Allerhand Gedanken über deutsche Cultur,* Wissenschaft, Kunst und Gesellschaft von Mehreren empfunden (Parsifal-Resonances: Miscellaneous Thoughts of a Small Group on German Culture, Science, Art, and Society). Leipzig: Fritzsch, 1883.

———. *Richard Wagner als Begründer eines deutschen Nationalstils mit verschiedenen Blicken auf die Kulturen indo-germanischer Nationen* (Richard Wagner As Founder of a National Style with Diverse Mention of the Cultures of Indo-Germanic Nations). Chemnitz, Ger.: Schmeitzner, 1880.

———. *Richard Wagner in seiner nationalen Bedeutung und seine Wirkung auf das Culturleben* (The National Importance of Richard Wagner and His Effect on Cultural Life). Leipzig: Fock, 1886.

———. *Über nationale Erziehung* (On National Education). Leipzig: Fock, 1882.

———. *Der Vegetarismus: Ein Theil der sozialen Frage* (Vegetarianism: A Part of the Social Question). Hanover: Schmorl and Seefeld, 1882.

———. *Das Verhältnis des modernen Judenthums zur deutschen Kunst* (The Relationship of Modern Jewry to German Art). Berlin: Schulze, 1881.

———. *Zur Frage der "nationalen Erziehung"* (On the Question of "National Education"). Leipzig: Fritzsch, 1883.

Förster-Nietzsche, Elisabeth [as Elisabeth Nietzsche]. "Coffee-Party Gossip about Nora." 72/99/100, Goethe-Schiller Archive, Weimar.

———. "Cosima Wagner," *Nord und Süd,* 8 Dec. 1927.

———. "Cosima Wagner und Friedrich Nietzsche: Wahrheit und Dichtung" (Cosima Wagner and Friedrich Nietzsche: Truth and Fiction), *Der Tag,* 15 May 1930.

——— [as Eli Förster]. *Dr. Bernhard Förster's Kolonie Neu-Germania in Paraguay* (Dr. Bernhard Förster's Colony Neu-Germania in Paraguay). Berlin: Pioneer, 1891.

———. *Der einsame Nietzsche* (The Lonely Nietzsche). Leipzig: Kröner, 1913.

———. "Friedrich Nietzsche über Weib, Liebe, und Ehe" (Friedrich Nietzsche on Women, Love, and Marriage), *Neue deutsche Rundschau* 10 (1899).

———. *Friedrich Nietzsche und die Frauen seiner Zeit* (Friedrich Nietzsche and the Women of His Time). Munich: Beck, 1935.

———, ed. *Friedrich Nietzsches Briefe an Mutter und Schwester* (Friedrich Nietzsche's Letters to Mother and Sister). 2 vols. Leipzig: Insel, 1909.

———. "Das geheimnisvolle Manuskript" (The Mysterious Manuscript), *Naumburger Tageblatt,* 20 Dec. 1929.

———. *Der junge Nietzsche* (The Young Nietzsche). Leipzig: Kröner, 1912.

———. *Das Leben Friedrich Nietzsche's* (The Life of Friedrich Nietzsche). 3 vols. Leipzig: Naumann, 1895–1904.

———. "Nietzsche—Frankreich und Deutschland." 1915. TS 72/17, Goethe-Schiller Archive, Weimar.

———, ed. *Nietzsche Worte über Staaten und Völker* (Nietzsche: Words on States and Peoples). Leipzig: Kröner, 1922.

———. "Nietzsche, Frankreich, und England" (Nietzsche, France, and England). *Neue freie Presse,* 11 June 1916. TS 72/16, Goethe-Schiller Archive, Weimar.

———. *Das Nietzsche-Archiv: Seine Freunde und seine Feinde* (The Nietzsche-Archiv: Its Friends and Foes). Berlin: Marquardt, 1907.

————. "Nietzsche und der Krieg" (Nietzsche and War), *Der Tag,* 10 Sept. 1914, and *Hamburgischer Correspondent,* 15 Sept. 1914.

————. "Nietzsche und Deutschland," *Berliner Tageblatt,* 5 Sept. 1915, supp.

———— [as Eli Förster]. "Ein Sonntag in *Nueva-Germania*" (A Sunday in New Germania). Pp. 7–20 in *Bernhard Förster: Eine Schrift zum Andenken und zur Rechtfertigung* (Bernhard Förster: A Memorial Publication and Justification). Leipzig: Fritzsch, 1889. Expanded version published as pp. 30–52 in *Dr. Bernhard Förster's Kolonie Neu-Germania in Paraguay* (Dr. Bernhard Förster's Colony New Germania in Paraguay). Berlin: Pioneer, 1891.

————. *Wagner und Nietzsche zur Zeit ihrer Freundschaft* (Wagner and Nietzsche at the Time of Their Friendship). Munich: Müller, 1915.

————, ed. *Der werdende Nietzsche* (The Developing Nietzsche). Munich: Musarion, 1924.

————, ed. *Der Wille zur Macht* (*The Will to Power*). Leipzig: Naumann, 1901.

Francé-Harrar, Annie. "Nietzsche—gesehen durch die Familienbrille. Elisabeth Förster-Nietzsche" (Nietzsche—Seen through the Family Spectacles: Elisabeth Förster-Nietzsche). Pp. 184–89 in Francé-Harrar, *So war's um Neunzehnhundert: Mein Fin de Siècle* (This Is How It Was at the Turn of the Century: My Fin de Siècle). Munich: Langen/Müller, 1962.

Gabel, Gernot U., and Carl Helmuth Jagenberg. *Der entmündigte Philosoph: Briefe von Franziska Nietzsche an Adalbert Oehler aus den Jahren 1889–1897* (The Disenfranchised Philosopher: Letters of Franziska Nietzsche to Adalbert Oehler from the Years 1880–1897). Hürth: Gabel Verlag, 1994.

Galindo, Martha Zapata. *Triumph des Willens zur Macht: Zur Nietzsche-Rezeption im NS-Staat* (Triumph of the Will to Power: On Nietzsche-Reception in the National Socialist State). Hamburg: Argument, 1995.

Gleim, Betty. *Erziehung und Unterricht des weiblichen Geschlechts* (Education and Instruction for the Female Sex). 1810. Paderborn, Ger.: Huttemann, 1989.

Goch, Klaus. "Elisabeth Förster-Nietzsche (1846–1935): Ein Biographisches Porträt" (Elisabeth Förster-Nietzsche [1846–1935]: A Biographical Portrait). Pp. 361–413 in *Schwestern berühmter Männer* (Sisters of Famous Men). Ed. Luise Pusch. Frankfurt am Main: Insel, 1985.

————. *Franziska Nietzsche.* Frankfurt am Main: Insel, 1994.

Heidegger, Martin. *Nietzsche.* 2 vols. Pfullingen, Ger.: Neske, 1961.

Herloßsohn, Carl, ed. *Damen-Conversations-Lexikon* (Ladies' Conversational Lexikon). 1834–38. Berlin: Union-Verlag, 1987.

Hoffmann, David Marc. *Zur Geschichte des Nietzsche-Archivs: Chronik, Studien, und Dokumente* (On the History of the Nietzsche-Archiv: Chronicle, Commentary, and Documentation). Berlin: de Gruyter, 1991.

Kessler, Harry Graf. *The Diaries of a Cosmopolitan.* London: Weidenfeld and Nicholson, 1971.

Klingbeil, Julius. *Enthüllungen über die Dr. Bernhard Förster'sche Ansiedelung Neu-Germanien in Paraguay: Ein Beitrag zur Geschichte unserer colonialen Bestrebungen* (Revelations about Dr. Bernhard Föster's Settlement New Germania in Paraguay: A Contribution to the History of Our Colonial Efforts). Leipzig: Baldamus, 1889.

Kreyenberg, Gotthold. *Mädchenerziehung und Frauenleben in Aus- und Inlande* (Girls' Education and Women's Lives at Home and Abroad). Berlin: Guttentag, 1872.

Lacan, Jacques. *Écrits*. Paris: Éditions du Seuil, 1966.

Lenz, Dr. Harald Othmar. *Kleine Naturgeschichte für Schul- und Selbstunterricht* (A Brief Natural History for School- and Self-Tuition). Gotha, Ger.: Beck, 1848.

Macintyre, Ben. *Forgotten Fatherland: The Search for Elisabeth Nietzsche*. London: Macmillan, 1992.

Marelle, Luise. "Elisabeth Förster-Nietzsche Dr. Phil." *Frauenweckruf: Organ des deutschen Frauenbundes* (*Women's Reveille: Mouthpiece of the German Women's Federation*) 17 (15 Dec. 1926): 183–84.

———. *Die Schwester: Elisabeth Förster-Nietzsche* (The Sister: Elisabeth Förster-Nietzsche). Berlin: Bischoff, 1934.

Neliba, Günter. *Der Legalist des Unrechtsstaates Wilhelm Frick: Eine politische Biographie* (The Legalizer of the Unjust State: A Political Biography of Wilhelm Frick). Paderborn, Ger.: Schöningh, 1992.

Nietzsche, Friedrich. *Briefwechsel: Kritische Gesamtausgabe* (Correspondence: Critical Complete Edition). Ed. Giorgio Colli and Mazzino Montinari. 24 vols. Berlin: de Gruyter, 1975–. Cited in the notes as KGB.

———. *The Complete Works of Friedrich Nietzsche*. Ed. Oscar Levy. 18 vols. Edinburgh: T.N. Foulis, 1909–13.

———. *Gesammelte Werke: Musarionausgabe*. (Collected Works: Musarion Edition). Ed. Richard Oehler, Max Oehler, and Friedrich Christian Würzbach. 23 vols. Munich: Musarion, 1920–29.

———. *Sämtliche Briefe: Kritische Studienausgabe* (Collected Letters: Critical Study Edition). Ed. Giorgio Colli and Mazzino Montinari. 8 vols. Berlin: de Gruyter, 1986.

———. *Sämtliche Werke: Kritische Studienausgabe* (Collected Works: Critical Study Edition). Ed. Giorgio Colli and Mazzino Montinari. 15 vols. Berlin: de Gruyter, 1980.

———. *Werke: Kritische Gesamtausgabe* (Works: Critical Complete Edition). Ed. Giorgio Colli and Mazzino Montinari. 30 vols. Berlin: de Gruyter, 1967–. Cited in the notes as KGW.

———. *Werke und Briefe: Historisch-Kritische Gesamtausgabe*. Ed. Karl Schechta. 9 vols. Munich: Beck, 1933–42.

Oehler, Adalbert. "Die Mutter von Friedrich Nietzsche: Lebensbild einer deutschen Mutter" (Friedrich Nietzsche's Mother: Biographical Portrait of a German Mother). TS. 100/ 1335, Goethe-Schiller Archive, Weimar.

———. *Nietzsches Mutter*. Munich: Beck, 1940.

———. *Nietzsche's Werke und das Nietzsche-Archiv* (Nietzsche's Works and the Nietzsche-Archiv). Leipzig: Kröner, 1910.

Oehler, Richard. *Friedrich Nietzsche und die deutsche Zukunft* (Friedrich Nietzsche and the Future of Germany). Leipzig: Armanen Press, 1935.

Oeynhausen, Wilhelmine. *Worte mütterlicher Liebe an meine Tochter: Eine Gabe für christliche Jungfrauen* (Words of Motherly Love to My Daughter: A Gift for Christian Maidens). Frankfurt am Main: Brönner, 1844.

Otto, W. F. Afterword to *Ansprachen zum Gedächtnis der Frau Dr. Phil. H.C. Elisabeth Förster-Nietzsche bei den Trauerfeierlichkeiten in Weimar und Röcken am 11. und 12. November 1935* (Speeches in Memory of Frau Dr. Phil. H.C. Elisabeth Förster-Nietzsche at the Ceremonies in Weimar und Röcken on 11 and 12 November 1935). Weimar: Wagner Verlag, 1935.

Peters, Heinz Frederick. *Zarathustra's Sister: The Case of Elisabeth and Friedrich Nietzsche.* New York: Crown, 1977.

Podach, Erich F. *Friedrich Nietzsche und Lou Salomé: Ihre Begegnung 1882* (Friedrich Nietzsche and Lou Salomé: Their Meeting in 1882). Zurich: Niehans, 1937.

———. *Gestalten um Nietzsche: Mit unveröffentlichten Dokumenten zur Geschichte seines Lebens und seines Werks* (People around Nietzsche: With Unpublished Documents on the History of His Life and Work). Weimar: Lichtenstein, 1932.

———. *Nietzsche's Zusammenbruch* (Nietzsche's Collapse). Heidelberg: Kampmann, 1930.

Raumer, Karl von. *Die Erziehung der Mädchen* (The Education of Girls). 1853. 2d ed., enl. Stuttgart: Liesching, 1857.

Salis, Meta von. *Philosoph und Edelmensch: Ein Beitrag zur Charakteristik Friedrich Nietzsches* (Philosopher and Gentleman: A Contribution to the Description of Friedrich Nietzsche). Leipzig: Naumann, 1897.

Salomé, Lou von. *Friedrich Nietzsche in seinen Werken* (Friedrich Nietzsche in His Works). 1897. Published in English as *Nietzsche.* Trans. Siegfried Mandel. Redding Ridge, Conn.: Black Swan Books, 1988.

Schaberg, William H. *The Nietzsche Canon: A Publication History and Bibliography.* Chicago: University of Chicago Press, 1995.

Schlechta, Karl. *Der Fall Nietzsche* (The Case of Nietzsche). Munich: Hanser, 1958.

Schoedler, Friedrich. *Das Buch der Natur* (The Book of Nature). 1846. 2 vols. Braunschweig: Vieweg, 1875.

Sigismund, Ursula. *Zarathustra's Sippschaft: Pikante Enthüllungen aus Friedrich Nietzsches Familie* (Zarathustra's Kith and Kin: Piquant Revelations about Friedrich Nietzsche's Family). Bastei-Lübbe: Bergisch Gladbach, 1981.

Simon-Ritz, Frank, and Justus H. Ulbricht. "'Heimstätte des Zarathustrawerkes.' Personen, Gremien, und Aktivitäten des Nietzsche-Archivs in Weimar, 1896–1945" ("Home for *Thus Spoke Zarathustra*": People, Committees, and Activities in Weimar, 1896–1945). Pp. 155–76 in *Wege nach Weimar* (Paths to Weimar). Ed. Hans Wilderotter. Berlin: Jovis, 1999.

Vaihinger, Hans. "Johanna Schopenhauer und andere Philosophenmütter" (Johanna Schopenhauer and Other Mothers of Philosophers). *Jahrbuch der Schopenhauer-Gesellschaft* (Yearbook of the Schopenhauer Society) 15 (1928): 240–46.

———. *Nietzsche als Philosoph* (Nietzsche As Philosopher). Berlin: Reuther and Reichard, 1902.

———. *Die Philosophie des Als Ob* (The Philosophy of "As If"). Berlin: Reuther and Reichard, 1911.

Welch, Claude. *Protestant Thought in the Nineteenth Century.* 2 vols. New Haven, Conn.: Yale University Press, 1972.

Wollkopf, Roswitha. "Elisabeth Nietzsche—Nora wider Willen? Ein bisher unentdecktes Manuskript" (Elisabeth Nietzsche—Nora against Her Will? A Hitherto Undiscovered Manuscript). *Nietzscheforschung: Eine Jahresschrift* (Nietzsche-Research: A Yearly Publication) 1 (1994): 261–66.

Index

CAROL DIETHE, a former lecturer and research fellow at Middlesex University in London since 1997, is one of the founders of the British Friedrich Nietzsche Society. She is the author of *Nietzsche's Women: Beyond the Whip, Historical Dictionary of Nietzscheanism,* and *Aspects of Distorted Sexual Attitudes in German Expressionist Drama with Particular Reference to Wedekind, Kokoschka, and Kaiser.* She is also the translator of *Nietzsche on the Genealogy of Morality and Other Writings.*

International Nietzsche Studies

The University of Illinois Press
is a founding member of the
Association of American University Presses.

Composed in 10.5/13 Minion
by Jim Proefrock
at the University of Illinois Press
Manufactured by Thomson-Shore, Inc.

University of Illinois Press
1325 South Oak Street
Champaign, IL 61820-6903
www.press.uillinois.edu